Praise for other books b...

Great Australian Places

'Seal reveals much about Australia—and Australians—on a storytelling tour from iconic destinations to tiny settlements, remote landmarks and little-known corners.' —*The Senior*

Great Australian Mysteries

'Seal brings to life the enigmas and puzzles behind unsolved crimes, lost treasures and strange phenomena . . . a fascinating read.' —*Canberra Weekly*

Australia's Funniest Yarns

'Full of songs, stories, poems, rules and quizzes. It is a lovely book for those who want to catch a glimpse of the old characters who used their stories and language to make the Australia of the past much more colourful than it is today.' —*Glam Adelaide*

Great Bush Stories

'Takes us back to a time when "the bush" was central to popular notions of Australian identity, with the likes of Henry Lawson and "Banjo" Paterson serving to both celebrate and mythologise it.' —*Writing WA*

Great Convict Stories

'With a cast of colourful characters from around the country— the real Artful Dodger, intrepid bushrangers . . . *Great Convict*

Stories offers a fascinating insight into life in Australia's first decades.' —*Sunraysia Daily*

Great Australian Journeys

'Readers familiar with Graham Seal's work will know he finds and writes ripper, fair-dinkum, true blue Aussie yarns. His books are great reads and do a lot for ensuring cultural stories are not lost.' —*The Weekly Times*

Great Anzac Stories

'. . . allows you to feel as if you are there in the trenches with them.' —*Weekly Times*

Larrikins, Bush Tales and Other Great Australian Stories

'Another collection of yarns, tall tales, bush legends and colourful characters . . . from one of our master storytellers.' —*Queensland Times*

The Savage Shore

'A gripping account of danger at sea, dramatic shipwrecks, courageous castaways, murder, much missing gold and terrible loss of life.' —*Queensland Times*

Great Australian Stories

'A treasure trove of material from our nation's historical past.' —*Courier Mail*

GRAHAM SEAL

ALLEN&UNWIN
SYDNEY·MELBOURNE·AUCKLAND·LONDON

First published in 2023

Allen & Unwin
Cammeraygal Country
83 Alexander Street
Crows Nest NSW 2065
Australia
Phone: (61 2) 8425 0100
Email: info@allenandunwin.com
Web: www.allenandunwin.com

*Allen & Unwin acknowledges the Traditional Owners of the Country on which we
live and work. We pay our respects to all Aboriginal and Torres Strait Islander
Elders, past and present.*

A catalogue record for this
book is available from the
National Library of Australia

ISBN 978 1 76106 903 1

Set in 11/17 pt Stempel Schneidler by Bookhouse, Sydney
Printed and bound in Australia by Pegasus Media & Logistics

10 9 8 7 6 5 4

MIX
Paper from
responsible sources
FSC® C008194

The paper in this book is FSC® certified.
FSC® promotes environmentally responsible,
socially beneficial and economically viable
management of the world's forests.

CONTENTS

AUTHOR'S NOTE

The stories in this book span several centuries. Over that time much has changed, including language, points of view and the value of money.

Some of the direct quotations from historical sources may contain terms and reflect attitudes no longer viewed as appropriate and should be read within the context of their time and place.

Where relevant, for historical amounts of money (mostly stolen) I have provided an approximation of their value in today's dollars. Unless otherwise specified, all amounts are in Australian dollars.

INTRODUCTION

nick—to steal; to apprehend; a police lock-up or prison

'Nick' is a useful bit of slang, especially in relation to the underworld. In one form or another, it can mean to steal something, as in 'they just nicked the money'; or it can mean being caught and arrested for a crime. As well as those connected meanings, 'the nick' is slang for a police station or gaol, as in 'she's in the nick for a couple of years'. The word has other uses, too, but *Australia's Most Infamous Criminals* is not about those; it's about some of Australia's many crimes and a few of the bold robbers, sharp con artists and otherwise colourful 'identities' who carried them out.

Crime and criminals literally came to Australia with the First Fleet and its cargo of mostly British convicts. Not that it took long for people to begin violating the new colonial rules. The earliest recorded crimes included stealing food from the common stock of scarce rations. Convicts and soldiers were flogged and hanged for these offences. Food filching was quickly followed by murder and other violent crimes, as well as property theft, fraud, deception and all the many other crooked activities that humans inflict on each other. After another 80 years of penal transportation delivered around 160,000 convicts, some began to call Australia 'a nation of convicts'. Untrue though this is, we have a rich history of bold heists, clever deceptions and more than a few grisly murders. In this bubbling stew of greed, inequality and cunning are many great stories.

Some of those stories have been sensationalised, romanticised or even fictionalised by writers. There has always been a shaky relationship between some criminals, the press and the police. Sometimes this has worked to the advantage of the law and justice; at other times, not so much. The fascination with crime and criminals that fuels press reporting, true crime books and detective fiction reflects the uneasy tensions and murky connections between these significant elements of society. High drama, violence and mystery are bound to attract public attention and interest and, in some cases, even celebration of crime and its perpetrators. Then, as now, it was sometimes difficult to separate real crime scenes from fiction and some of the world's earliest authors of stories about clever sleuths, devious wrongdoers and chilling deeds lived in Australia.

Robberies are one of the most common illegal activities. Sometimes this is simply more or less opportunistic thieving, but a few sensational heists have been masterpieces of planning, logistics and audacity. Banks, payrolls and bookies' takings are the favoured targets, but even supposedly secure mints are not immune. Some of the most notorious jobs have never been solved and the loot is still missing. The underworld code of silence has often protected the robbers, even when police have strong suspicions about who was guilty.

Modern Australia may well have begun as an importer of crime, but since then we have also exported it far and wide. Australian con artists have long played above their weight in many parts of the world and today's intricate flows of crime and money continue to involve some of our citizens. Confidence tricksters are the criminal elite. Even the most basic 'short con', such as the three-card trick, requires skill and daring to succeed. At the more lucrative heights of the game, those men and women who practise the deceptive arts of the 'long con' are accomplished swindlers who operate among the well-heeled 'marks' in the spheres of business, finance and opulent leisure. Among them are some of the underworld's more intriguing characters, as well as some suffering from afflictions that compel them to impersonate and defraud people, sometimes including themselves.

Contrary to popular belief, Australia is a relatively law-abiding country. But even so, we have no shortage of murderers, past and present. Many murderers have been caught, though a good many homicides remain unsolved, some of them very 'cold cases' indeed. The deliberate ending of another human's life takes many forms and has many causes. Jealousy, fear, hatred and greed are among the most usual spurs to murder. Less frequent are political assassinations and serial murder cases, though we have had our fair share of these as well.

Criminal behaviour and its consequences range from the dramatically grotesque to the plain old sneaky and everything in between. *Australia's Most Infamous Criminals* finishes with a selection of more unusual crimes and some recent developments. Those who break the law professionally are nothing if not adaptable. New methods of deceit, deception and underhand enrichment are constantly being added to the lengthy list of possible wrongdoings, sometimes exploiting the possibilities of the internet, sometimes just fresh variations on the old 'smash and grab'.

Surveying the broad expanse of illegal activity inevitably raises questions about the nature of crime and the motivations of criminals. Illegal acts are committed across all fields of human endeavour, communities and ways of life. All societies evolve laws to regulate behaviour, property and wealth. Those who break those laws must be caught by a police force of some sort, brought to justice in some kind of legal system and, if found guilty, punished accordingly. Other than those unfortunate enough to receive death sentences, most criminals are eventually released. Many begin the cycle of crime all over again.

These realities mean that enormous resources must be devoted to legal systems, policing, prisons, rehabilitation and to researching the causes and, we hope, cures for criminal behaviour. To date, Australia, along with every other country, has not found the answer to the intractable problem of crime. It's a problem that's been around for a very long time.

Well over two thousand years ago the ancient Greek philosophers, Plato and Aristotle, addressed their thoughts towards the crimes of their era. Plato concluded that the problem was basically moral. Some people were simply not inclined or able to observe the law. Aristotle thought that people did the wrong thing because they desired wealth, property or something else they lacked. Both philosophers had some rather severe prescriptions for the punishment of criminals that were later echoed in the harsh penal codes of the medieval era and well into the eighteenth century. The convicts transported to Australia from Britain and its empire were latter-day victims of this method of controlling lawless behaviour.

Centuries after the Greek thinkers grappled with the problem of crime, the philosophising Roman emperor Marcus Aurelius Antoninus, said that 'poverty is the mother of crime', an observation as true today as when it was first made. Later theories suggested that certain types of people, identifiable by their supposedly inherent criminal features, were the most likely to commit crimes. This discriminatory nineteenth-century approach, known broadly as 'phrenology', has long been debunked. Today, crime is usually seen to be largely the result of social and economic inequality and, ideally, the guilty should not be so much punished as rehabilitated to become useful members of society on their release.

Philosophers and scientists will continue to debate the nature of crime, but everyday folk have also developed a body of wisdom about the problem. A Russian proverb holds that 'It's only a crime if you get caught.' A more recent saying sounds a cautionary note: 'Do the crime, do the time.' And, of course, everyone has heard that 'crime doesn't pay'—or does it? Whether criminals profit from their misdeeds or not, sayings like these from all periods and places indicate how frequently crimes are committed, always have been and probably always will be.

PROLOGUE

Four years before the First Fleet sailed to the place we now call Australia, nine-year-old John Hudson stood alone and undefended in the dock at London's Old Bailey court. He was charged with breaking and entering the house of a chemist in East Smithfield to steal goods worth over £2. As well as a linen shirt, five silk stockings and two aprons, he was also charged with stealing a pistol.

At a time when youth was rarely taken into account during criminal proceedings, the judge was concerned about John and asked him: 'How old are you?'

JOHN: Going in [sic] nine.
JUDGE: What business was you bred up in?
JOHN: None, sometimes a chimney sweeper.
JUDGE: Have you any father or mother?

JOHN: Dead.
JUDGE: How long ago?
JOHN: I do not know.

The judge told the court that he 'wanted to see whether he had any understanding or no, we shall hear more of him by and by'. As it turned out, nothing more was heard from John during the proceedings.

But there was plenty from several witnesses called to prosecute the charges, the first being the chemist, William Holdsworth. On the morning of 17 October 1783, his maid told him that his house had been robbed. The thief or thieves entered through a broken skylight and one of them, barefoot, slid down the shutters. Holdsworth found the imprint of 'small toes' on the shutters and on a nearby table. He 'took the impressions of the foot and toes that were on the table upon a piece of paper as minutely as I could'. The piece of paper was produced as evidence at the trial.

A local lodger, Sarah Baynes, then testified that she had encountered John about ten the same morning at the communal water tub: 'he was all sooty'. She then found most of the loot, hidden after the shirt had been pawned earlier in the morning.

John had then been apprehended by John Saddler who testified that the prisoner at first denied the theft, then said that there had been another boy involved, which was probably true. When brought before a local justice, John's foot was shown to match the imprint on the chemist's piece of paper. He was made to confess to the crime.

'Did the boy seem to want understanding before the justice?' the judge queried.

'He said very little.'

'Did he appear to you to want understanding?'

Saddler replied that he seemed to understand what was happening and that he had already been caught by the 'runners', the early London police body, three times over the previous ten days.

The judge was still unhappy. He reluctantly allowed John Hudson's forced confession:

> but we must take it with every allowance, and at the utmost it only proves he was in the house . . . I think it would be too hard to find a boy of his tender age guilty of the burglary; one would wish to snatch such a boy, if one possibly could, from destruction, for he will only return to the same kind of life which he has led before, and will be an instrument in the hands of very bad people, who make use of boys of that sort to rob houses.

John Hudson was found not guilty of burglary but guilty of the felony charge of breaking and entering. Possibly hoping to remove the boy from his criminal connections, the judge sentenced him to seven years transportation.

A few months later, John was one of the convicts aboard the transport ship *Mercury*, all bound from Torbay in Devon for hard labour in the American colonies, then still in British possession. The convicts mounted a violent attack on the crew and managed to take over the ship but were forced back to harbour by bad weather.

Along with most of the other escapees, John was recaptured in Devon and ended up on a hulk, or prison ship, in Plymouth harbour. John spent three years on the notoriously brutal and depraved hulks before being loaded aboard the First Fleet transport ship, *Friendship*. During the voyage he was reportedly a well-behaved prisoner but he was also a graduate of the hulk school of crime.

He landed with the rest of the First Fleet convicts and their keepers and remained at Port Jackson until he was sent to the first penal settlement at Norfolk Island in 1790. The next year he was caught outside his hut after 9 pm and suffered fifty lashes. He was back in Sydney by 1795 where he was last recorded as being no longer dependent on the government stores, presumably now able to fend for himself in the colony of crime.

How well John Hudson did, or not, we don't know, there are no further records of the sweep's boy who was one of Australia's first criminals. There have been many since.

Flogging a convict in Moreton Bay, Queensland, one of Australia's first penal settlements. In the 'nation of convicts' floggings and hangings were common. Illustration by William Ross, from The Fell Tyrant, *1836.*

1

A NATION OF CONVICTS

THE FIRST BANK JOB

Australia's first proper banking operation was the Bank of New South Wales, established in 1817. A few years later a cashier embezzled £12,000 in one of the country's earliest white-collar crimes. But it was another six years before an Australian bank attracted the interest of working-class criminals.

In 1826 the Bank of Australia started up in Lower George Street in Sydney to compete with the earlier institution. Of course, the new enterprise needed a secure location for the money and so its basement was converted into a stone strongroom. The mason who did the job was Thomas Turner, a convict. He had also worked on a sewer drain that ran very near to the new bank vault. It proved difficult for the mason to resist temptation.

Turner knew that he could not carry out the robbery himself so he floated the idea with a few convicts and ex-convict mates. One of these men, John Creighton, had also worked on laying the floor of the bank's basement conversion. The knowledge of Turner and Creighton, together with the skills of blacksmith William Blackstone (Blaxtone) and help from ex-convicts James Dingle and George Farrell, made the group an effective team for the well-planned bank job they carried out over several weekends in September 1828.

Firstly, they needed a way to remove bricks and stones from the walls and floors of the drain and the vault itself. Blackstone the blacksmith came up with a simple but effective gadget, which he later described as 'similar in shape to a file, with a round handle, a crow-bar, a gimlet about two feet [60 cm] long, to pierce the joint of the stone'. He also made a 'dark lantern', featuring a hood able to conceal the light from a burning candle.

Around 4 am one Saturday, Blackstone met Dingle and Farrell near the bank. They needed to locate the exact position of the vault so they would be able to break into it from the drain. Dingle tied a line to a broomstick and reached across the fence to the wall of the bank from where Farrell guided the line into the drain in the passageway beside the bank, known as 'Redman's Yard'. Farrell then

> carried the line into the grating over the drain near Redman's; we then went down Redman's yard, and got to the end of the drain, where we entered, and proceeded on till we came to the part immediately under Redman's arch, where we took the end of the line through the grating, and run [sic]

it down the wall between the two buildings, by which we found the front of the Bank building, allowing two feet six [75 cm] for the thickness of the foundation, two feet six for the extra-thickness of the strong room, and five feet [1.5 m] more to bring us in the centre of the room.

By the hidden light of the dark lantern, they began removing bricks with the aid of Blackstone's device. They were able to work all day until dark, undisturbed. By then they were through the drain wall and had five stones out of the bank building. The next Saturday morning, the three men returned to the crime scene they were creating together with Creighton, the floor-layer. As they approached the drain a man came out of the bank and asked them what they were doing. He apparently believed their vague story that they were doing some necessary work on the building. Blackstone and Creighton went back into the drain and continued working while the other two robbers kept watch. By day's end they were partly through the foundations of the bank.

On the third Saturday they repeated the procedure, though a heavy stone fell on Blackstone and put him out of action, along with the lantern. They were rattled by the accident but were now through the outside wall and removing stones from the wall of the vault. It was decided that they would need another day to complete the job and that it would have to be Sunday. As serving convicts, Blackstone and Dingle would be expected at the church muster but Dingle knew someone who could arrange an exemption for them, for a small consideration, of course. The robbers then made their way to the pub, unwisely becoming involved in a brawl along the way. They attracted the attention of the constables but managed to escape and celebrate at one of Sydney's many drinking dens.

At daylight on Sunday, Blackstone, Creighton and Farrell went through the drain while Dingle kept lookout. Twenty minutes into the last stage of the excavation, an unknown man suddenly appeared beside them in the drain. At first, the robbers were alarmed, but the stranger, named Val Rooke (Rourke), was a last-minute recruit to the gang. He had promised to 'keep counsel', so they carried on a little faster. As the drums signalled the start of the church muster, the sweaty diggers broke through the thick floor of the vault. Farrell, the smallest, crawled through the hole they had made and brought out two tin boxes of notes and coins. More tins and bags of loot were brought out and the robbers busily sorted them into parcels of different value.

At one point, Creighton unaccountably defecated in one of the tin boxes. Blackstone 'told him he was a scoundrel for so doing, that there was no need to aggravate the offence'. The unrepentant Creighton replied that 'he would have the pleasure of using a bank note on the occasion' and, presumably, did.

The robbers divided the loot and as the bells rang for evening service returned with what they could carry to the waiting Dingle, leaving his share of the silver. They then went to his house where they had arranged to stash the first tranche of the money. Returning early the next rainy morning, Blackstone and Dingle retrieved another load of silver. Avoiding the constables, Blackstone managed to get it back to his place, fearing that Dingle had been taken. Dingle had indeed been stopped by the constables but managed to talk his way free by saying he had been 'at a merry-meeting on the Rocks'. The job netted around £14,000, estimated in today's value to be more than $30 million.

After news of the sensational robbery came out, the bank withdrew its notes from circulation and had to rapidly print new ones. They offered a £100 reward for the capture and conviction of the thieves. Governor Darling also offered a free pardon to any informer, which the bank boosted further with a promised passage back to England. Several hoards of notes were discovered hidden around the settlement but the robbers could not be found. It was not until 1830 when Blackstone, then serving a long sentence on Norfolk Island for another crime, decided he'd had enough and informed on his accomplices.

By then, Creighton was dead and Rooke was long out of the country. Dingle and Farrell were tried and found guilty, both receiving life sentences on Norfolk Island. Another man named Thomas Woodward had received some of the stolen notes and was tried and found guilty. He was sentenced to fourteen years. The 'approver', Blackstone, got his reward money and kept his freedom but declined the passage home. A couple of years later he was found guilty of more robberies and sent to Norfolk for life where he was reacquainted with Dingle and Farrell who were undoubtedly very pleased to see him.

The mastermind of the crime? There was no evidence against stonemason Thomas Turner. He'd managed to discreetly dispose of his share of the proceeds and was never prosecuted.

This audacious heist was not only an historical first, it also passed into folklore. Only some of the haul was ever recovered, leading to speculation that the rest must be hidden somewhere around Sydney. Darling Harbour and other harbour sites were favoured locations, though, as far as anyone knows, nothing has ever been found there. Acting on a tip that the gold was buried near Mrs Macquarie's Chair, the then premier had the area dug up in the early 1890s, with no result. The treasure hunters haven't given up though. In 2017 it was suggested that bays along the North Shore might be hiding a few of the coin boxes. There are sure to be at least one or two hopefuls still looking for the loot.

THE NIGHT WATCH

Once basic survival has been assured, the next task of a new society is to police itself. As the young colony at Sydney Cove struggled to grow enough food, even humble vegetable gardens were targets for night-time pilfering. By the end of 1789, rations had been reduced and the colony was approaching starvation. Stealing food and provisions became a potential life-and-death issue as well as a property crime. A night patrol of marines failed to stop what had become a serious problem for every colonist, bound or free. John Harris, a convict, suggested to the judge advocate that a night watch of convicts might be helpful. Putting the foxes in charge of the hen house was an idea that the authorities would not have previously tolerated. But the situation was becoming so bad that Arthur Phillip agreed to it.

The night watch was a crude form of civil policing 'appointed for the more effectual preservation of public and private property, and for preventing or detecting the commission of nightly depredations'. This was the official proclamation establishing the watch, though it was already in operation by the time the order was published.

Made up of twelve male convicts meant to be of the 'fairest character', the watch was divided into four district groups.

The convicts' huts and the public farm on the east side of the cove to be the first division. Those at the brick-kilns and the detached parties at the different farms in that district the second division. Those on the western side, as far as the line that separates the district of the women from the men, the third division. The huts occupied from that line to the hospital, and from thence to the observatory, to be the fourth division.

Armed with short staffs, the men of the night watch were to make sure nobody was out after 'tapto' (tattoo), the drum signal for the start of curfew and 'the discovery of any felony, trespass, or misdemeanour, and for the apprehending and securing for examination any person or persons that may appear to them concerned therein, either by entrance into any suspected hut or dwelling, or by such other manner as may appear expedient'. The men were specifically tasked to report unsanctioned bartering of clothes and food among the convicts, and any soldiers or sailors straggling after curfew. Robberies were to be investigated and offenders tracked down.

The night watch received no payment for these duties 'but their diligence and good behaviour will be rewarded by the Governor'. The job was a good one for those looking for a remission of their sentences. But the proclamation concluded with a stern warning that 'Any negligence on the part of those who may be employed on this duty will be punished with the utmost rigour of the law.'

Recorded members of the night watch numbered between nine and twelve, suggesting that it might have been difficult to find a dozen convicts of the 'fairest character'. The founder of the watch was John Herbert Keeling (also John Kellan or Keelan) who had been transported for life. His contribution to the civil society of the colony was rewarded with a pardon in 1800 after he had also been on Norfolk Island between 1790 and 1793. A man of strong will, he provoked the lieutenant-governor there, Major Robert Ross, and was flogged for his impertinence. Six years after receiving his freedom, Herbert Keeling was found guilty of forging promissory notes and executed.

Others of the watch went on to follow various paths. John Harris, who had originally suggested the idea and briefly served in it before going to Norfolk Island, later became a constable. At least one other later took to the bush. The well-known Henry Kable was also a member and received a pardon for his work. He was appointed head constable though was later dismissed from service over a conflict of interest between his duties and his flourishing enterprises. He would become one of early Sydney's most successful businessmen.

This rickety police force was judged to be reasonably successful at first, though the marines would not submit to being detained by convicts. Phillip had to amend his orders to exclude soldiers from the jurisdiction of the night watch after tapto or if they were caught committing a crime. By March of 1790, the colony was in even more serious trouble and even closer to starvation. Night watch successes fell away and 'robberies of gardens and houses were daily and nightly committed', as David Collins wrote in his diary. Despite this, the watch continued and its hours extended to the full day and night. The system was also introduced in the outlying settlements.

In 1796 Governor Hunter, concerned at constant public disorder and crime, introduced a system allowing free settlers to elect their own watchmen. It seems that these complemented the convict watch and the system of paid constables who, together, formed the first of Australia's many police forces.

As the colony grew, so did its troubles. Governors after Hunter also struggled to regulate and control a host of issues, including roaming pigs, dogs and water pollution. Vagrancy became a problem as people wandered between the various settlements and forgery was also rife, along with early bushranging. Attendance at church was required, though widely flouted. Such was the dissatisfaction with this rule that a church was set alight on at least one occasion.

But the most intractable matter was alcohol. Whether smuggled ashore from ships, illegally brewed in backyard stills or simply available through more or less legitimate outlets, the grog and its social consequences gave governors the biggest headache of all. One of them, William Bligh, lost his position through the Rum Rebellion of 1808. No matter how many edicts were issued or policing arrangements made and remade, Sydney continued to float on rum.

It was not until the coming of Governor Lachlan Macquarie that an effective solution was found. Macquarie simply increased the excise on spirits and used the proceeds to fund a more effective policing system and a more efficient magistracy. From 1810, he instituted a stream of reforms and initiatives in line with new ideas about controlling crime. Policing evolved from a convict-conceived and convict-staffed organisation that, despite its failings and contradictions, helped the colony survive its early challenges.

THE FLASH MOB GOES EXPLORING

It wasn't as if Thomas Mitchell didn't have enough to deal with in 1845. The surveyor-general of New South Wales was leading a party of soldiers and convicts on a long trek into largely unknown lands to find a route from Sydney to the Gulf of Carpentaria. Notoriously insubordinate and glory-seeking, Mitchell was out to cement his reputation as an explorer. There were rivers, mountains and plains to discover and name, as well as new species and ancient fossils. If successful, the trek would open up the north of the eastern coast of the country. A train line would then follow his route, allowing direct connection to the British possessions of India, stimulating trade and, although only implied, facilitating strategic empire interests. That was the plan.

This wasn't the first time Mitchell had travelled overland but on his previous journeys the convicts selected to go with him 'had acquired good recommendations from their immediate overseers'. On this trip though, his men were 'for the most part chosen from amongst those still remaining in Cockatoo Island, the worst and most irreclaimable of their class'. The Cockatoo Island prison and dock works were a noted centre of skilled trades. Bad though they might have been, many convicts were also blacksmiths, carpenters, wheelwrights and shoemakers, all essential to keeping a nineteenth-century group of travellers, with their horses and carts, in working order.

When Mitchell called for volunteers from among the Cockatoo Island felons to go exploring, by his own account, 'All pressed eagerly forward with their claims and pretensions,' anxious to earn their freedom through one year of good behaviour in the bush. Mitchell found that 'it was not easy to find one without a catalogue of offences, filling a whole page of police-office annals' but after examining their physical features according to the then-popular pseudo-science of phrenology, together with a close look at their records, Mitchell made his selection and 'With them, I mixed one or two faithful Irishmen, on whom I knew I could depend, and two or three of my old followers on former journeys, who had become free.'

He was pleased with the group he chose, stating that 'the greater number, as on all former expeditions, gave the highest satisfaction, submitting cheerfully to privations, enduring hardships, and encountering dangers, apparently willing and resolved to do anything to escape from the degraded condition of a convict'. But Mitchell's initial approval would change, at least when it came to a group of six men among his convicts. They were known as 'the flash mob' and even the other convicts avoided them, so black was their reputation. These men

> spoke the secret language of thieves; were ever intent on robbing the stores, with false keys (called by them SCREWS). They held it to be wrong to exert themselves at any work, if it could be avoided; and would not be seen to endeavour to please, by willing cooperation. They kept themselves out of sight as much as possible; neglected their arms; shot away their ammunition contrary to orders; and ate in secret, whatever they did kill, or whatever fish they caught.

The term 'flash mob' turns up in newspapers from the 1830s, though it has a longer lineage stretching back to the street criminals of London and other English industrial cities in the eighteenth century. To be 'flash' was a criminal slang term for arrogant defiance and manipulation of the law and its representatives in any form, whether police, judges, prison guards or soldiers. Those who were flash lived entirely by criminal enterprise. Their secret slang, also known as the 'flash language', or just 'the flash', was designed to obfuscate those who did not speak or understand it and to allow them to communicate their illegal plans without fear of prying ears. A 'flash mob', also referred to as 'the fancy', was a closed criminal confederacy dedicated to self-protection and self-gratification. Insular though this group were, they were always looking for recruits, whether in the slums of London, the penal establishments of New South Wales or the mobile community of explorers as Mitchell discovered in the vastness of the lands he sought to explore and exploit:

> Professing to be men of 'the Fancy,' they made converts of two promising men, who, at first, were highly thought of, and although one of them was finally reclaimed, a hero of the prize ring, it was too obvious that the men, who glory in breaking the laws, and all of whose songs even, express sentiments of dishonesty, can easily lead the unwary and still susceptible of the unfortunate class, into snares from which they cannot afterwards escape if they would. Once made parties to an offence against the law, they are bound as by a spell, to the order of flash-boys, with whom it is held to be base and cowardly to act 'upon the square,' or HONESTLY in any sense of the word; their order professing to act ever 'upon the cross.'

The flash mob could not be trusted around the food stores, which had to be constantly guarded. Despite this security measure, they still managed to steal flour and use it to satisfy their hunger as well as to entice other convicts of the exploring party into their wiles.

Although it is hard to tell from Mitchell's published account, his expedition was only partially successful. Threatened by traditional owners and near starvation on the Barcoo in far west Queensland's channel country, he turned back. He had not found a way for a steam train from Sydney to the Gulf of Carpentaria or the northward-flowing river he had long believed should be there. But he and his companions had endured for more than twelve harsh months without losing a man and with no major problems—despite the machinations of the flash mob.

In his journal of the expedition, Mitchell reflected on the nature of criminals and their crimes:

Convicts, in fact, consist of two distinctly different classes: the one, fortunately by far the most numerous, comprising those whose crime was the result of impulse; the other class consisting of those whose principle of action is dishonesty; whose trade is crime, and of whose reformation, there is much less hope. The offenders of the one class, repented of their crime from the moment of conviction; those of the other, know no such word in their vocabulary. The one, is still 'a thing of hope and change'; and would eagerly avail himself of every means afforded him to regain the position he had lost; the other, true to his 'order', will 'die game'.

'Dying game' was the ultimate proof of 'flashness'. According to tradition, Ned Kelly asked his mother to 'tell 'em I died game' shortly before his execution in 1880. At his trial he had an exchange with judge Sir Redmond Barry, claiming 'There is no flashness or bravado about me . . .'

By then, Sir Thomas Mitchell was long dead. After his failure to reach the Gulf, he went on to continued ups and downs related to his refusal to be told what to do by anyone, including governors. In 1851 he fought one of Australia's last duels over an issue arising from these controversies. Fortunately, both men missed. Out on a surveying trip in 1855, Mitchell developed pneumonia and died.

His legacy is a mixed one, though he is today generally thought of as an enlightened man of his time and one of the hardy explorers whose efforts underpin the development of modern Australia. Despite his faults, Mitchell was an outstanding surveyor and had progressive views on the culture of First Nations people and the possibility of redemption for the convicts he uniquely recruited to his expeditions. Though it isn't likely that any of the flash mob that accompanied his 1845 expedition ever turned over a new leaf.

A Child of Misfortune

No man was better qualified to gather the criminal lingo of colonial Australia. Ne'er-do-well, spendthrift, gambling carouser, thief, swindler—James Hardy Vaux was all these things by the time he was in his teens. And things went downhill from there. After the second of his three transportations from England to Australia, Vaux's spectacular, if mostly misspent, career did produce at least one positive result. His famous dictionary of criminal slang was compiled mainly while he was serving time in New South Wales. How he got there and how he got out— more than once—is one of the great tales of colonial crime.

In his memoirs, Vaux describes himself as 'a child of misfortune'. Like many of the excuses in his fascinating life story, this is difficult to credit. He was born into a middle-class English family in 1782, received a solid education and was raised primarily by his grandparents. He does not seem to have had a deprived childhood, though he felt that intergenerational family tensions led to a breaking of the relationship with his parents and 'As the kindness and liberality of my grandparents towards me increased, the affection of my father and mother diminished; and, as they had several children afterwards, I soon became an object, if not of aversion, at least of indifference.' A little later in his memoirs, Vaux refers to himself as 'the darling of his parents'—a seeming contradiction that is a constant theme in his colourful life.

Vaux went to work at age fourteen, not unusual at that time, and was apprenticed to a linen draper in Liverpool. Here he came under the influence of the older apprentices and quickly slipped into bad ways. His 'irregular mode of life' revolved around drink and sex, both expensive pastimes when taken to excess. Funding these pleasures led to gambling on cockfights, increasingly supported by pilfering from his employer's till. He was discovered and, generously, sent on his way rather than prosecuted. From there it was a succession of mostly brief occupations punctuated by obtaining goods and credit by false pretences and midnight flits to avoid paying rent. There was a brush with the law in London, a strategic retreat to Portsmouth, then a return to London where Vaux was convinced to join the Royal Navy.

The life suited him for more than a year, until he became 'enamoured of a fair Cyprian' and deserted to pursue her. When her outraged father forcibly took the girl back to the family, Vaux soon fell into poverty, relieved by playing billiards and card sharping. More short-term employment and defrauding employers followed until Vaux was again apprehended and charged, though acquitted for lack of evidence. He was soon after arrested again, tried and convicted, though claiming that he was innocent of pickpocketing a handkerchief. He was transported for seven years.

In Sydney, Vaux had an odd interview with the eccentric Governor King who dispatched him 'up the country' to work as a clerk to a storekeeper on the Hawkesbury. After three unblemished years, King called him back to Sydney to work in the Secretary's Office, a plum position. But here, Vaux was again tempted into 'a dissipated life' and became involved in a scheme to defraud the government stores. The scheme was discovered and a greatly displeased governor ordered him to be 'double-ironed, and put to the hardest labour, in common with those incorrigible characters composing what is called the jail-gang'. Vaux was then 'set to work at mending the public-roads, &c. &c., and as I had never before used a heavier tool than a goose-quill, I found this penance to bear hard upon me, and repented me of the evil which had brought me to this woeful condition'.

Vaux did not have to repent or labour for very long. After ten months or so he was appointed as clerk to the camp superintendent. He then worked for the Reverend Samuel

Marsden as magistrate's clerk and returned to King's favour. When the governor departed for England, he took Vaux with him to copy and arrange his many official papers. Vaux also received a free pardon. But there was a catch. He was still wanted by the Royal Navy for desertion and would have to return to that service upon his return.

After a momentous and harrowing voyage, Vaux arrived back in England, though as a sailor, not as a clerk. He had offended the irascible King and been sent 'before the mast' for punishment. The enterprising adventurer soon found a way out of his naval predicament and returned to London where he obtained government employment on his grandfather's recommendation. As usual, Vaux soon moved on and, despite resolving to 'live a strictly honest life', was tempted back to crime. During this time he formed a relationship with a prostitute who soon became pregnant. They married but the baby was premature and died. After another narrow escape from justice Vaux, this time under an alias, was arrested for stealing jewellery, convicted, condemned to death, reprieved and transported again, this time for life.

After a four-year absence, Vaux returned to Sydney where Governor Macquarie was now in charge and had him again sent to the Hawkesbury. After being mistreated by the settler in charge of him, he contrived to return to Sydney where he became an overseer and again resolved to 'reform my Life, and become a new Man'. This did not last long and after being convicted of receiving stolen property he ended up at Coal River, Newcastle, for an indefinite stay in 1811. After several years of good behaviour, he was returned to Sydney but his hopes of again working in an office were soon dashed and he attempted to escape. Vaux and his fellow escapees were betrayed, taken and received fifty lashes each: 'certainly as lenient as could be expected for such an attempt', he wrote. Then it was back to Coal River where he again worked as a clerk rather than a miner.

During this period Vaux put together the materials that were eventually published as *Memoirs of the First Thirty-Two Years of the Life of James Hardy Vaux, A Swindler and Pickpocket; Now Transported for the Second Time, and For Life, to New South Wales.* He concluded this account of his life to that point with more good resolutions:

> I am not without hope, that when I am permitted to quit my present service and return to Sydney, my good conduct will be rewarded with a more desirable situation. I have now been upwards of seven years a prisoner, and knowing the hopeless sentence under which I labour, shall, I trust, studiously avoid in future every act which may subject me to the censure of my superiors, or entail upon me a repetition of those sufferings I have already too severely experienced. I have thus described (perhaps too minutely for the reader's patience) the various vicissitudes of my past life. Whether the future will be so far diversified as to afford matter worthy of being committed to paper, either to amuse a vacant hour, or to serve as a beacon which may warn others to avoid the rocks on which I have unhappily split, is only known to the great Disposer of events.

That was not the end of this rogue's colourful tale. He married ex-convict Frances Sharkey in 1818, received a conditional pardon in 1820 and worked honestly for the government for six years. Then he was suddenly dismissed on suspicion that his criminal background made him unsuitable to hold such a position, even though he seems to have done no wrong. Bitter at this injustice he fled the colony and went to Ireland. There, under an assumed name, he was convicted of forging banknotes and transported for seven years. His real identity was unmasked as soon as he returned to the colony where his previous life sentence began again. He spent six years at Port Macquarie and was back in Sydney clerking by 1837. Two years later he was sentenced to two years prison for indecently assaulting an eight-year-old girl.

After his release, the 59-year-old thief, lexicographer and paedophile conducted his final scam and vanished from history. His raffish legacy is a rogue's memoir spattered with cant, or flash language, and collected into an A–Z of technical terms for crime and criminals. A few have entered Australian folk speech, including 'cove' for the boss; 'flash' in the sense of ostentatious dress and demeanour; 'mug' meaning a face; 'swag' in the sense of a bundle; and to 'spin a yarn':

> . . . a favourite amusement among flash-people; signifying to relate their various adventures, exploits, and escapes to each other. This is most common and gratifying, among persons in confinement or exile, to enliven a dull hour, and probably excite a secret hope of one day enjoying a repetition of their former pleasures . . . A person expert at telling these stories, is said to spin a fine yarn.

Few finer than those of 'Flash Jim' Vaux.

GENTLEMEN CONVICTS

James Hardy Vaux was not the only 'gentleman' convict in colonial New South Wales. Among the seething masses of murderers, fraudsters, rapists and robbers who made up most of the transported convict population were a number of upper-class men. Whether born into position and wealth or subsequently attaining it by fair means or foul, this assortment of oddities formed a small but very visible group in early Australian society.

Gentleman convicts were usually sentenced for white-collar crimes or for acts of violence associated with their class and culture. In the case of John Grant, his attempt to court an aristocrat's daughter were blocked by her family solicitor. The enraged suitor unwisely tried to shoot the solicitor. Grant was sentenced to death, though this was commuted to transportation for life through the appeals of his sister to the daughters of George III. He reached Sydney in 1804 on the transport *Coromandel*, aboard which his social status earned him a seat at the captain's table and a comfortable berth in his quarters. Armed with letters of introduction to the authorities, this pampered transportee had reasonable expectations of being offered an official posting and, as was sometimes the case, a ticket of leave or even a pardon shortly after.

But it was not to be. Governor King was not sympathetic to Grant because his connections were with the previous governor's allies. Grant had to fend for himself in the rough and tumble of life in a penal colony. Although he enjoyed support and some financial assistance from friends, his circumstances were much reduced, as they then used to say. His views of King and his administration were decidedly negative and he set about causing the governor as much trouble as possible.

While he was in the colony, Grant fell in with another gentleman convict. The only knight ever to be transported was the Irish Sir Henry Browne Hayes. Like Grant, Hayes's troubles came about through an affair of the heart. In 1797 he abducted a wealthy heiress and forced her to marry him. She was rescued shortly after and Hayes, outlawed, went into hiding. In 1800, by then in his late thirties, the fugitive decided to hand himself in, apparently believing that he would be treated leniently. He was tried and sentenced to death. After a commutation to transportation for life, he arrived in the colony in 1802. On the voyage out aboard the *Atlas*, he enjoyed the full privileges that his money enabled him to buy and frequently antagonised other gentlemen travelling on the same ship.

Hayes kept up his antipathy to authority by joining Grant and others in their opposition to Governor King. Hayes was banished to what is now the suburb of Vaucluse, where he built a grand house and plotted against the governor. Grant kept him informed of the politics of the town and in return enjoyed a sumptuous lifestyle of cultured opulence beyond the wildest fantasies of the average convict. After goading King too far, Hayes and Grant were punished with sentences to Norfolk Island and Van Diemen's Land respectively as common convicts.

Both men returned to Sydney after finishing their sentences. Hayes was later sent to the coalmines at Newcastle on several occasions for supporting King's successor, Governor Bligh, against the Rum Rebellion leaders. Fortunately, he had secured a pardon from Governor Bligh and when the rebels were replaced by Governor Lachlan Macquarie in 1810, he was free to leave. He departed two years later and, after a shipwreck in the Falkland Islands, retired to Cork, Ireland, where he died in 1832. Macquarie gave Grant a pardon and he returned to England in 1811.

Mostly forgotten today, Hayes was the focus of an enduring Sydney legend. His Vaucluse property was troubled by snakes. And, as the story goes, the Irish knight was of course familiar with the tale of St Patrick ridding Ireland of reptiles and concluded that it would be helpful to surround his colonial home with soil from the old country. With his great wealth Hayes was able to arrange for a large cargo of Irish peat to be dispatched to him in Sydney. The peat was unloaded, along with numerous barrels of Irish whiskey that Hayes was smuggling into the colony. They say that the peat was duly placed all around his house and had the desired effect. As, no doubt, did the whiskey.

A generation or so later, gentlemen were still being transported to New South Wales. Charles Cozens was a sergeant in the Royal Horse Guards sentenced to seven years (some sources say fourteen years) for using threatening language to a senior officer. Although a non-commissioned officer, the Welsh Cozens was educated, opinionated and considered himself to be a gentleman. He kept a diary of his experiences aboard the transport *Woodbridge* and of his subsequent adventures in New South Wales where he disembarked in 1840 aged 24.

Cozens' background set him apart from the common ruck of prisoners and his military skills were quickly put to use as a mounted policeman stationed in the Cooma district of New South Wales. At over 1.82 metres (6 feet), Cozens was an imposing figure and carried out his duties with distinction. The further-flung regions of the colony could still be wild places at this period, as Cozens recalled in his memoir, *Adventures of a Guardsman*:

> few men travel in the bush without being armed; and the mounted police have to question every doubtful or suspicious-looking person they meet as to his civil condition, whether free or bond, and very often they find some very uncivil parties. All free persons are supposed to carry credentials about them certifying their freedom. The emigrant must be able to produce a certificate of his ship's clearance; the emancipist one who has served his conditional term, of his 'emancipation;' the 'free by servitude,' he who has served his full sentence, is required to show his 'certificate of freedom;' and the ticket of leave-holder, his printed ticket.

Cozens was fortunate that a childhood friend, Reverend Charles Brigstocke, rector of Yass Church of England, used his influence to gain him a ticket of leave. Cozens, then in Sydney, took six weeks to walk from there to Yass where he joined the local police. Cozens gained his own certificate of freedom in 1846 and returned to Britain where he published his memoir in 1848. What happened to him after that, nobody knows.

Although Cozens was, technically, a 'gentleman', he was clearly not as much of one as Hayes and Grant, an inevitable reality of the finely graduated system of class and status that British society, and so colonial Australian society, supported. When members of the gentlemanly class were punished for their crimes, they were usually able to evade the worst aspects of the convict experience. Unless, that is, they took the dangerous path of dabbling in local politics, which led Hayes and Grant to far less comfortable locations than the now affluent suburb of Vaucluse.

An Artful Dodger

In 1824, twenty-year-old William Grady went with the surveyor-general of New South Wales, John Oxley, to found a settlement at Moreton Bay. It was to be a penal establishment for the most recalcitrant convicts and, in short time, it would gather a fearsome reputation for brutality. At just 1.62 metres (5 feet 4 inches), the fair-haired Grady was listed among the convicts of the expedition variously as a 'cutter' and a 'carpenter'—a far cry from his beginnings in London's underworld just a few years earlier. It had been an eventful start to life as a convict.

At around sixteen years of age, Grady fell in with a mob of London thieves known as the West End Mayfair Gang. All the industrial cities of Britain suffered from criminal street gangs, London in particular. These organisations were the result of rapid and mostly uncontrolled urbanisation and industrial-isation. They grew out of the vast slums of working poor not paid enough to escape the grim brutality of nineteenth-century life and labour. Many young men, women and even children from this background ended up in New South Wales, usually for extended stays.

Along with others, William Grady was arrested for stealing a man's watch in 1820. The prosecutor failed to appear in court and Grady was found not guilty. But it wasn't long before he was back in court on a similar charge of 'feloniously assaulting Josiah Walden on the King's Highway'. Walden described the crime at Grady's trial:

On Saturday evening the 6th of October, about a quarter before eight o'clock, I was in James-street, Oxford-market, walking home, the prisoner came up to me under a very large lamp, he looked me in the face, and struck me a violent blow in the chest, with his fist, he then snatched my watch out, and ran away with it, I pursued him down Chandler-street, and saw him go from there up the steps into Grosvenor-market, I there lost sight of him—I saw him in custody within three or four minutes after, two men had taken him. I am confident he is the man. There was a crowd about him, I afterwards saw him at the watch-house, my watch was found by Mrs. Stanfield, I went to her house, and she gave it to me. I have it here, the glass is not broken.

Various bystanders tried to stop the young thief as he made his getaway through side streets and into the market where two men eventually apprehended him after a chase and a struggle. The policeman who took him into custody found only a small knife on him after Grady ditched his loot in the chase. He also denied that he had an accomplice in the crime.

In the face of this damning evidence, Grady simply declared, 'I am innocent. I never saw the gentleman before I was taken.' He was found guilty and sentenced to death. His gang tried, unsuccessfully, to break him out of prison but once again he was lucky and his sentence was commuted to transportation for life.

Grady arrived in Sydney in 1822 and was sent to the new facility for youthful offenders known as Carter's Barracks, where he was taught the trade of a wheelwright. His knowledge of timber cutting made him a good choice of volunteers for Oxley's Moreton Bay enterprise with the promise of a ticket of leave as reward for his services.

By 1826, Grady was back in Sydney, narrowly escaping the tenure of the notorious Moreton Bay commandant, Captain Logan. Grady did not receive his promised ticket of leave, despite petitioning the authorities through letters written on his behalf by clerks at the Hyde Park Barracks. Apart from being punished for drunkenness and absconding in 1830, earning him a week at the treadmill, Grady seems to have behaved himself and in November that year finally gained the ticket of leave he had earned. In 1837 he received a conditional pardon. This allowed him to operate essentially as a free man as long as he did not leave the colony.

What happened after that is not known but there is a surviving photograph of William Grady. It shows a wizened old man dressed in good clothes for the camera with sharp features, unsmiling lips and a hard stare.

William Grady's story was typical of thousands more youngsters dragged by the circumstances of industrial Britain into lives of desperate crime and with no expectations other than prison and possibly execution. Charles Dickens famously fictionalised these 'artful dodgers' in the classic *Oliver Twist*. It was published fifteen years after William Grady sailed for New South Wales but picked up on the same circumstances that led him to that fate.

In those years and for the rest of the nineteenth century, Britain's youthful criminals continued along the same path as William Grady. Criminal gangs proliferated, frequently battling each other in the streets and fuelling the fears of the respectable classes. The courts continued to banish many while the penal transportation system lasted. After that, a growing market for orphaned and unwanted children developed. Children feared to be at risk were gathered up by philanthropic and religious groups, often supported by governments, and sent to institutions around the empire, particularly in Australia. Although times and circumstances changed, unaccompanied child immigration programs continued into the 1980s. The crimes committed in many of those places against some of those children are still coming to light.

RED TAPE AND BLUE DOTS

The convict system was full of what we would call 'red tape', involving record keeping, lists and forms for everything and anything, including rewarding those who captured runaway convicts. The Colonial Secretary's Office in Sydney regularly published information of this sort in the *New South Wales Government Gazette*, in this case misnumbered by some long-forgotten clerical error:

COLONIAL SECRETARY'S OFFICE, SYDNEY, 13th APRIL, 1832.
REWARDS FOR APPREHENDING RUNAWAYS.

HIS Excellency the Governor in Council having taken into consideration the system of pecuniary rewards hitherto adopted in this Colony for the apprehension of Runaway Convicts, is pleased to direct that the following regulations be established, and those now in force annulled, from and after the 30th day of April instant :—

There followed a detailed list of crimes and fines as well as not one but two forms to be completed by a justice of the peace and a magistrate.

Faced with these rules and regulations, many would-be bounty hunters might have decided to let absconding convicts run free. Lists of convicts who did make a break for freedom, also published in the *Government Gazette*, contained detailed descriptions of those wanted. These give an insight into a very different, closed world that existed at the opposite extreme of the official system.

Thomas Sullivan, number 36-1506, was a 26-year-old groom who went missing from Hyde Park Barracks in September 1836. His description reflects the level of bodily detail typically documented in the records of the system. He was:

> 5 feet 2 and a half inches [1.59 m], fair ruddy comp, light sandy brown hair, grey eyes, red whiskers, perpendicular scar over right eyebrow, I N R I and crucifix inside lower right arm, Ts IHS inside lower left arm, ESTSPS in German Text, and anchor, back of same, four blue dots back of left hand, ring on middle and third fingers of same, from Hyde Park Barracks, since September 7.

Others were similarly described, sometimes down to the distinguishing feature of a 'hairy chest'.

It was not only male convicts who attempted to escape. Fanny Conly (probably Connelly), number 33-11 from County Mayo in Ireland, took off for the second time in October 1836. The 1.5 metre (4 foot 11 inch) housemaid was 34 years old with a 'sallow and freckled comp., dark brown hair, hazel eyes, nose cocked, three blue dots back of right hand'. She had fled from an R. Williams in Sydney.

Fanny's 'blue dots' were typical convict tattoos. These, like some of the numerous tattoos on Thomas Sullivan, were often of personal, secret or otherwise obscure significance. These included names of loved ones, religious symbols, astrological signs, ships, anchors, mermaids, birds, snakes, flowers, skeletons and just about anything else, including a vagabond's map with advice for tramps on the road. They might appear on any part of the body, including areas usually hidden such as the backside, groin and even the penis in some cases.

Exactly what the blue dots represented is unclear, despite speculations that they signified membership of particular criminal fraternities. All that is known is that dots were a popular tattoo motif on eighteenth- and nineteenth-century convicts, a very different way of marking identity compared with official red-tape forms.

THE FELONRY OF NEW SOUTH WALES

One of the many differences between the British and Australian legal systems was that in colonial New South Wales it was possible for convicted felons to practise law after their 'emancipation'. During the first 30 years of settlement, legal practitioners in New South Wales were all ex-convicts. That changed as British judges arrived in the colony and began applying English legal principles to the administration of colonial justice. By then, there were complaints about corruption, which were given support in the publication of a book titled *The Felonry of New South Wales*

(1837) by an ex-soldier, agriculturist and one-time magistrate named James Mudie.

By 'felonry', Mudie meant the entire convict and ex-convict population of the colony, which was itself a unique society, as Mudie put it: 'The population of New South Wales, in its constituent parts, forms a community essentially differing, morally, legally, and politically, from any other community in the world.' Mudie was highly critical of the governance of the colony, basing his opinions on his extended residence from 1822 to 1836 as a farmer in the Hunter Valley. There, he was a heavy employer of convict labour and spent seven years as a magistrate, hearing cases and dispensing his brand of justice. He came to the very strong opinion that, basically, once a convict always a convict and railed against the many financial and social successes of those who had been transported to the penal colony.

Mudie was a supporter of Governor Ralph Darling, a stern disciplinarian and mightily unpopular with convicts and ex-convicts. When Darling finished his term in 1831 and returned to England, he and his wife were pursued by a mob of convicts yelling insults and waving a bloody boar's head on a stick at the porthole of Mrs Darling's cabin. The convicts were said to be working for the noted emancipist, William Wentworth, a prominent member of the ex-convict fraternity then engaged in what was effectively a power struggle between the 'emancipists' and the governor.

Darling was succeeded as governor by Major-General Sir Richard Bourke who, Mudie claimed, was too soft on the convict and ex-convict population and who had not renewed his term as a magistrate. Would the felonry take over the prison? This was the nub of Mudie's concerns. He believed they had already done so and his book was designed to bring this to the attention of the monarch, parliament and anyone else who might take notice.

Mudie's book is a product of colonial politics in the early nineteenth century. It brims over with his moral outrage and his dislike of almost everyone except Governor Darling. He rakes over old gossip, scandal and crimes, including one case that especially galled him involving a convict named William Watt.

Born in Scotland but convicted in England of embezzlement, Watt arrived in 1828. His education and clerical experience immediately placed him in a desirable clerical position in which he soon earned his ticket of leave. He was then employed as the subeditor of the *Sydney Gazette* newspaper, which he soon came to run due to the owner's alcoholism. Watt pursued a policy of publishing articles arguing that other convicts and free emigrants were moral equals, a position that infuriated many, especially Mudie. When Watt obtained some libellous copy about Mudie from another newspaper, he mailed it anonymously to Mudie in an attempt to embarrass the rival newspaper. The ploy backfired and Watt was tried for stealing. A jury composed mostly of discharged convicts soon found him not guilty but, in his defence, Watt charged his rival with 'the most malignant and false aspersions upon the character of the author of this work'. Mudie had him dragged before the magistrate and:

> charged him, with being a man of infamous character and a habitual liar, living in a state of adultery with a female runaway convict, and with having falsely slandered the complainant during his defence before the supreme court,

on which occasion he not only attributed his own situation to the persecutions of the complainant, but even alleged that the complainant had been guilty of murdering his convict servants.

But this pursuit of Watt was unsuccessful, enraging the ex-magistrate even more. Mudie then sued Watt's boss, the publisher of the *Sydney Gazette*, for libel.

During that case, it came out that Watt was conducting a long-term relationship with convicted highway robber, Jemima (Mary) Chapman during which they 'had issue!'. Such relationships were commonplace in the colony, but were technically illegal, a point made much of by a vengeful Mudie in his book, pointing out that Jemima, Watt's 'lewd companion was a runaway convict and (an Amazonian who had been convicted in England of the unfeminine crime of highway robbery) a transport for life'.

Mudie raked over the entrails of these colonial controversies and proceedings in obsessive detail, most of which would have been of little interest to his intended readers. He accused Watt of bigamy, which may or may not have been the case, but he was most incensed with the very unlikely proposition that 'through his *secret connection with functionaries of the government,* Watt actually *ruled the colony*' (original italics).

In the end, Watt was banished to Port Macquarie where, in a move that further provoked Mudie's spleen, he married the widow of his old newspaper boss. He continued to make trouble for the government, eventually losing his ticket of leave and being sent to labour in a road gang, a dire punishment for a gentleman convict. He tried to escape, was captured and flogged. Watt was drowned in 1837, aged 30. Jemima would later marry a convict in the Bathurst area, with whom she would have three children. She died in 1845 aged 32 years.

Mudie also raged against other convicts who had done well in the colony. Like most of the upper classes of the period he was a moralist: 'Each convict ship carries out a herd of females of all ages, and of every gradation in vice, including a large proportion of prostitutes of all grades, from the veriest trull to the fine madam.' He slandered the paid magistrates, police, military guards, the composition of colonial juries, the political system and crown law officers. Mudie himself, of course, 'has always been in the condition of a gentleman, and in the habit of associating with gentlemen'. He provided numerous references and endorsements to support his immodest assertion.

The Felonry of New South Wales was, unsurprisingly, not well received in Sydney. It was widely known that Mudie had himself arrived in the colony as a free but penniless business failure and, through his well-placed connections, soon amassed a large amount of granted land in the Hunter region. This he developed through exploitation of convict labour provided mostly at government expense. During his tenure as a magistrate under Governor Ralph Darling he was known as an enthusiastic flogger. So there was a deep reservoir of local resentment waiting for him when he unwisely returned to Sydney in 1840. He was publicly horsewhipped by the son of a judge he had defamed in his book. The damages awarded against Mudie's assailant in the ensuing prosecution were quickly paid by public subscription, a measure of the man's low standing in the community. Still fulminating about the felonry of New

South Wales, Mudie returned once more to England and died there in 1852, little lamented.

'I AM NOT A BAD MAN AT HEART'

In October 1867 the Sydney newspaper *Empire* carried a story that purported to be the autobiography of a convict. The man was not identified but the tale he told, true or not, included just about every twist and turn a criminal life might take at that time.

The convict said he was serving time in Darlinghurst Gaol for an unspecified robbery. His story began with the frequent mistake of falling into bad company, in his case in Norwich, England. He was transported for seven years after being found guilty of a robbery there:

> From Norwich I was removed to the Justitia hulk, Woolwich, thence to the Eurylus hulk at Chatham, thence on board a convict ship which conveyed me, twelve months after conviction, to Point Puer, Tasman's Peninsula, Van Diemen's Land. Point Puer was then the penal receptacle for juvenile offenders. I was fifteen years of age when I landed at Point Puer, where I remained for six years . . .

At Point Puer, the young convict suffered 'a total number of 528 lashes, and 74 days solitary confinement on bread and water'. Eventually turned loose in Hobart at the expiry of his sentence, the convict engaged with a ship's captain to work his passage back to England. But before he could embark, he met an old prison acquaintance who fooled him into being an accomplice in a mugging. He was nicked for another seven years to be served at Port Arthur. After a few months, he escaped:

I was the leader, rushed the constable, and took away his firelock, and succeeded in getting to Norfolk Bay, nine miles [14.5 km] from Port Arthur. But we were still on Tasman's Peninsula. We had to elude not only the constable sent after us and the out-station constables, but the vigilance of sixteen bloodhounds and mastiffs, besides a detachment of military and police at Eagle-hawk Neck before we could reach Forester's Peninsula. We had to pass another constable's station at the Sounds, and another at East Bay Neck before we could reach the mainland. Even then, if successful, we should be in rags and tatters, compelled to hide ourselves in the bush by day, and rob the first farmhouse we came to at night for clothing and food. We resolved to reach the main land, or perish in the attempt.

The convict and his three companions were forced to swim or float through shark-infested waters to avoid the line of dogs guarding Eaglehawk Neck, Port Arthur's forbidding disincentive to escape attempts. He was the only survivor of the sharks and the cold waters. Too exhausted to run, the police found him on the shore and took him back to prison. He was given eighteen months to be served in chains and removed to the feared Norfolk Island.

My first sentence at this 'Ocean Hill' was ten days solitary confinement for talking to a fellow prisoner on the works. My second was six months in heavy 36lb. [16 kg] leg irons for talking to a soldier of H. M. 99th regiment. My third sentence was 150 lashes and fifty six days solitary confinement, three hours on the gag—a sort of choking arrangement—seven weeks fastened to a massive ring bolt in a dark cell, besides being severely beaten by constables, for striking an overseer named H—s. I pleaded the overseer's tyranny in extenuation of my offence but was laughed at. After this I was removed from the gaol to the settlement, but was compelled to work in long trumpeter iron (18lb [8 kg]) with the gaol gang.

These punishments were interspersed with others for minor infractions of the many rules on Norfolk:

During the time I was under these sentences I received inter-mediate sentences of flogging and solitary confinement, too numerous to particularise. Throwing down my cap at the gaoler, fifty lashes. Having the sign of tobacco in my mouth, fifty lashes. Being in possession of a bar of highly-polished steel, to wit, a needle, fifty lashes. For insolence in looking significantly at a constable, fifty lashes. Fighting, fifty lashes. For unlawfully holding possession of three needlesful of thread, six days solitary confinement. For having possession of a copper button, thirty-six lashes. For talking in school, first offence thirty-six lashes; second offence, fifty lashes, and, so on.

After attempting to murder a tyrannical overseer with an axe, the convict was given twelve months in heavy irons.

At this time, Norfolk Island was under the control of John Price, known to convicts as 'the Demon'. He would be beaten to death on a Melbourne hulk a few years later after unwisely allowing a mob of prisoners to form too close by. On Norfolk, his reign was typified by belittling prisoners and absurd punishments:

If any prisoner had a toe rag in his boot, one month in irons. For swearing at bullocks when driving them, fifty lashes. For smiling at yourself, or to any one, fourteen days solitary confinement. For passing an overseer without saluting him, thirty six lashes. It was difficult to distinguish a constable from an overseer. There was no distinctive uniform. Wearing shoes without being marked, two months in irons. For sewing a button on your clothing thirty-six lashes.

After nearly five years of this, the convict was unexpectedly transferred back to the Hobart Penitentiary where he was hired out to a settler as a labourer. Overworked and kept on starvation rations, he stole some potatoes and was sent back to the Penitentiary for six months, including a couple of months on the cruel treadmill. After this, he was again hired out:

> to a Vandemonian 'Soogee Settler' on the usual passholder terms. A soogee settler is one of the respectable class who wants as much as possible for as little as possible. On the second day of my service at this place a large basketful of dirty linen was brought to me to wash. I suggested to my mistress the impropriety of a man washing this soiled linen. I was at once taken before a magistrate. 'Do you refuse?' roared the magistrate. 'I do' said I. 'Three days solitary confinement, and,' said the justice, 'sorry I am that I can't flog you.'

He escaped and 'took to the bush', robbing stores until he was caught and sentenced to transportation for life at Port Arthur. Here, he was forced to work in chains and suffered solitary confinement. After another escape attempt, the now broken convict was again punished with solitary and working in heavy chains.

> At this time Mr. Boyd, the Commandant, began to notice me, and certainly treated me in a manner that, years before, would have done good. I was now too old, hard, and callous. My spirit had been broken at Norfolk Island. I had no faith in humanity, in kind words I anticipated treachery.

After another eight years, the convict received a ticket of leave and was again hired out, only to finally succeed in absconding. He managed to reach Sydney and after 'months wandering about restless, sometimes in work, but I came across some companions, fell, and now I am where I shall be safe for eighteen months to come'. While this sounds almost 'too bad to be true', it paints a picture of the miseries that could be inflicted on victims of the penal system in New South Wales, Norfolk Island and Van Diemen's Land.

An Habitual Criminal

Mercevina Caulfield, known as Mina, was the servant of a wealthy Dublin merchant's wife when she was transported in 1848. She was a pretty young woman, around 1.65 metres (5 feet 5 inches) tall, with black hair and light hazel eyes. Her crime was stealing the rich fabrics and jewels of her mistress, bringing her a seven-year stretch in Van Diemen's Land.

Like many, if not all, convicts, Mina did well in the colony. She kept out of trouble, married free sailor Frances Jury a few years after her arrival and received a ticket of leave in 1851. She and Frances would produce many children during their marriage, which sadly ended with Frances's accidental death. The family was then living in Adelaide and immediately fell into poverty. By 1868 she and the children were struggling to get by in Melbourne. Then, something happened that changed their lives forever.

In 1855, Roger Charles Tichborne, son of Sir James Tichborne, Bart., disappeared when his ship sank while sailing to England from Rio de Janeiro. There had been survivors, some of whom were rumoured to have been taken to Melbourne after their rescue. Roger Tichborne's grieving mother, unwilling to accept that her beloved son and heir was dead, placed an advertisement on the front page of *The Sydney Morning Herald* in July 1865 promising 'A handsome reward will be given to any person who can furnish such information as will discover the fate of Roger Charles Tichborne.'

A few months later, Lady Tichborne heard from a butcher in Wagga Wagga, New South Wales, by the name of Tom Castro. Although the rotund Tom was larger than the slight Tichborne and spoke no French, in which language Tichborne was fluent, he insisted on the truth of his story. Lady Tichborne asked Castro to come to England. He arrived there in December 1866 and convinced many family and friends that he was the missing heir. He began living in style with the English elite on Lady Tichborne's bounty.

But not everyone was convinced. Investigations revealed that Castro was, in fact, Arthur Orton from Wapping in East London. When Lady Tichborne died in 1868, some family members brought a civil case against Orton. The trial and accompanying press frenzy lasted almost a year and led to Orton being charged for perjury. It was necessary for witnesses to be brought to England from Australia to testify for or against the identity of the Tichborne claimant, as Orton was usually called.

Mina had a connection by marriage to Orton and was paid to journey to London to testify in his trial. She had known Orton in Hobart—though he claimed never to have been there—and had even lent him money that he had never repaid. She testified, 'He is Arthur Orton, sir, to whom I lent the money.'

Orton was found guilty and controversially sentenced to fourteen years hard labour, of which he eventually served ten. He only once confessed to his imposture, and quickly recanted, insisting until he died in poverty that he was the rightful heir to the Tichborne fortune. In 1898 he was buried as 'Sir Roger Tichborne', the name appearing on his death certificate and on the coffin plate.

During the trial, Mina had taken up with another witness and lodged with him at the Ship hotel. The couple left without checking out and stole belongings as they went their separate ways. Mina travelled north with her share. The rest of her life was a succession of crime, capture, imprisonment and reoffending, including some bold deceptions.

Under one of her many aliases, she wrote to both the Earl of Kilmorey and the Duke of Edinburgh with a convincing sob story and managed to extract from them the then very substantial sum of £20 (about the equivalent of $3000 today). This earned her a year of hard labour, a relatively short term compared with the usual seven-year sentences she received for most of her other infractions.

Mina's assumed names kept her true identity from the authorities in the many different locations where she was apprehended. But she eventually became an officially registered 'habitual criminal', claiming her birthplace as Australia. In 1885 she was in prison again for more stealing and imposture, this time targeting the Freemasons and the mayor of Stoke-on-Trent. She was discharged just before Christmas in 1889. Her dark hair had turned to grey, her face and arms scarred, and she was missing some teeth. Her occupation was entered in the discharge records as 'pianoforte teacher', though she seems to have preferred robbing to teaching music and continued to offend.

By 1890 she was wanted in her native Ireland as well as for thefts in England. But, as far as the records go, she was never apprehended and no more is heard of her. Perhaps she continued deceiving under other aliases? Or perhaps she gave up her life of crime and became a respectable citizen?

It would be nice to think that she managed to return to Australia to be reunited with her surviving abandoned children. Her oldest son 'who was the principal support to me' died before Mina left for England. Some of the children went into care or became wards of the state, several absconding when they got the chance. Those who survived into adulthood went on to various careers in the railways, farming and mining. It seems unlikely that Mina and her surviving children were ever reunited and she probably died in Ireland.

Police mugshot of Phil 'the Jew' Jeffs, a canny crook who built a small fortune as the proprietor of numerous sly grog clubs in 1920s and '30s Sydney.

2

CRIME SCENES

MURDERING GULLY ROAD

Table Cape is an extinct volcano near Wynyard in north-west Tasmania. The area was developed by the Van Diemen's Land Company in the 1820s and thirty years or so later was home to a small community of settlers. But not everyone got along. Samuel Oak(es) and his family had an ongoing feud with their neighbour, William Bannon. Tensions reached a fatal climax in 1858.

Samuel Oakes, said to be a quiet and respectable man, left home around six on the morning of 5 May. His wife, Lydia, accompanied him far enough to see William Bannon at work on his property before she said goodbye to her husband and returned home. The next time she saw Samuel he was a bloodied corpse.

Bannon and Oakes had been at odds for two years. The main issue seemed to be about Oakes's pigs, which sometimes wandered onto Bannon's land. Most properties were unfenced at this time and roaming stock were a common feature of colonial bush life. But Bannon, incensed by the trespassing swine, had developed a dark enmity towards Oakes. Only a few weeks earlier he had been 'bound over to keep the peace', an early form of apprehended violence order, after threatening to shoot his neighbour.

After leaving his wife that morning, Samuel Oakes made his way to the property of George Shekelton, a local justice of the peace, where he was given three sovereigns, presumably for work done. He left Shekelton's around 10 am, heading home but never reached his house. Next morning Lydia, concerned that Samuel had not returned, went looking for him. Along the road she found his hat, spotted with blood. She rushed to Shekelton's with the hat and he quickly set off with two other locals to find out what had happened.

> I noticed a tract leading from the road as if made by some substance being dragged through the ferns, and following it we discovered the body of the deceased; when we found the body none of us touched it; we only removed some ferns with which it was covered; the ferns had been partially burnt; the first part of the body I saw was the legs, over which the fire had burned and gone out; I did not uncover any other portion of the body then; the legs were scorched; we then left the body . . .

Bannon was the obvious suspect and was quickly arrested. At the trial the examining doctor testified to the brutality of Samuel's murder:

I made an examination of the body externally; a portion of the flesh and muscles of the legs and thighs were burnt away, and the bones of the legs were charred; there was a wound on the lower part of the wrist on the right arm; the same wound extended along the inner side of the fore arm, having all the appearance of a gun-shot wound; I saw a mark under the right breast, 3 or 4 inches [8 or 10 cm] in length, and ½ an inch [1 cm] in width, presenting the appearance of having been produced by a ball which had glanced off from the body; the face was much shattered, apparently from gun-shot wounds, and the blows of some heavy instrument; one of the principal gun-shot wounds entered under the left ear and passed out under the right eye; another mark of a shot or ball I observed had passed through the substance of the brain.

The doctor then described:

several marks on the face, as if made by the muzzle of the gun; one of them in particular had fractured the lower jaw, on the left side, and had driven several teeth into the mouth. I opened the scull [sic] and found the external injuries had broken up the substance of the brain, so that death must have been almost instantaneous; the shot hole over the right eye would probably have been caused by a small bullet; the gun produced in Court I should say might have caused the marks on deceased's face; the stone which was found might have caused the battered appearance of the scull [sic]; the wound on the right side might have been caused by the butt end of a gun.

Samuel Oakes had been shot several times and also brutally beaten with the butt of an angry murderer's gun and a stone.

Perhaps not surprisingly, Lydia gave a confused testimony, though she was clear about Bannon's dislike for her dead husband and his family:

> My husband and the prisoner had not been on good terms this two years. One day, about a week before the 5th May, the prisoner met me on the road, and said, 'You —— old faggot; I'll murder you, I will.' With that I ran away. He said he would make a total massacre upon me and my family.

Other locals testified that they had seen Bannon burning a pair of moleskin trousers on the day in question. Police had later found buttons of the type used on these trousers in the ashes of his fireplace. Although the evidence was circumstantial, it did not look good for Bannon. His solicitor addressed the jury, rebutting the evidence given. He must have been convincing. The twelve-man jury did not even retire to consider their verdict after the judge directed them to find in favour of the prisoner. William Bannon was declared not guilty of the brutal murder and immediately discharged.

No one else was ever brought to justice for the slaughter of Samuel Oakes. He was 'interred in the burial ground on [sic] the township (Wynyard) on Sunday morning, and was attended by all the respectable people in the neighbourhood'. His only memorial seems to be the name of the place where he was killed—Murdering Gully Road.

DANGEROUS DIGGINGS

There are conflicting views of life on the colonial goldfields. It was mostly a pretty rough-and-tumble affair, with driven men obsessed about finding their fortunes. On the other hand, a good many diggers went prospecting with wives and families and people were usually quick to establish at least a semblance of law, order and civil society. But some goldfields were notoriously violent, with names like Choke 'em Gully, Deadman's Flat and Murderer's Hill in Victoria giving a hint of what went on at these places and others like them all around Australia.

Policing and authority were sometimes slow to catch up with the hordes of hopeful diggers rushing to isolated locations where a nugget had been found, or simply when a rumour of gold arose. Diggers were forced to take their security into their own hands to protect whatever they had won from the many who wanted to take it away from them.

A Polish digger on the Victorian goldfields, Seweryn Korzelinski, recollected an attack on some Dutch miners. One night, he and others heard a commotion and ran to the tent where the Dutchmen were camped. When they arrived they found:

> They had one bushranger tied up with ropes, his head split open with a pickhandle and the other bushranger was dead. The Dutch boys told us that they had spent the night behind their beds instead of on them and when the strangers armed with knives entered, surprised them with a sudden attack. The dead man was unceremoniously buried and the other handed over to the police commissioner.

And that, it seems, was that.

Korzelinski also wrote about the dangerous practice of 'shooting off' that could result in criminal charges. Diggers often went armed during the day with a pistol containing one bullet. After work they were in the habit of firing off the round:

> [sending] bullets in all directions, even into other miners' tents. Sleeping miners have been killed by stray bullets. I nearly had it happen to me in Bendigo. By the sound of the passing bullet I knew it was close to my head for it did not moan like a high flying shot, rather it whispered by and suddenly the sound ceased as the bullet hit the ground.

Mia Mia, just over 50 kilometres (30 miles) south of Bendigo, was another hazardous spot. A First Nations man named Buckley was brutally beaten and drowned in a waterhole by two diggers in 1862. Three years earlier, a digger named—among other monikers—Bowen got into a fight with a man named Dandow. The fisticuffs went better for Bowen, so Dandow left the tent and went to fetch an American axe, a tool with a short, broad blade. He rushed back to Bowen's tent and plunged the weapon into his opponent's chest. Bowen went down and the axeman stuck him again, this time across the skull. The wounds inflicted were terrible. As well as losing part of an ear, the victim's head was cleaved apart and a great gash split his chest. Not expected to live, Bowen was given medical attention. A few days later an astonished doctor reported on his condition:

> Notwithstanding that the brain protrudes through the opening made in the skull by the axe, he is perfectly sensible,

and converses in as rational a manner as though he had not been touched. In order to convey a clear idea of this astonishing fact, it must be stated that the size of the wound is about equal to the top of an average sized basin. On the bandages being removed by Dr Candiottis the other day, we could plainly see the pulsation of the blood in the vessels of the brain. The wound in the chest is healing rapidly, and all danger from that source is at an end.

Claim jumping was another source of goldfields violence. The jumpers entered a mine at night, while the legal lessees were in their tents. Next morning there was usually a confrontation, difficult for the proper miners to win as the thieves were well entrenched inside. A variant of this method was 'undermining', digging a tunnel into the mine and taking over that way. Violence was an almost inevitable consequence of this lawless behaviour.

As well as violence, swindling was endemic to goldfields life. The *Argus* newspaper published a guide to the kinds of sharp practices that hopeful diggers could expect to encounter. There were plenty. Dishonest scales were a favourite. The beam scales used to weigh gold were easily fiddled by lightly moving the balance point:

In a matter of such value as gold, one eighth [3 mm], or even a sixteenth [1.5 mm], of an inch difference in this respect would yield a most enormous profit to a man purchasing numerous small parcels every day; and we hear that there are many such scales in use by which extensive fraud are practised.

The writer of the article, obviously well versed in the scams described, also outlined another trick, 'a sort of gold buying leger-de-main'. This one worked when the digger threw his bag of dust and, possibly, nuggets, on one end of the buyer's scales. The buyer was a busy man, picking up weights and dropping them on the other end of the scale and keeping up a patter designed to confuse the unsuspecting digger:

> . . . for the express purpose of swindling him out of a few ounces of his precious metal. 'Seven—and four's eleven— and three's fourteen—and six is nineteen'—says the broker in his rattling off-hand style—'and six is twenty-three—and eight's thirty-one—and nine's thirty-nine ounces—and ten pennyweights—thirty-nine ounces ten pennyweights, Sir; one hundred and eighteen pounds ten shillings; here's your money, Sir;' and the gold is summarily pitched upon another heap previously purchased; and the poor, bustled, hurried digger leaves the shop, staring and doubtful, but swindled out of eight or ten pounds worth of his hard earnings.

Official licensing of gold brokers was the only way to stop these frauds and, it was argued, 'afford a very fair chance of checking the rascalities of some of the trade'.

The most dramatic goldfields crimes were hold-ups of the gold escort. Diggers with a strike had to transport their gold to a city to get a decent price for it. This meant they had to leave their claims, losing valuable working time and also increasing the likelihood of claim jumping. The government and private interests organised armed gold escorts to give the gold safe carriage to market.

In 1853 the escort from the McIvor field near Heathcote, Victoria, was relieved of at least £6000 worth of gold near Mia Mia, Victoria— a significant amount in today's money. Enraged diggers soon heard the news and formed a large posse to retrieve their hard-won treasure. But without success. Leaving four badly wounded guards behind them the bushrangers simply vanished. Most were later captured as they attempted to flee the colony, apart from the leader who was never caught.

The most famous escort robbery took place at Eugowra, New South Wales, in 1862. Led by Frank Gardiner, the gang got away with £14,000 worth of gold and banknotes. Three years later, some members of the same gang, together with new recruits tried to rob the Araluen goldfields escort near Braidwood but were detected and the attempt failed. There were many others. Wherever significant quantities of gold were found and extracted, there were those keen to steal it.

Were the colonial goldfields as violent and crime-ridden as they are often portrayed? Opinions differed, then and now. It seems that some fields were more violent than others. It is also likely that a lot of criminal activity was simply unreported, particularly before policing the fields became more organised. As the Russian proverb goes: 'It's only a crime if you get caught.'

SYDNEY COVES IN 'FRISCO

Gold has been at the root of crime ever since the precious ore was first used as a store of value. Australia's fascination with extracting the stuff began in the early 1850s and has continued ever since, producing crimes and criminals in abundance. But before that, some Australian criminals exported themselves to America where they established a notorious criminal underworld in the heaving gold-rush city of San Francisco.

The Californian rushes exploded from 1848 and attracted large numbers of optimistic prospectors from around the world, Australians among them. It is estimated that more than 11,000 people sailed from Australia to California from April 1849 to May 1851. Many of these emigrants lived in a squalid clutch of ramshackle wooden shanties and abandoned hulks at the bottom of San Francisco's Telegraph Hill. This waterfront area of pubs, brothels and cheap lodgings soon became known as Sydney Town or Sydney Valley and was populated by a diverse community of sailors, wharf labourers, tradesmen, washerwomen and domestic servants, all struggling through gritty lives. It was also home to a notorious criminal gang known as the Sydney Ducks or the Sydney Coves.

In their distinctive duck, or canvas, trousers, cabbage tree hats and speaking the 'flash' lingo, the Australians were a distinctive group among the multicultural mayhem of the neighbourhood. Almost half the gang were of Irish origin, casualties of the Great Irish Famine of the 1840s and early '50s. Most of them had been convicts in Australia and they wasted no time getting down to business in their new surroundings, including extortion, shanghaiing sailors, thieving, gambling and all varieties of violence. They were also heavily involved in the sex trade.

The Ducks followed the well-tried truth of speculative mineral rushes—the best way to get rich is not to dig holes in the ground but to provide necessities and services to those who did. The large number of mostly male miners passing through San Francisco wanted to be sheltered, fed and provided with prostitutes. The Australians were only too pleased to supply the demand. One of their shipments of women from Australia caused a near riot when the *Adirondack* docked in July 1851. Miners fought each other to get aboard the ship where a hundred women were said to be waiting to greet them.

As well as their more or less legal activities in the sex trade, the Ducks had more dubious sidelines. They became especially notorious for the novel technique of setting fire to buildings and stealing their contents after the residents had fled in terror. This not only deprived victims of their belongings but caused vast amounts of damage as flames roared through the highly flammable buildings that made up most of the city.

In December 1849 a high-class saloon refused to pay the Ducks protection money. The fire they set in retaliation destroyed large sectors of the city and caused more than a million dollars in damage. Police arrested seventy suspects; forty-eight of them were from Australia. Another conflagration later wreaked havoc to the tune of $12 million, destroying eighteen city blocks and more than 2000 buildings. The Ducks had now gone well beyond the usual confines of crime and had become a threat to the existence of San Francisco and its citizens.

Dissatisfied with the efforts of corrupt and inept city authorities to contain the Ducks, the seriously disgruntled people of the city took matters into their own hands. A letter was sent to the newspaper suggesting a 'committee of safety' should be formed because 'it is now rendered positive and beyond a doubt, that there is in this city an organized band of villains who are determined to destroy the city'. This eventually became the Committee of Vigilance and the vigilantes who formed it wasted little time in carrying out their self-appointed duties.

Sydney Duck John Jenkins was hanged in June 1851 after being found with a stolen safe. James 'Long Jim' Stuart, a leader of the gang, was executed the following month for murder. In August Samuel Whittaker and Robert Mackenzie (McKinley) were dispatched together for 'various heinous crimes'. Thousands came to watch. All four were ex-convicts from New South Wales. Before they were executed, the prisoners were made to confess. They all lied about their convict pasts. As well as the hangings, other Ducks were flogged, run out of town or handed over to the proper authorities. Fourteen were deported back to Australia.

One of those arrested, though not hanged or deported, was Mary Ann Hogan. She spun the vigilantes a yarn about being taken to New South Wales by her English parents as a toddler and later operating a pub in Sydney before travelling with her husband to San Francisco. Some of this was more or less true, but her real name was Mary Collier, transported at the age of seventeen in 1831 with a seven-year sentence for stealing three sovereigns from a man. She married ticket-of-leave holder Michael Hogan in 1836.

Short, with a fair complexion, brown hair and brown eyes, Mary was now in her late thirties and kept public houses in San Francisco. By her own account, when Hogan lost their money on bad land deals and departed 'on business' to Oregon, she took up with two of the Sydney Ducks who would suffer the ire of the vigilantes. Her confession, together with those of the others, painted a murky picture of gambling, theft, violence and sex, fuelled mostly by the greed for gold.

Violent and illegal though this rough justice was, it worked. By 1852 the Ducks were mostly gone and the crime rate went right down. For a while. The committee was revived in 1856 to deal with another crime wave, though not one created by Australians. They had been mostly forgotten and the area once known as Sydney Town was more usually being called the name it has since become known by—the Barbary Coast, a reference to the area of North Africa notorious for slave trading and piracy.

MIDNIGHT IN MELBOURNE

What behaviour should be criminal? This question has troubled all societies and each has answered it in different ways. Apart from acts of violence and robbery there are many human pastimes and pleasures that may or may not be legal at any particular time and place.

In 1860s Melbourne, the mingling of everyday—or every night—life and illicit goings-on was frequently noted by many, especially the press. In 1868, Marcus Clarke, destined for fame as the author of the classic *For the Term of His Natural Life*, accompanied the police on a tour through the gaslit main streets and darker alleys of midnight Melbourne. He vividly reported the swirling carnality and crime played out in the flickering shadows.

By this time, the rowdy gold-rush era was in the recent past and newly enriched diggers were no longer watering their horses with champagne or washing themselves in expensive

French wine. Nor were they reeling from pub to pub or being found stabbed to death with their pockets emptied. There was now a greater sense of public order and 'The dens of infamy and vice, which were for a long time the disgrace of the city, and which were used as schools to train the young of either sex for the gallows and the hulks, are rapidly being destroyed by the demand made upon house-room by the respectable working population.'

These civilising influences had the effect of confining 'the most degraded and utterly criminal' to the dark alleys and now-famous Melbourne lanes. But the main streets still provided plenty of opportunity for licensed and unlicensed behaviour. Casinos and theatres lined Bourke Street, all amply served by bars that provided various services. The series of bars known as the Portico was one of the most popular. Entering through iron gates:

> . . . we find ourselves in a large hall, open at one end to the street, and closed at the other by the pit and stall entrances to the theatre. The curtain has just fallen upon the piece of the evening, and the crowds from gallery, pit, and stalls are refreshing themselves before the farce. On each side are covered bars, where some twenty or thirty girls dispense, with lightning rapidity, the 'brandies hot,' 'glass of ale,' 'cold without,' 'colonial wine,' 'nobblers for five,' 'whiskeys hot,' 'sherry and bitters,' 'two glasses claret,' 'nobblers for two,' 'dark brandy,' &c, which expectorating crowds of men and boys call for on all sides. White-coated waiters shoot like meteors through the mass, bearing coffee to some of the more quiet frequenters of the place.

Some patrons made use of the establishment's other possibilities, which included fencing stolen goods and:

> [a] little door where a woman in blue silk and white lace is standing. That door leads to the 'ladies' refreshment-room,' but is known to its fast frequenters by another name. The women who assemble there are well dressed and orderly. They live for the most part in adjacent streets, paying a high rent for their houses, which are usually leased and kept in order by some old woman, who is too old to attract.

The Portico was a more or less respectable establishment compared with the 'shy houses' where:

> lights glimmer through the shutters, while in some of the doorways flaunting but shabbily-dressed women peer forth, like spiders from their webs, on the look-out for prey. Most of these women are thieves as well as prostitutes; and in the fetid and dingy back premises lurk ill-looking ruffians, who are prepared to silence any opposition on the part of the not sufficiently stupefied victim.

Out in the street, bushmen from the Murray who were delivering their cattle to the metropolitan markets 'booted, breeched, and smoking violently' were 'goin' on the bust'. They jostled with groups of sewing girls and milliners' apprentices 'neatly and sometimes handsomely dressed' parading up and down the streets, reeling sailors and 'pigtailed, blue-coated, and mandarin-capped' Chinese on their way to the opium dens and gambling joints of Little Bourke Street.

All along the streets were coffee vendors, ballad sellers screeching 'noo and fav'rite melodies' while a man with a telescope sold views of Jupiter for a penny. A street preacher held a small crowd singing hymns. Before the singers finished the last chorus, urchins picked their pockets and slunk back to the shadows of Little Bourke Street where 'Dirty and draggle-tailed women begin to appear at the ends of right-of-ways, and the popular music halls have just vomited forth a crew of drunken soldiers, prostitutes, and thieves.'

Horse-drawn cabs thronged the main street, though these could be hazardous to wealth and health because the cabmen were often working with prostitutes. When a gentleman or drunken sailor took a ride, the driver would pick up the prostitute and 'frequently [succeed] in inveigling the pigeon into her house'.

The police were most interested in illegal gambling and the whereabouts of loot stolen by thieves like Nosey Samuels and fenced by the likes of Old Jacob, the most 'artistic' fence in Melbourne. His shabby pawnshop had 'a back entry, where many a case of jewellery or watches has entered, never to return again'. He negotiated a dual relationship with the thieves and the police and 'his old wife—a Tasmanian Jewess—professes much affection for the members of the D division'.

As well as monitoring the pawnshops, the detectives were careful observers of premises supposedly selling tobacco:

Tobacconists still are ablaze with lamps, and anyone who took the trouble of watching the doors closely would see many persons enter and not come out again. A great many of these shops are 'blinds.' The real trade of the place is done upstairs. The upper rooms are fitted up as gambling saloons, and the arrangements for communication with the shop below are so perfect that on a stranger attempting to enter the penetralia the 'office' is at once given by means of a wire, and all signs of the occupation removed.

The officer accompanying Clarke was Detective Fox of D Division. He was investigating, among other things, the theft of £30 from an unwary sailor as well as making his round of 'the cribs', seeking information from the likes of Dandy Sal and other well-known criminal identities. These included 'magsmen' whose 'occupation', as Fox tersely puts it, was 'kidding on the flats'. They will 'follow a man from up the country, and engage him in cards, drinking, or betting, and end by fleecing him of his money'.

Eventually, this throbbing scene of pleasure and crime fades away. By two-thirty the shops have closed and:

The streets are tenanted only by a few wretched creatures, who still wander disconsolately up and down, on the look-out for some stray victim. A few 'bar loafers' are shudderingly creeping down into the back slums, and wondering if they can get another 'nobbler o' P.B.' shouted, before they finally turn-in to their private gaspipe for a night's repose. The 'coffee stalls' are nearly deserted, and their owners are taking a snooze, preparatory to their 'early morning's business.'

A few cabs still hover about the main street but the police are no longer outnumbered by revellers and rookers. Now 'The shutters are up, and the lights in the "newspaper offices" are the only signs of industry. Melbourne is asleep, and street life is over for one night.'

WHO WAS MARY FORTUNE?

The woman who wrote some of Australia's and the world's first detective stories was long a mystery herself. Decades before Arthur Conan Doyle began penning his Sherlock Holmes tales, Mary Fortune was publishing her detective yarns in Australian newspapers. She would go on to write 500 or so crime stories, as well as novels, articles, poems and a memoir. Yet she has been almost totally forgotten. It was not until researchers began delving into the history of crime fiction that the author whose pen name was 'Waif Wanderer' (and 'WW') was slowly revealed.

Belfast-born Mary Wilson went to Canada with her parents at an early age and while still a teenager married and gave birth to a son, Joseph, in 1852. A few years later Mary and Joseph followed her father to the Victorian gold rush. Her husband did not come with her, though she continued to use her married name when she gave birth to George in 1856 while working on various goldfields and establishing herself as a writer. Before she left Canada, Mary arranged with *The Ladies' Companion* magazine to write about her experiences in Australia. She never delivered the promised articles for, as she wrote later, 'Who would write pages at fifteen shillings . . . when one paid nine shillings per day for milk, and for a "woman's" magazine, too! Nay, there was nothing of the namby-pamby elegance of ladies' literature in our stirring, hardy, and eventful life on the early goldfields.'

Mary was clearly a woman of strong character. She needed to be. It was a time when journalism and writing were seen as male activities. When she was offered a job on a goldfields newspaper on the basis of her mailed contributions, the editor cancelled the offer on discovering that she was a woman.

Joseph died in 1858, possibly from meningitis, and Mary then entered into a brief marriage to a policeman. This furthered her interest in crime as a subject for stories. Along with her many other writings of poetry, gothic romance and even a co-authored pantomime, she began to develop what would be the longest-running crime series of the period. By 1868 and a single mother, Mary was in Melbourne writing for *The Australian Journal* and developing her long-running series titled 'The detective's album'. All the time her true identity was known only to her editors and her occasional co-author, who plagiarised some of their joint efforts and published them in Britain under his own name. To the reading public Mary was just another pseudonymous, if prolific, scribbler.

Many of Mary's crime stories featured the detective Mark Sinclair, who usually narrated his cases to the readers as he leafed through albums of mugshots. Sinclair was portrayed from his youthful police cadetship in 1855, his rapid elevation to detective three years later and his subsequent career as a senior detective in the Metropolitan Force of Detectives. Like Mary, he was deeply influenced by his experience on the goldfields, where he served as a trooper policeman at Avoca. Reminiscing on this time in his life, Sinclair says, 'If I had such a thing as a heart I should fancy "Avoca" printed on it indelibly.' Despite his hard-bitten style and a touch of anti-heroic self-loathing anticipating the modern fictional detective, Sinclair was a gentleman. He dealt just as effectively with the street thugs of Melbourne as he could with crimes involving well-bred young ladies from the squattocracy.

In the story titled 'The detective's dream', published in 1886, Sinclair is recovering from a serious illness—'unhinged both in body and in mind'—when an old dream recurs from Christmases past (the story was published in the Christmas edition). His doctors insist he has a rest and a change of air and a young university student he once helped out of 'a not over respectable mess he had got into in one of our Town slums' fortuitously invites him to visit the family property at Werrimona where the young man's sister is about to be married. Werrimona is 'one of the loveliest spots the sun of Victoria shines on', but it is to be the scene of Sinclair's dark dream and an even darker tragedy.

At Werrimona, Sinclair meets the bride-to-be, the startlingly beautiful but oddly pale, cold and sad-eyed, Evelyn Pemberton. She has broken off her long-standing relationship with a local man, Edward Corwyn, in favour of Charles Kingsley, a wealthy man her own age: nineteen. Sinclair describes the groom-to-be dismissively as 'a common-place boy' and as 'a fair haired and empty-headed boy, full of chatter and vanity, good tempered, doubtless, and proud of his beautiful fiancée but no more suited as guide, guardian, and companion to such a woman than a school boy of twelve'. By contrast, the jilted Corwyn, is 27 years old, 'tall and strongly built, yet gentlemanly—nay, distinguished looking. I have seen such a man in a cavalry regiment, with a sword in his hand, and the air of one born to do great deeds.'

Why has the queenly Evelyn dropped the manly Corwyn for the well-heeled but feckless youth, Sinclair wonders? And why is Corwyn taking it so well, remaining good friends with Evelyn and Kingsley? At dinner, he observes hidden tensions at play between the guests, particularly between Evelyn and her mother, whom Sinclair suspects of having forced her daughter into the match with the wealthier younger man.

With these puzzles playing on his mind, Sinclair retires to his room and contemplates the darkening vista from his window. Pleasant though Werrimona is in the day, at night it is all 'gloomy shadows' and 'silent hills'. To the depressed Sinclair it is 'a land of ghosts'. He is about to go to bed when he spots the silhouette of a woman gliding through the bushes towards a hillside. Halfway to the top she stops under a tree where she is joined by a tall man—'that was all I could be certain of, though my eyes were keen from years of detective duty'.

After a brief conversation the couple part and the woman returns to the house. Sinclair gets a sight of her in the moonlight. She is a short woman in her early twenties who the detective assumes is one of the house servants out for a midnight tryst with a lover, a tall man whom Sinclair cannot identify in the darkness. He goes to bed and sleeps well despite his brooding state of mind.

It turns out that the wedding has to be brought forward to Christmas Eve and preparations are sped up. Sinclair takes a solitary stroll up the hill where he witnessed the moonlight meeting and finds an onyx shirt stud he had seen Corwyn wearing at dinner. He picks it up but drops it again when he sees the short woman of the previous night looking for something in the grass. He hides and sees her find the stud and take it away with her. Why was Corwyn meeting another woman at midnight? In Sinclair's estimation, 'The man that could do so was a low villain no matter how noble or gentlemanly the appearance with which he deceived a shallow world.'

Back at the house, Sinclair discovers that the short woman on the hillside is Evelyn's helper, Milly Werner, leading him to wonder if she had been sent up the hill with a secret message for Corwyn. Late that night he searches for some bedtime reading in the drawing room and stumbles upon Evelyn there. She is staring intently out of the window into the darkness beyond. 'Never can I forget that beautiful face with the whiteness of death on it, and almost the shadows of death beneath the heavy eyes.' He can hardly fail to notice that Evelyn is very lightly dressed:

> a half-fitting wrapper of white cashmere tied with a silken cord. Her golden brown hair was gathered back in wavy and glossy masses, and fastened with a large comb behind, beneath which loops and long tresses fell down carelessly on her shoulders. Her small slender foot, as it peeped from under the cashmere skirt, showed a white silken stocking and shoe of black satin; and that was all—there was not a bit of lace at her fair neck or wrists, or a ring of gold on the perfect fingers.

The deathly Evelyn tells the detective that she is unhappy at having to leave Werrimona after her marriage and that she has had a 'presentiment' of an early death. Ever the gent, Sinclair comforts her and offers his help which she gracefully refuses, though suggests there is 'some strange, solemn tie' between them and that her 'honour and good name' somehow lay in his hands.

Sinclair returns to his room, puzzled. He is woken by Evelyn's distraught mother telling him that her daughter has disappeared. Sinclair now goes into full detective mode and takes command of the messy situation. The suspicion is that Evelyn has eloped with Corwyn, though Sinclair has his doubts and continues his masterful investigation, which soon results in him handcuffing the maid who refuses to answer his questions.

The detective is convinced Evelyn has met with foul play. But where can she be? That night he has a gothic dream of Evelyn in a dishevelled state and languishing in a deserted house somewhere. Questioning her brother about any such place nearby, the two men rush there to find 'the form of Evelyn Pemberton, with some folds of her stained robe covering her dead face!' Outside they find the dying Corwyn, fallen from his horse after committing the deed: "'I've had my revenge you see, and all is well" he murmured, "she will play no man false again."' The revenge of the jilted lover.

Despite her role in organising Evelyn's fatal last meeting with her killer, the red herring Milly Werner is released. Sinclair, now reflecting on these events, wonders if Evelyn's mother should bear the blame for forcing her to marry one she did not love 'for the sake of his wealth'. If so, she 'carried the secret of her sin with her to the grave'. The detective concludes his recollection of the case with some cryptic reflections on the power of 'excitement' to move humanity forward in interesting ways.

Detective Mark Sinclair continued in reprints and syndication to pursue his quarries across the pages of Australian newspapers until 1919. But Mary gradually lost much of her sight and had to give up writing, dying in her late seventies in 1911. Despite her productivity, she always struggled to make ends meet. Around age forty she was already pale and thin, poorly dressed and had been locked up more than once for drunkenness. She was living with a man in Collingwood on the ironically named 'Easy' (Easey) Street and was wanted by the Russell Street police as 'a reluctant witness in a case of rape'. Her second son would fall into a life of habitual crime, including 'robbery under arms', something she could never understand.

'Wandering Waif' ended her years in public institutions, long forgotten even by those who once read her tales with relish. Author Lucy Sussex, building on earlier research, eventually found Mary's unmarked and unmourned resting place in Springvale Cemetery. It was only then that 'The mother of Australian crime writing' received her overdue recognition as the prolific creator of some of Australia's earliest fictional crime scenes.

COLLINGWOOD CRIMES

In the nineteenth century, Melbourne's Collingwood was known as a dangerous place to live and work. A growing population mostly slogged away in the factories and workshops that mushroomed everywhere, with very little official regulation. By the 1870s the area was notorious for the larrikin 'pushes', or gangs, that roamed the streets, engaged in large and often lethal brawls and terrorised respectable citizens.

Public holidays were especially dangerous times for gang violence. The young men who made up the pushes were mostly employed in local industry and relished their days off as opportunities for drinking, fighting and defying the police. On New Year's Eve 1884 and into the following day, there was trouble in the town. When publicans tried to close up that night, the crowds of drunken larrikins and other revellers turned nasty. At midnight and after, 'Auld Lang Syne' was celebrated by smashing windows. When a few policemen tried to arrest one of the larrikins the crowd, estimated to be around 600 strong, attacked them with stones and wooden pickets in an attempt to free the prisoner. Several of the police were badly wounded, one receiving a lifelong injury that probably contributed to his eventual death, possibly by suicide.

It was not only the police who were unsafe in Collingwood. It could also be a hazardous place to bank your money. Just after ten in the morning of 14 June 1864, three men entered the Collingwood branch of the English, Scottish and Australian Chartered Bank. One waited by the door while the other two, armed with pistols, went looking for the manager, a Mr Dowling, and the ledger keeper, Mr P. de J. Grut. The manager was counting out the silver when he noticed a short thin man coming towards his office door:

> Struck with the peculiarity of his appearance, and instinctively apprehending the felonious designs of his visitor, when the man had opened the door, Mr Dowling, who had rushed round, at once collared him. They grappled, and in the struggle they gyrated round the room. The man drew a pistol when first seized, and said 'I'll shoot you.'

Dowling called for help as he grappled with the robber and his brother came running from another part of the bank. He grabbed the robber's collar and hit him. The man threatened to shoot. He did, and the manager's brother was wounded in the right hand.

While this struggle was going on, the ledger keeper was dealing with the second armed robber. From behind, Grut had grabbed the robber by the scruff of his neck and started to strangle him. The thief got one shot off over his shoulder, the powder scorching Grut's cheek, collar and hair. Then he ran off as the ledger keeper first raised the alarm, then went to the assistance of the manager and his brother and began beating the other robber with a brass candlestick until it broke. The battered robber drew a knife but a neighbouring shopkeeper, alerted by the gunshots, had run into the bank with a large cheese knife of his own. He 'raised the weapon he had brought from the shop, and exclaimed. "You beggar, if you stir an inch I'll cut you down," which so cowed the scoundrel that he instantly succumbed, exclaiming "don't kill me outright;" and three policemen coming in at the moment pounced upon him, and secured him.'

The man who had grappled with Grut got away with £2 to £3 of silver. Detectives were quickly on the case and soon tracked down some suspects, mostly in and around Little Bourke Street, then notorious for criminal activity.

The bank closed for the rest of the day to allow the brave employees to recover from their defence of depositors' funds. They were hailed as heroes, displaying true British 'pluck'. Even the governor, Sir Charles Darling, paid the bank a visit. He 'received from Mr Dowling a narrative of all the circumstances as they occurred, and appeared much interested while observing the scene. He complimented the manager on the presence of mind he had displayed, and on his gallant resistance, and examined the cheese knife with which Mr Ross had terrified the man who seems to have led the attack.'

A generation later, Collingwood banks were still attracting desperate characters. On 3 June 1885, the National Bank in Simpson's Road was attacked by three disguised and pistol-packing robbers also hefting iron bars. Although the robbers were inordinately polite in requesting the bank's money, their methods were rough. The manager and two clerks were made to kneel down on the floor, tied and gagged. One of the thieves jumped on the manager and took a pistol from his pocket. A clerk managed to get to the door and unlock it, even though his hands were tied behind his back. A passer-by untied the bankers and the alarm was raised, though the robbers escaped with more than £1000 in notes, gold and silver—a solid swag.

There was great excitement at the news of this robbery. The heroism of the bank employees in the 1864 heist was recalled, particularly the beating administered to the luckless thief by Mr P. de J. Grut with the brass candlestick. An ex-detective from the earlier era was interviewed for his recollections of the English, Scottish and Australian bank job over twenty years before.

While locals were recollecting, the police were hunting the villains and soon made some arrests. Five men eventually went to trial, though one was mysteriously discharged before the proceedings began. He had informed on his accomplices. The remaining four were found guilty. Three received surprisingly light sentences of six years in prison each and the fourth, an accomplice not involved in the robbery itself, was imprisoned for one year.

Today, Collingwood is a desirable near-city residential area renowned for its heritage buildings, nightlife and retail strip. In 2022 the main thoroughfare, Smith Street, was voted 'the coolest street in the world'. But the area has not quite shaken off its earlier reputation. In 1977, two women were savagely knifed to death in Easey Street. The murders of housemates Suzanne Armstrong and Susan Bartlett remain unsolved, despite a $1 million reward being offered in 2017. The case is often called 'Victoria's most brutal crime'.

INSIDE STARVINGHURST

No stranger to institutions of correction and rehabilitation, Henry Lawson wrote some verses on his prison experiences when he was sent to Sydney's Darlinghurst Gaol for many short periods between 1905 and 1909. His crimes included drunkenness, family desertion and failure to pay child support to his estranged wife, Bertha, and their two children. Although Lawson's sins were relatively minor, he was subject to the same discipline as other prisoners and wrote of the tough conditions in the place he called 'Starvinghurst'.

He was not allowed pen and paper, an especially cruel punishment for a writer, so was forced to memorise his poem until he had a chance to write it down and, with the help of a friendly guard, or 'screw', smuggle out the poem to his publishers.

Now this is the song of a prison—a song of a gaol or jug—
A ballad of quod or of chokey, the ultimate home of the mug.
The yard where the Foolish are drafted; Hell's school where
    the harmless are taught;
For the big beast never is captured and the great thief never
    is caught.

A song of the trollop's victim, and the dealer in doubtful eggs,
And a song of the man who was ruined by the lie with a
    thousand legs.
A song of suspected persons and rouge-and-vagabond pals,
And of persons beyond suspicion—the habitual criminals.

'Tis a song of the weary warders, whom prisoners call 'the
    screws'—
A class of men who I fancy would cleave to the 'Evening
    News.'
They look after their treasures sadly. By the screw of their
    keys they are known,
And they screw them many times daily before they draw
    their own.

It is written on paper pilfered from the prison printery,
With a stolen stump of a pencil that a felon smuggled for me.
And he'd have got twenty-four hours in the cells if he had
    been caught,
With bread to eat and water to drink and plenty of food for
    thought.

And I paid in chews of tobacco from one who is in for life;
But he is a decent fellow—he only murdered his wife.
(He is cherub-like, jolly, good-natured, and frank as the skies
    above,
And his Christian name is Joseph, and his other, ye gods!
    is Love!)

The Governor knows, and the Deputy, and all of the warders
    know,

Once a week, and on Sunday, we sit in a sinful row,
And bargain for chews of tobacco under the cover
   of prayer—
And the harmless Anglican chaplain is the only innocent
   there.

Staircase and doors of iron, no sign of a plank or brick,
Ceilings and floors of sandstone, and the cell walls two feet
   thick;
Cell like a large-sized coffin, or a small-sized tomb, and
   white,
And it strikes a chill to the backbone on the warmest
   summer night.

For fifteen hours they leave you to brood in the gloom
   and cold
On the cheats that you should have cheated, and the lies that
   you should have told;
On the money that would release you, you lent to many
   a friend,
And the many a generous action you suffered for in the end.

Grey daylight follows softly the heartless electric light
That printed the bars of the window on the wall of the cell
   all night
The darkness has vanished 'hushing' when there is nothing
   to hush—
And I think of the old grey daylight on the teamster's camp
   in the bush.

I think of the low bark homestead, the yard and the sinister
   bail,

And the shed in a hole in the gully—a pigsty compared with
    gaol;
The drought and the rows and the nagging; the hill where a
    flat grave is—
The gaol of my boyhood as dreadful and barren and grey
    as this.

We rise at six when the bell rings, and roll up our blankets
    neat,
Then we pace the cell till seven, brain-dulled, and with
    leaden feet.
Bolts clank, and the iron doors open, light floods from an
    iron-barred arch—
And we start with a start galvanic at the passionless, 'Left—
    Quick march!'

Down the crooked and winding staircase in the great wrong-
    angular well,
Like the crooked stairs that of late years we have stumbled
    down to Hell;
We empty the tubs and muster, with the prison slouch and
    tread,
And we take to the cells our breakfast of hominy and
    of bread.

The church in its squat round tower, with Christ in His
    thorny wreath—
The reception house is below it, so the gates of Hell are
    beneath,
Where sinners are clad and numbered, when hope for a
    while has died
And above us the gilded rooster that crowed when Peter lied.

What avail is the prayer of the abbess? Or the raving of
  Cock-eyed Liz?
The holy hermit in his cell, or the Holy Terror in his?
Brothers and sisters of Heaven, seen through the bars in
  a wall,
As we see the uncaught sinners—and God have mercy on all.

Lawson also composed another poem in 1908 based on his prison experiences. He called it 'One Hundred and Three', his prison number. It gives a picture of prison life and the killing drudgery of doing time:

They shut a man in the four-by-eight, with a six-inch slit
  for air,
Twenty-three hours of the twenty-four, to brood on his
  virtues there.
And the dead stone walls and the iron door close in as an
  iron band
On eyes that followed the distant haze far out on the level
  land.

Bread and water and hominy, and a scrag of meat and a spud,
A Bible and thin flat book of rules, to cool a strong man's
  blood;
They take the spoon from the cell at night—and a stranger
  might think it odd;
But a man might sharpen it on the floor, and go to his own
  Great God.

It was not uncommon for prisoners to pass out in church from lack of food:

The great, round church with its volume of sound, where we
  dare not turn our eyes—
They take us there from our separate hells to sing of
  Paradise.
In all the creeds there is hope and doubt, but of this there is
  no doubt:
That starving prisoners faint in church, and the warders
  carry them out.

Even remand prisoners were malnourished:

I've seen the remand-yard men go out, by the subway out of
  the yard—
And I've seen them come in with a foolish grin and a
  sentence of Three Years Hard.
They send a half-starved man to the court, where the hearts
  of men they carve—
Then feed him up in the hospital to give him the strength
  to starve.

Tobacco was the currency at Starvinghurst, as in every prison
before or since:

They crave for sunlight, they crave for meat, they crave for
  the might-have-been,
But the cruellest thing in the walls of a gaol is the craving for
  nicotine.

As usual, Lawson found an opportunity to make a barbed
comment on the state of society, as he saw it:

The clever scoundrels are all outside, and the moneyless
  mugs in gaol—
Men do twelve months for a mad wife's lies or Life for a
  strumpet's tale.
If the people knew what the warders know, and felt as the
  prisoners feel—
If the people knew, they would storm their gaols as they
  stormed the old Bastille.

Henry Lawson died in his mid-fifties in 1922. He was accorded the unusual honour of a state funeral, attended by many. He was, and remains, one of Australia's most popular poets, short story writers and criminals.

At the Fifty-Fifty Club

Phil 'the Jew' Jeffs was one of the smarter thugs of 1920s and '30s Sydney. He was a thorough villain, but one who was smart enough to survive the gang wars and to retire rich. Like most of the crims of his era, Phil began his career as a small-time thief, serving some time for larceny in the early 1920s. By the second half of the decade, he was shooting other toughs in the series of gang wars that raged through the Sydney underworld, mainly over disputes around drugs and prostitution.

The enactment of laws against prostitution and the removal of cocaine from unregulated sale created new criminal enterprises. Loopholes in the relevant legislation allowed women to run brothels, so Tilly Devine and Kate Leigh did just that. Cocaine had long been available as a pick-me-up and many people were already addicted to it. The crims were only too happy to supply the need. Sly grog had been a problem since the earliest years of the colony, widened now by the ban on legal drinking after 6 pm. Few were prepared to stop at six and so establishments providing illicit alcohol blossomed. Into this mix of vice and sin, as the papers might have described it, came the standover man demanding money from those plying illicit trades—or else.

Jeffs grew to maturity in this stew of vicious crime and shoot-outs between the mobs of Tilly Devine and Kate Leigh. He was acquitted of malicious shooting and rape charges and was badly wounded in 1929 by a gunman he refused to identify. Narrowly cheating death, he went on to a couple of other brushes with the law, then more or less disappeared.

But Jeffs was not out of the game, just laying plans for new and slightly more legal ventures. He was wise enough to see that the old-style razor gangs and underworld vendettas were no longer a productive form of criminal enterprise. A far better approach was to develop what looked like legitimate businesses and cultivate a veneer of respectability. The canny crook got out of cocaine and brothels and established after-hours nightclubs financed largely by his sly grog business rather than the old-school standover tactics.

Jeffs had begun purchasing venues in the 1920s, but now, assisted by his contacts in the police and politics, he was able to expand. He maintained the appearance of a businessman and kept a low profile by having others appear to be the proprietors of his clubs. On the rare occasions when public outrage provoked a half-hearted police raid, Jeffs could claim that he was just an employee of the business and depend on his well-paid stooge to answer the charges laid. The few fines levied on his clubs were much less than the licence and taxes Jeffs would have paid on a legitimate hotel.

With some politicians and police in his pocket, Jeffs prospered. His clubs were well patronised by revellers from a variety of social backgrounds. A 1932 newspaper report of his Fifty-Fifty Club in Darlinghurst was headlined 'Riotous all-night orgies at the Fifty-Fifty Club' followed by 'Scions of society seek shocks in this sordid den'. The article described the denizens of the club in colourful style:

> The Fifty-Fifty disgorges, half-fearfully, its freight of human flotsam into the night.
>
> The fair girl with the beautiful skin and the scared, stricken eyes, steps daintily into a taxi.
>
> The woman of the scent and bedraggled finery, steps wearily, but with a touch of proud defiance—into the street.

Couched in the ethnic and moral prejudices of the period, the overheated piece ranted on:

> Orientals, thugs, half-castes and painted women of the streets rub shoulders and mingle with well-known scions of Society, prominent actors and actresses and the leading lights of our legal and medical profession. The place has even had Vice-Regal connections. Unofficially, of course.

The club was awash in illegal alcohol being consumed at an astonishing rate by 'a dark-skinned foreigner' thought to be a white slave trader, a crim just out of gaol, a couple of drunken young marks being further inebriated by a 'suicide blonde' and a host of respectable and unrespectable citizens. A 'white-faced youth, sitting bolt upright and staring sepulchrally before him' plays a grand piano as people dance like 'puppets' to the 'mechanical' but 'rhythmic music'.

The grand master of this bacchanal, Phil Jeffs, is described:

> Sartorially Immaculate and affecting a quiet elegance of dress, he may be seen reclining easily against a polished oaken pillar or conversing in earnest undertones with one or two associates . . . Rarely does he lose that suave dignity so befitting the owner—official or otherwise—of the Fifty-Fifty Club.

And what was the effect of 'the abandoned orgies, utterly degenerate and depraved, held nightly at the Fifty-Fifty' on public—and private—morality, wondered the journalist?

> What would these anxious guardians of the public morals say if they knew their own daughters, may, or might frequent the Fifty-Fifty . . . Legislation should be enforced against the latter, not solely because of the unfortunate degenerates who go there, but in view of the corrupting influence it must have on the morals of our youth.

The answer to this rhetorical question was that most people were more than happy to enjoy the transgressive pleasures of Phil the Jew's sly-grog joints. Nothing ever came of the calls for legal and moral retribution, or even regulation. The sinners and the hedonists partied on.

Towards the end of the 1930s, Jeffs began selling off his clubs. As well as the Fifty-Fifty Club, he ran a higher-class joint called the 400 Club, and Oyster Bill's Club near Tom Ugly's Bridge on the Georges River. By 1942 he was out of the sly-grog racket and retired to a luxury property he had built at Ettalong on the New South Wales Central Coast. Surrounding himself with thousands of books and attractive blonde women, he lived well on his rumoured fortune of £250,000 (more than $20 million today).

After a brief return to crime in the 1944 baccarat craze, Jeffs died the following year. Some said the wound he bore from the gang wars of the 1920s had finally caught up with him. There were, apparently, only around £65,000 of his riches left to pay for his funeral and, the papers said, for the blonde women who were among the few mourners.

TRUE DETECTIVE STORIES

Her beauty was the magnet that drew him to . . . murder! Was there any significance in the fact that the gown she wore for the first time he met her was black?

This was the headline paragraph for the story of 'The Beautiful Lady in Black' that appeared in Number 88 of *True Detective Stories*. The crime recounted was the 1952 murder of Alfred Dahlberg by Miroslav Tuma, the lover of Kathleen Biliski. She was a woman described by the press as having 'the screen-star looks of a youthful Rita Hayworth', a noted Hollywood beauty of the era, a fact contributing to the intense press interest in the murder.

Biliski had taken up with the suave American Dahlberg when her previous husband, also American, left her after only three weeks of marriage. Tuma ran a nightclub where he first saw Biliski in company with Dahlberg and fell fatally in love. He wooed her, as they used to say, and they lived together. After this relationship fell apart, Biliski left to live alone. Tuma later discovered she was again seeing Dahlberg. In a jealous rage, he got his rifle, broke into Biliski's flat and shot Dahlberg in the stomach. Dahlberg later died of his wounds.

Police arriving at the crime scene found Biliski partly conscious on the bed after struggling with Tuma who had then fled the scene. She was wearing a black nylon nightie, a detail the press rushed to headline. After a revealing trial, Tuma was found guilty and given a death sentence, later commuted to life imprisonment. The retelling of these sensational events in *True Detective Stories* was typical of the 'pulp' true crime magazine that titillated and shocked readers from the mid-1940s until the late 1950s.

When the Australian government restricted the entry of American periodicals to the country in the early 1940s, publisher Frank Johnson saw a business opportunity. Trashy fiction, comics and lurid true crime yarns were lapped up by a local public enthralled by the sensational and, compared with Australia at the time, racy stories and illustrations featured in these publications. Johnson set up a company to publish similar material but using Australian rather than American locations and stories. *True Detective Stories* was the most successful of the many regular publications his business churned out through railway station kiosks and newsagents. People could easily carry the flimsy pocket-sized booklets and enjoy reading them as they went to and from work by public transport. And what tales they read, both new and old.

The account of 'Looney' McDouall's Ghost dealt with a murder in mid-western New South Wales in the 1860s. The magazine introduced it in typical style:

> What strange hypnotic spell was cast over murderer John Wood to draw him back to the scene of his ghastly crime and surrender him into the waiting hands of the law? Was it the mysterious compulsion that drives a slayer to return . . . or was there something more?

Hard to resist reading on. When you did, you discovered that shepherd 'Looney' McDouall had been foully murdered on his way to Carcoar, New South Wales, by a travelling companion, John Wood. The killer took all the money the young man was carrying before burying the body in a shallow grave. Then he went off to spend his loot in the grog shanties around the district. Just a few weeks later, circling crows alerted Looney's replacement to the dead man's whereabouts. The curious shepherd followed the carrion birds and found, as the story described the scene, 'a human skull, surely the whole world holds few more heart-chilling sights! There was no visible skeleton, but only a skull, upright on its neck, peering from vacant eye-sockets—northward!' The dingoes had been at the body as well.

Wood was eventually identified as the killer but, despite an intensive search, could not be found. It turned out that he was serving a six-month sentence in Mudgee Gaol for another crime. It was not until after his release that he was apprehended in unusual circumstances. Two trooper police were out one night in the area where Looney had been buried. They saw a light where none would normally shine and went to investigate. They came upon John Wood 'nodding his head in sleepy stupor on the grave which once held all that was mortal of "Looney" McDouall'.

Apparently unable to live with his actions, Wood's guilt had driven him back to the scene of the crime. The author of the article, F.J. Lynch, had it that 'Looney's ghost had haunted Wood and drawn him back to the grave.' Wood was later hanged and the murder avenged as 'the ghost of "Looney" McDouall brought Wood to his death by the rope'. Other sensational narratives appearing in *True Detective Tales* included some epic colonial cattle stealing, serial poisoners, blackbirders, executions and assorted murders, all with grisly details lovingly provided. They were presented inside garish covers featuring desperate-looking characters, dramatic moments and, often, attractive young ladies in what would then have been considered revealing clothing. Issue 1 Number 74 of the new series was titled *Blood in the Bagnio*—meaning a brothel—and lured readers with a picture of a young woman about to have a dagger plunged into her bosom.

True Detective Stories finally folded in the late 1950s, victim to a lifting of the ban on even more sensational American publications and the arrival of television. Over its lifetime, the magazine, and its sister publications, had provided work for dozens of authors, illustrators and printers.

Johnson wasn't the only one producing this material and between his output and that of his rivals, this period was a golden age for Australian literary workers providing more opportunities than previously or since. The focus on Australian rather than imported stories made them firm favourites with local readers. Great literature it was not, but the fast-paced and conversational style of this pulp magazine provided reading for many who may not have had access to more serious work. The stories were also surprisingly well researched by their authors, providing historical context and social and political details with a degree of educational value. Readers were given sharply drawn sketches of the main characters and their motivations, along with the inevitably grisly details of each crime and the dramatics of the trials that followed.

Although *True Detective Stories* has long passed from the publishing scene it can still be read online. The National Library of Australia has digitised many issues and made them available through Trove. Like to find out about 'The hideous career of Sally Arsenic' or 'The sacrifice of the death-bowl'? Just look up issue 3 (New Series), titled *Corpses and Candles*. Who could resist?

MURDER CITY

'Give a dog a bad name', as the old saying goes. Adelaide was dubbed 'murder city' in 2008 based on a misleading statistic and the title stuck. It's not true, of course. Adelaide is one of the safest cities in the country. But the stately metropolis of churches does seem to produce some of Australia's most bizarre and mysterious crimes. As well as the unsolved disappearance of the Beaumont children these include the Family murders, the Truro murders and the Snowtown murders.

During the 1970s and '80s five young men were tortured to death by a shadowy group known as 'the Family'. Only one person was ever convicted of one of these murders and police have an open brief on the case. Also in the 1970s the remains of seven young girls were found mainly in Truro and two other locations. Two men were identified as the murderers, one dying before the killers were revealed. His accomplice was convicted of six of the seven murders and sentenced to six consecutive life terms. In the 1990s, eleven people were killed and their dismembered bodies packed in barrels and hidden at Snowtown. One individual, believed to be the ringleader of the gang of killers is serving a life sentence.

These are only some of the more recent grisly cases. At the time they took place and since, they have received extensive and intensive media coverage in South Australia, around the country and internationally. The still unanswered questions around the Snowtown and Family cases continue to generate speculation and to keep the cases in the public eye.

Going back a little further in time the still unsolved disappearance of the Beaumont children in 1966, presumed murdered, is still remembered in folk memory and is frequently revisited by mainstream media. It also features in the proliferation of cold case sites and podcasts on the internet. The intensive coverage of these cases tends to imply that they are unprecedented. But Adelaide had its fair share of murders in earlier times, some almost as grisly as the more recent cases.

In August 1906, William Manson was staying with his sister at their mother's house in Tynte Street, North Adelaide. Around 10.30 on the night of Sunday, 12 August, two youths turned up at the house with a pony and trap (small open buggy) that belonged to Manson's brother-in-law, Notele (Natalla, Notalle) Habibulla. The boys had found the wooden carriage partly capsized on King William Road. Puzzled, Manson examined the trap and was 'amazed to find blood stains on the footboard, and a torn white shirt and two sugar mats covered with blood'. Accompanied by his sister, he drove the gory conveyance into the city centre, picked up a policeman and proceeded with him to the Habibulla home in Bristol Street at the south-eastern end of the city.

The front door was opened by a young woman who had been working for several weeks as a servant to Habibulla's 21-year-old wife, Edith Ellen Mary. The servant took the three visitors through the three-room house. Inside, all seemed as it should be. But when they went out into the backyard they found a large pool of blood and 'fatty substances of the body'. The policeman secured the premises and sent Manson and his sister to the Adelaide police watchhouse to inform detectives that a serious crime had been committed.

But where was the body?

Next morning, with the assistance of a First Nations tracker, police found a trail that led from the Habibulla house to the Torrens Lake. Land and water searches were carried out, revealing wheel tracks probably made by the trap, and a scrap of bloodstained paper. Police dragging the river then found a sugar bag. Protruding from the hessian sack were a pair of human legs. They continued searching for the torso.

By now, police had Habibulla in custody. Shortly after twelve on the night of the murder, he had reported to police that his pony and trap were missing. Police later took him to the house in Bristol Street where they conducted a full search. Clothes found under the bed were identified by the servant girl as belonging to Edith, or 'Nellie' as she was usually known.

Habibulla was charged with murder despite the absence of a complete body. Police found the missing part on 15 August, in another sugar bag beneath water near the Morphett Street bridge. Inside was a woman's head, trunk and arms. They were quickly identified as the remains of Nellie Habibulla. She had been pregnant when she died.

The case was a press sensation around the country. Habibulla's background as a Punjabi immigrant cameleer was investigated, as was his troubled relationship with his much younger wife who had previously left him for an affair with another cameleer. All these facts, gossip, prejudice and innuendo, together with the 'ghastly details' of Nellie Habibulla's last moments, were revealed at the inquest and endlessly rehashed by the newspapers.

Habibulla had firstly tried to strangle his wife in their house, then taken her naked into the backyard where he had murdered her and dismembered the body with an axe and a knife. There were bloodstains on the weapons, along the verandah and on the suspect's clothing. He was committed for trial on a charge of wilful murder and found guilty on 18 October. Despite a strong recommendation for mercy from the jury, impressed by Habibulla's defence of limited culpability due to Nettie's adultery, he was sentenced to death.

Petitions for mercy and letters to editors against the execution were futile. In 'white Mohammedan habit and turban', Notele Habibulla was taken to the scaffold on 16 November. Before the noose was tightened around his throat, he thanked his

warder and was 'extremely brave and resolute, a remarkably slight tremor at the knees being all that was noticeable'.
Then the trapdoor was opened. Fortunately, the hangman had
correctly calculated the condemned man's body weight and the
height of the drop. Habibulla died instantly.

Telegrams flashed the news across the country to be reported
in dozens of metropolitan and rural newspapers. The press
squeezed the last drop of sensation from the case in their
round-ups for the year 1906. Then the killing and butchery
of Nellie Habibulla faded into the mostly forgotten homicidal
history of Adelaide, a city founded on progressive views of
religious tolerance and also known as 'the city of churches'.

Safe-cracker and robber Bertie Kidd, pictured here with a lady friend identified only as 'Cindy', is regarded by some as Australia's most complete criminal. He spent 27 years in prison, was involved in many criminal ventures in his heyday and claims to have masterminded the famous Murwillumbah bank robbery of 1978.

3

HEISTS AND HEAVIES

PIRATING THE *NELSON*

Ex-convicts from Van Diemen's Land, later Tasmania, were perceived in other colonies as villainous crims responsible for most of the crime in their jurisdictions. Whether this was true or not (evidence suggests that it probably was), the 'Vandemonians' were usually the first to get the blame for criminal activity, particularly during the gold-rush era in New South Wales, Victoria and Queensland. In the case of one of the most spectacular heists of the early gold-rush era, most of the robbers were actually ex-convicts from the 'Land of lags', as Van Diemen's land was also sometimes known to those who unwillingly spent some time there.

When Captain Walter Wright departed London for Melbourne in 1851, he had not heard the news of the wild rush unfolding down under. His ship, *Nelson*, docked at Melbourne in October and, as happened with many ships at the time, the crew mostly disappeared to seek their fortunes on the diggings. With not enough sailors left to sail the *Nelson*, it was towed to Geelong, loaded with wool and a lot of gold and then towed back to Melbourne where Captain Wright hoped to find a new crew to return to England after five difficult months of delay. He went ashore to look for men, leaving a skeleton watch aboard his ship to guard more than 8000 ounces (227 kilograms) of gold, worth over $24 million today. Early that morning, the pirates struck.

With muffled oars, two stolen boats full of men 'armed to the teeth' rowed out from Sandridge (Port Melbourne) Beach to where *Nelson* was lying off the Williamstown lighthouse. Thinking themselves far enough offshore to be secure, those crew aboard posted no guards and the robbers easily boarded the ship, capturing three of the crew before any alarm could be raised.

Having dispersed themselves over the vessel, some went aft and seized the chief officer and a friend, together with the carpenter, who were asleep in the cabin, whilst others employed themselves in throwing overboard all the small arms within their reach, as well as the swivel-guns mounted on the poop deck. Mr Draper, the chief officer, received a slight wound in the thigh, from a shot fired by one of the robbers, before they succeeded in overpowering him and his companions, which they soon did, and having lashed their hands together, they commenced plundering the Lazarette, of the position of which they appeared to be well acquainted.

After stashing the loot in their boats, the pirates locked up the crew in the lazarette, a specially strengthened part of the ship's cargo area, and rowed away into the darkness. Fortunately, a crewman who had managed to hide from the pirates was able to release the prisoners, and the chief officer rowed to Williamstown with the bad news. The Water Police set out immediately but saw nothing until daylight, when they found one of the boats and the tracks of the dray the robbers used to haul the gold away. The other boat was discovered abandoned soon after. The police rode out in search of the robbers and within a few days began rounding up suspects.

The ringleader was a runaway convict from Van Diemen's Land going by the name of John James. He had previously been a police constable at Hamilton, near Hobart, where he was known as William Johnson. He had received a sentence of fifteen years hard labour, the first three years to be served in chains, as did several of the others eventually tried for the crime. Many of the twenty or so robbers who had boarded the *Nelson* were never captured and only a fraction of the gold's value was ever recovered.

The robbery of the *Nelson* was well planned and generally well executed. The robbers had good knowledge of the valuable cargo aboard the ship and knew exactly where it was held. They knew there were only a few crew members aboard on the night of the attack and they had gathered the arms and transport needed for the heist. They also had a fence lined up to dispose of the loot, for a large premium. The suspect, a St Kilda publican, was never charged.

Agitation for the end of penal transportation was at a high level during this period. The fact that many of the convicted robbers were convicts provided anti-transportation advocates with useful ammunition to further their cause. Other interests did not do so well out of the *Nelson* piracy. The losses incurred were so large a blow to the insurance industry that gold insurance premiums rose

The memory of the robbery lingered on in Melbourne folk memory, according to Marcus Clarke's version of events:

So far, the story of the robbery as given in the official records. But there are circumstances connected with business, which, though well-known to Melbourne residents at the time, and remembered by many folks who are now residing there, were never published in Court. For instance, there were two female passengers in the 'Nelson' at the time of her seizure. These ladies were named Kidd, one is the sister of the editor of a leading medical journal in London, and the other, married to Mr. Robert Evans, the brother of the City Inspector in Melbourne. When the robbers broke open the cabin doors, a masked man, 'who had the air of a gentleman,' begged the ladies not to be afraid, and handed them politely into the cuddy where champagne was waiting! After the transhipment of the gold was made everybody had a glass of champagne, even the bound men, to whose lips the courteous robber held the glass.

There were also some strong suspicions about who was behind the heist:

A curious story concerning the enrichment of numerous influential citizens was mooted at the time, but for obvious reasons it is unwise to repeat it here. The remarks of Duncan and Morgan that they would 'get a thousand a piece for the job' was held to confirm the opinion that they were but the agents of scoundrels less daring in action, but more ingenious in contrivance. The 'gentleman' who conducted the proceedings of the robbers was said to be identical with a well-known and respected colonist. It was whispered that more than one financial concern profited by the 20,000 pounds which remained to the 'firm' which paid 5000 pounds to its agents for the forced loan.

Clarke was writing many years after the robbery and concluded that 'So many years have passed that it is now unlikely that the true story of the "Nelson" gold robbery will ever be told. That which I know I am constrained to conceal. Readers can but weigh and surmise.'

Indeed.

THE CRIMS CAME BY MOTORCAR

The first mention of a motor vehicle in connection with crime seems to be in the *New South Wales Police Gazette* of December 1897. But it was almost another twenty years before some enterprising crooks hit on the idea of getting away from the scene of their robbery in a car.

The conveyance in question was a now long-forgotten Moline brand. Cars were not a common sight in 1914 and seeing one moving at speed was even rarer. As the car hurtled down the street, a bystander was intrigued enough to note down the registration number. This made the work of the police very easy in tracking down the men who had been inside the vehicle.

They were in haste after snatching the payroll at the Eveleigh Workshops of the New South Wales Railways, netting well over £3000 in cash, worth hundreds of thousands of dollars today. The sensational heist itself was well planned and well executed. It was after the crooks made their motorised getaway that it all began to unravel.

The story of the Eveleigh Workshops raid is one studded with the dark criminal stars of that time and one destined for bigger things in the future. The main players were the robbers, Samuel 'Jewey' Freeman and Ernest 'Shiner' Ryan, Arthur Tatham owner of the getaway car and Norman Twiss, the inside man. A young woman named Kate Leigh, at the early part of a long and high-profile criminal career, also featured in the events following the heist and the getaway.

On 10 June 1914, the payroll was being delivered to the workers at the Eveleigh Railway Workshops. Two employees of the sprawling industrial complex usually met the wagon carrying the money and transported it to the office where it was prepared for payment. Norman Twiss, who had been at the workshops for some time, was one of those men. The other was a man named Miller.

As the second cash box was being taken to the office, a grey car skidded to a halt beside the cart. The two men inside the car wore driving goggles and handkerchiefs across their lower faces. One, later identified as Freeman, cried out 'bail up' as he leapt from the car, pointing a revolver at Twiss and Miller, the other man handling the cash. He was pushed to the ground by the gunman who told Twiss to give him the money. Twiss had been lifting the second cash box from the cart and immediately did as he was told. Freeman slung the chest into the car, jumped in and Ryan drove rapidly away. The driver of the payroll cart, Albert Andrews, bravely gave chase but his horse-drawn vehicle was no match for the motorised villains.

With the registration details from the astute bystander, police soon located the car. Inside was an empty cash box and the revolver used by Freeman. The bullets were charged only with pepper. The car's owner, mechanic Arthur Tatham, claimed the car had been stolen. The police did not believe him. In the meantime, Miller reported his suspicions of Twiss, who had seemed to him to be unaccountably cool when threatened with the gun. The government quickly posted a £400 reward for 'the apprehension and conviction of the two masked and armed offenders, who absconded in a motor car'.

The police got lucky. An underworld informer quickly fingered Freeman. Ryan unwisely left a highly visible trail of cash, expensive jewellery purchased for his girlfriend, and general high living. Perhaps not the sharpest pencil in the box, Ryan sent some of the cash to a mate in Melbourne. When he wanted it back, Ryan eluded the cops hot on his trail and took the train to the southern capital to retrieve his dough. The mate, of course, had disappeared with it. The overly trusting crim was soon cornered in Melbourne with £600 of the stolen payroll—the only proceeds of the crime ever recovered.

Freeman was arrested trying to board another train to Melbourne and the four accused were brought to court in September on charges of assault and stealing. Considered by police to be an especially desperate character, Freeman was also up on a charge of shooting and wounding a man in another robbery four days before the Eveleigh heist. On this charge, his girlfriend, Kate Leigh, tried to coerce a man at the point of a tomahawk to testify on Freeman's behalf. Leigh, described by one policeman as 'a very shrewd and dangerous woman', was later tried for this perjury and sentenced to five years in gaol. For the Eveleigh heist, Freeman and Ryan each received a ten-year sentence. Tatham and Twiss were both acquitted.

The main culprits served their time and continued their criminal careers. Leigh went on to dominate the Sydney under-world for a good many years. In later life, she and Shiner Ryan got back in touch through correspondence and were married in 1950, after Ryan was released from his latest gaol term. They separated after a few months.

Dubbed 'the heist that shocked the nation', the Eveleigh job was a sensation in its day, as just one of the many headlines suggests.

MASKED MOTOR BANDITS RECORD HAUL AT EVELEIGH. ROBBERS TAKE £3300 AT REVOLVER-POINT. DARING DAYLIGHT CRIME. PAY CLERK WITH MEN'S WAGES BAILED-UP. HIGHWAYMEN DASH AWAY WITH BOOTY IN FAST CAR. STOLEN VEHICLE USED.

Several other newspapers recollected robberies of a similar kind. The *Sunday Times* of Sydney described a heist in Brisbane almost ten years earlier:

About 2 o'clock one Friday afternoon the pay clerk of the North Brisbane Gas Company got out of a tram carrying a bag containing a large sum of money wherewith to pay the company's employees. When the pay clerk had walked about half-way down the fenced-in path leading to the Gasworks, he heard a call, and, turning, saw 'a man coming up behind him on an old white horse, who ordered him to "drop that bag." The clerk did so, and the brigand dismounted, and, seizing the bag, cantered away. Though a police station was quite close, and a hue and cry started quickly, it was not until late in the afternoon that the white horse was found in a blind street in Bowen Hills. No one had seen him arrive there, and the rider and the bag of money had, apparently, been just as invisible.

Sydney was clearly leading the way in applying new technology to the business of crime.

FLASH AS A RAT WITH A GOLD TOOTH

It is not well known that one of Melbourne's, and Australia's, most notorious criminals was the star of a lost movie. *Riding To Win* was produced in the early 1920s by amateur director, Eric Harrison. It was a comedy drama in which a heroic jockey saves the daughter of a horse trainer from criminals intent on making him lose a race. When police found out about the film they tried—only with partial success—to have it banned in Victoria and New South Wales in a similar way to the restriction of the first Ned Kelly movie of 1906 and a subsequent ban on bushranger movies in general. Authorities were still fearful of the corrupting power of film and the romanticisation of a leading man tempting others into a life of crime.

The star of *Riding To Win* (originally titled *Emergency Colours*) was the career criminal known as 'Squizzy' Taylor. His girlfriend of the moment, Ida Pender, played the damsel in distress. The film was eventually screened to good houses in Queensland in 1925. Two years later, Squizzy was dead, victim of a still murky gangland vendetta. The movie is now one of Australia's long-forgotten 'lost films' but the life and legend of Melbourne's most colourful career criminal continues to fascinate us.

Taylor's origins were those of many petty criminals. A tough childhood in a poor neighbourhood, the suburb of Richmond. He was in trouble early and continually appeared in court and in the newspapers until his death. Unlike most crooks of his era, Squizzy did not slink in the shadows. He was a flashy dresser, drove expensive cars and was a highly visible figure, flashing gold teeth and a large diamond tiepin in and around his principal places of business, including racetracks, brothels and drug dens. His willingness to engage in a movie was typical of his American-style gangster image. But despite many charges and trials, he rarely went to gaol, and when he did, it was not for long. This understandably enraged the police who often believed they had him dead to rights for all manner of crimes from loitering with intent, to murder.

What was his secret? He didn't have one. He had two.

Squizzy Taylor was, firstly, an especially devious crook. He usually managed to intimidate or influence others into carrying out bank robberies, murders and other crimes from which he benefitted and for which he usually avoided retribution while others 'took the fall'.

His second magic act was to build and maintain a clan-destine network of police, legal people and others likely to be useful in the kind of situations in which he and his henchmen were frequently embroiled. Squizzy Taylor was a master jury rigger. After fairly frequent early arrests and convictions, he was forever getting off the consequences of his crimes. Using bribery, intimidation and blackmail, he was able to undermine legal processes, not only for himself, but for others facing criminal proceedings. He could charge heavily for such a valued commodity and may have made as much, if not more, from this side of his illicit business than he did from gambling, prostitution, drugs and robbery. And it was far less dangerous.

But despite his craftiness, expensive cigars and celebrity image, Taylor was still a vicious thug who used friends and foes alike and would stop at nothing to achieve his ends.

Born in 1888, Joseph Leslie Theodore Taylor's slight stature suited him to an early career as a jockey. Horses were soon abandoned in favour of crime, though he continued his racecourse connections, mainly for illicit purposes. In 1913 he graduated from an early career phase of mostly petty thievery in Victoria, New South Wales and New Zealand. He was involved in several murders though managed to win acquittals when tried in court. In 1914 he was sentenced to nine months with hard labour for intent to commit a felony and was later imprisoned for thirteen months.

Taylor's heyday coincided with the gang wars between various crime groups in Melbourne. He was head of the Richmond push, their main rivals being the toughs of the Fitzroy push. Beatings, robberies and murders committed by members of both groups came to a head in 1919 and Taylor was sentenced to eighteen months for his part in the violence, though this was overturned on appeal.

Taylor was mostly in hiding during 1921–22 until caught breaking and entering. Bailed for the large sum of £600, ($50,000 today) Taylor failed to appear in court to answer the charges. He eluded capture for over a year, narrowly escaping the scene of a clothing store robbery in March 1922. The getaway car was driven by his then partner and co-star-to-be, Ida Pender. She and another accomplice were caught and police searched vigorously for the missing Squizzy. Ever the exhibitionist, Taylor wrote to the newspapers promising to give himself up which, to the surprise of the police, he did in September 1922. As usual, the jury could not agree on the gangster's culpability and a retrial found him not guilty.

The following year a Glenferrie bank manager was robbed and shot, later dying from his wounds. Police suspected Taylor was the mastermind of the crime. He was remanded for two months, then released on bail, using the time to engineer a rigged jury and plan a prison escape for one of his accomplices. Taylor was charged and tried on various counts, including conspiracy to murder and was acquitted on all but one relatively minor charge of occupying a house frequented by criminals. He was sentenced to six months but exasperated authorities moved to have him imprisoned indefinitely. Surprisingly, or perhaps not, the Supreme Court concluded that his record was not black enough to justify an indeterminate sentence.

By late 1924, Squizzy Taylor was back on the streets and back in business. This included an expansion of his drug dealings and trespassing on the New South Wales trade. In 1927 Sydney razor gang stalwart, John 'Snowy' Cutmore, an old foe of Taylor's, was sent to kill the troublesome Melbourne mobster. Taylor got word of Cutmore's arrival and, with a couple of henchmen, eventually tracked him down to his mother's house in Carlton where Snowy was in bed with the flu. Squizzy and one of his accomplices went into the bedroom and gunshots quickly followed. Snowy died quickly but not before he put a bullet into Squizzy's right side. Badly wounded, Taylor staggered to a waiting taxi and was taken to St Vincent's Hospital but expired soon after arrival.

Various accomplices and enemies were arrested for having a part in the killings but all were eventually discharged for lack of solid evidence. Unanswered questions about these events led to many speculations about the motives of those involved. Some claimed Melbourne business identity and political fixer of the era, John Wren, had Squizzy killed. Others said Snowy Cutmore's mother shot Squizzy after he killed her son. Various rivals were said to have wanted the gangster dead so they could take over his business. Or, inevitably, a woman was somehow involved. Even in death, the king of the Melbourne underworld could muddy already darkened waters.

Squizzy Taylor's spectacular and very public life of crime, together with his puzzling demise, provided the basis of a long afterlife. His ability to elude capture and to avoid conviction for his many crimes also endeared him to a public who were sceptical of police integrity and saw Taylor as something of a working-class hero, a role he was only too happy to fill. There has been a steady stream of biographies and books about him, as well as film and television productions, even a musical. Contemporary audiences became familiar with Taylor through the television series *Underbelly*. It will be a while before we hear the last of the high-living and cunning hoodlum who ruled Melbourne's gangland for a decade or more and corrupted police and officials with seeming impunity.

THE SHADOW AND THE KING

'I do not rob the poor . . . I ruin nobody. I am after the bigger money.' Giovanni Lucci unabashedly declared his philosophy in attempting to rob Sydney's Union Bank. He was the leader of a gang of international 'breakers' who attempted what would have been a sensational heist in August 1926. The job was a failure, but the tale of what happened intrigued the country. And there was another, secret story behind the headlines.

A series of bank jobs in New Zealand first alerted the Australian police that some highly skilled safe breakers were down under. Robberies in Melbourne quickly followed and Sydney police prepared for the inevitable arrival of whom they suspected were Continental crims onto their patch. They didn't have to wait long.

In July 1926 the ABC Bank in Oxford Street was hit. Police arrived to find the safe had not been blown in the usual way but had been literally cut open: 'The work had been done by what are referred to as "tin openers"—huge cutters that will go through steel plate as easy as the ordinary tin opener goes through a can.'

As well as the empty safe, the thieves had, rather unprofessionally, left behind a clue. A scrap of cloth found on the floor turned out to be of Italian origin. As the police puzzled over this piece of luck, the gang struck again at premises in the Haymarket. It wasn't long before the distinctively dressed Italians were spotted and placed under intense surveillance. The Italians lodged at different premises but they had a Fiat car that they used to transport pieces of equipment from place to place. One item was known as the 'tin opener', but the crooks had an even more exotic device, 'a huge wheel that could cleave the top off any safe built'.

Surveillance revealed that the Italians paid particular attention to the Union Bank in Castlereagh Street. When police discovered the gang had rented a room directly over the bank premises, two detectives spent an uncomfortable few days huddled under the manager's desk with only some bread, water and apples for sustenance. But their timing was premature. Nothing happened.

Police continued to shadow the thieves and their Fiat, wondering when they would strike. One morning, the car disappeared along with the thieves. The police began a desperate search throughout the city. The Fiat was eventually found and trailed into the night. Detectives relaxed; everything was under control again.

It wasn't.

Fortunately, a couple of detectives decided to check the bank building one more time, just to be sure. They arrived around 2.15 am. They had a key but were reluctant to use it as there were people inside the building and the detectives didn't want to attract attention. Eventually, around 2.30, they let themselves quietly in and crept along a darkened passage. Their torches revealed some clothing on the floor outside the door of the room over the bank. 'They're here,' whispered one to the other. Guns were drawn and one detective went back to the car that had brought them and told the driver to speed to headquarters for reinforcements. As he made his way back to join his colleague, he heard him shout, 'Throw up your hands, every man. Don't move or I'll shoot.' The room lights were switched on to reveal three robbers standing over a large hole they had made in the floor, giving them direct access to the bank strongroom containing around £9000 (around $800,000 today).

The men surrendered without resistance and police found 'drills, hacksaws, bolt cutters, huge tin openers with spare blades that could be set at various angles, keenly tempered snips, wrenches, torches, beeswax, master keys, and a huge circular hole cutter'. The rest of the gang were quickly rounded up, including the leader, whom police called 'the King', the 28-year-old engineer, Lucci. He 'was not in the least perturbed about the matter, and said that had he secured the 9000 pounds in the bank he would have had a very good breakfast. He denied that he was a professional criminal, claiming that he worked only for himself.'

The thieves were charged. They pleaded guilty and three of them served three years for attempted bank robbery. Two were eventually deported. A win for the Sydney cops. But while the press made heroes of the detectives involved in foiling the visiting breakers, an undercover police officer remained in the shadows, just as he and the police commissioner preferred. His name was Frank Fahy, known to most only as 'the Shadow'.

Frank Fahy joined the New South Wales Police in 1921. After training, he was ordered to become an undercover operator. Apparently, his relatively slight stature compared to the usual burly cops of the era was his main qualification for the job. But Frank took to his new role with what became an obsessive enthusiasm that lasted through an amazing thirty-year career. His identity was known only to the most senior police and, this, together with his legendary covert exploits, led to his well-deserved nickname.

Fahy kept well clear of the limelight, letting others take credit for much of his work. Newspaper reports on the police success in foiling the Union Bank job did not mention that Fahy had tracked the Italians to the small workshop where they were making and assembling the elaborate equipment they used in their attempt on the strongroom. Dressed in one of his favourite disguises as a down-and-out, Fahy kept the workshop under surveillance for days and nights, eventually discovering that the robbers had hired the office room above the bank, the information that ultimately cracked the case.

As well as his various vagrant disguises, the inventive Fahy sometimes dressed convincingly as a middle-aged woman, an itinerant knife sharpener and as a fruit-barrow boy. For avoiding detection while following criminals, he invented a double-sided coat with which he could quickly change his appearance. He had an old police motorcycle and sidecar customised to look like a knife-sharpening business transport, complete with signage. It was really a surveillance vehicle. Fahy would hunch for hours in the sidecar, spying on suspects until he discovered useful information. He could then leap on the powerful motorbike and follow motorised suspects.

Fahy's disguises and frequent fraternising with criminals saw him warned off by policemen on several occasions and one notorious detective even beat him up, thinking he was a crim. Later in his career, Fahy's expertise and experience were harnessed by the security services

All this contributed to the legend Fahy developed within the police force and with newspaper crime reporters, one of whom, Vince Kelly, wrote a best-selling biography of Fahy's exploits after the Shadow retired in 1952. He died at the age of eighty-two in 1978.

Dapper Desire's Last Escape

'I suppose the police will get me in the long run,' the dapper deceiver, escaper and robber who called himself Desire La Court once said. 'And they will get me by shooting me.' They did, putting a bloody end to La Court's extraordinary and colourful career in 1926.

Desire began life as George Ohl, born in Germany. He went to sea as a young man and came ashore in Australia only to be interned as an enemy alien during World War I. He was firstly imprisoned in Queensland where he soon began to display his ability to escape from captivity, often by simply jumping over fences. Although he was a fast runner, he was caught and later sent to Holsworthy camp in New South Wales from where he fled at least three times before being released after the end of the war.

There was still bad feeling in Australia about Germans so Ohl changed his name to Desire La Court to imply that he was French or Belgian. In 1920, the charming and always well-dressed La Court married retail worker and volunteer nurse, Anne Gertrude Salsberg, who went by her middle name. Gertrude and Desire soon started a family. A fitness enthusiast, La Court kept himself in top physical condition through a regime of exercise and a diet that included eating raw steak. He needed to be nimble. To keep his growing family fed and himself in silk shirts, expensive hats, gloves and a silver-topped cane, he took to thieving on a grand scale.

La Court's first brush with the law was in 1921 and the following year he went to prison for twelve months after being found guilty of six charges of receiving stolen goods. Despite his suave appearance and manner, La Court was considered by police to be 'the most "slippery" criminal that has ever operated in this State'. They said that he was not only difficult to capture 'but also when in court, he was a difficult man to convict. He was a careful criminal, and covered up his tracks so skilfully that it was not surprising that the police could not fit him on any of the big list of charges on which he was arrested.'

La Court was a speedy runner who often outran his pursuers. On the numerous occasions when police fired at him, he just kept going. But his ability to elude capture and slide out of most criminal charges laid against him came to a sudden end on 14 March 1926. The previous day, police had arrived at the family home at Manly in search of La Court on suspicion of robbery and car theft. At the inquest, Detective-Sergeant Sedgwick gave evidence:

On March 13, with a posse of police, he went to a house in Condamine-street, Manly. When a woman came to the door, he asked her whether La Court was there. The woman, who said her name was Dean, but turned out to be Mrs. La Court, said 'No, I don't know him. I know no one by that name.' Witness then said 'I am going to search your place as I have good reason to believe La Court is here, and I want him for burglary.' She answered, 'He is not here, and I would not like you to go inside, as my husband is away.'

While Gertrude engaged Sedgwick in conversation on the back verandah, La Court was spotted legging it, uncharacteristically dressed only in blue trousers and a singlet. The detective chased the speeding robber for a few kilometres but failed to catch him and returned to the house to confront Gertrude.

'You told me a lie,' he said to her.

'Yes,' she replied frankly, 'when I saw the police around the back of the house I woke my husband up and told him to beat it.'

When police searched the house they found silk shirts, rolls of silk and more than 300 pairs of silk stockings, together with other clothing, cigarettes and chocolate. They needed two cars to transport the loot to the North Sydney police station.

Meanwhile, the resourceful La Court was making good of what would be his final escape. He picked up a lift with William Stephens and was soon spinning him a yarn.

'You don't seem to be a bad sort of chap, I'll take you into my confidence. Can you keep a secret?'

'Yes, go ahead,' replied the hapless Stephens as La Court leaned into his spiel.

'I've had some trouble with the police—they are after me. I was asleep in bed last night and my wife awakened me. I noticed two detectives talking to my little children in the front of the house, jumped through the window and escaped in the bush.'

La Court said that he didn't carry a gun, but Stephens noticed the bulge in his passenger's hip pocket, which he took to be a pistol. He then went along with La Court's polite but firm requests to use some of his clothing and to take him to addresses in various North Shore suburbs, helped along the way with a few bottles of beer. La Court finally left his obliging lift near Pymble and Stephens last saw him rolling a cigarette in the bush.

It wasn't long before a local merchant's Peugeot went missing from his garage, along with three tins of benzine. La Court drove the car to the Black Horse Hotel in the then sleepy town of Richmond, New South Wales. He checked in under a false name and garaged the Peugeot. In the afternoon he was with the proprietor and others on a motor jaunt around the locality. Just another tourist. No one suspected the charming foreigner of anything untoward until they returned to the hotel where the police were waiting for him.

Now as nattily dressed as ever in freshly stolen clothes, La Court immediately spotted Constable McGeoch and Sergeant Cafe and moved hastily through the hotel without heeding commands to stop. As he reached the back door he broke into one of his famous sprints.

'Stand in the king's name, or I'll fire,' shouted Constable McGeoch. La Court again ignored the command and McGeoch cried out, 'Stop or I'll shoot you,' firing a shot into the air. The fugitive kept running down the long backyard of the hotel towards an open gate in the fence. Fearing they would lose their man, McGeoch raised his revolver and discharged it. The desperate shot caught La Court in the head and dropped him to the ground. A local doctor was called and the stricken man was taken to hospital where he later died.

La Court left behind Gertrude and two surviving children; his youngest child had died in a buggy accident some years earlier. At the inquest, Gertrude was frank about her attempts to aid her husband's escape. When asked if she ever questioned where Desire obtained all the goods he continually brought home she answered that she did but he just told her to 'mind her own —— business' and punched her.

Dapper Desire La Court was reportedly buried in the Catholic section of Rookwood Cemetery on 17 March 1926, next to his deceased son. Gertrude's complicity in his crimes brought her to court charged as an accessory to theft. Her situation as a widowed mother seems to have struck a rare note of sympathy from the legal system and she was discharged when no evidence was presented against her. Under the name La Court, she later remarried.

THE MOST VIOLENT WOMAN IN SYDNEY

An accordion-playing busker, petty thief and sly-grog seller seems an unlikely person to be labelled 'the most violent woman in Sydney'. But Iris Webber managed to attain this moniker in the midst of some of Sydney's most violent characters. She wasn't even born or brought up in the tough neighbourhoods of 'sin city', beginning life as a country girl.

Born Iris Shingles in Bathurst, New South Wales, at a Salvation Army institution in 1906, she grew up in Glen Innes, New South Wales, and Warwick, Queensland. She married Edwin Webber in 1925 and with him moved close to Byron Bay. Times were tough in the depression of the 1930s and when Edwin got a job in distant Hay, he had to leave Iris behind. It was now that she began to show the first signs of the behaviour that would earn her unenviable title.

Edwin repeatedly failed to send Iris any money and also owed her mother money. Packing a small-bore weapon known as a 'pea rifle', Iris travelled to Hay, tracked Edwin down and had it out with him. The argument ended when she shot him in the buttocks. Edwin went to hospital and Iris went to remand for a few months but was eventually acquitted.

A year or so later, Webber was living in the Sydney suburb of Glebe. She was apparently maintaining herself by busking with an accordion. At this time, busking was considered a form of begging and Webber was often charged for 'gathering alms', soon gaining a reputation for conducting her own fiery defences in court.

By the mid-1930s Webber was living in Surry Hills. Her neighbours included a cross-section of the city's most notorious crims, including Kate Leigh, who was destined, along with Tilly Devine, for the title Crime Queen, as their various empires expanded later in the decade. During this time, Webber was involved in a same-sex relationship that involved her in violent assaults and shootings. When one of these confrontations led to her killing a man with, again, a pea rifle, she was charged with murder, though she was eventually acquitted, pleading self-defence.

As the depression decade wore on, Webber continued to make frequent and dramatic court appearances related to her busking activities. 'How many innocent men must be in gaol! Is this the justice a citizen gets?' she demanded while on trial for begging, using bad language and assaulting a policeman in 1938. She was found guilty on all three counts. Although Webber tried professional legal representation, she usually returned to conducting her own defences, at which she was highly skilled. Even the homophobic police who hated her for her lesbianism as much as her criminality admitted that she had a 'brilliant brain'.

In November 1939, Iris Webber was in court with accomplice, Laurie Cole, charged with stealing a handbag from the Mark Foy's department store. Webber was also charged with severely kicking the shop inspector and assaulting a constable. The couple complained of having no breakfast at Long Bay Gaol, 'only a slice of bread and dripping', and asked the court to grant an adjournment of their case. The magistrate refused and Webber threatened to report the incident to the Minister of Justice. Cole pleaded guilty but Webber claimed she was innocent and had only tried to keep her friend out of trouble. Both women were fined £3, though Webber said she would appeal. On the charge of assault, Webber received two months imprisonment, together with another two months for assaulting a constable.

In 1940 Webber was carrying a knuckleduster and served time for assault. She got out of prison at the right moment to turn a profit from the large number of American servicemen seeking the delights of Sydney's nightlife. Webber sold sly grog in Woolloomooloo and continued her usual violence, sometimes using a tomahawk. She married briefly, possibly to allay police persecution for her lesbianism, and continued her frequent encounters with the law. She also took a new lover, Vera May Sariwee, with whom she carried out several robberies.

Under her new married name of Mrs Eileen Furlong, the former Iris Webber was arrested for murder in 1945. She and her accomplice alleged they had been beaten by police and forced to confess: 'The police are merely making statements and are producing no evidence, and, in consequence, are depriving me of my liberty,' Furlong complained. The two accused were eventually bailed and acquitted.

But times were changing. The war was over and the easy marks were mostly gone. Furlong and Sariwee fell on hard times. They were involved in another domestic argument that ended in Furlong attacking a couple of randy visitors with a tomahawk. The two women were charged but 'bush lawyer' Furlong 'argued points of law with loquacious aplomb'. When a Crown witness failed to appear Furlong and Sariwee 'romped out of the charge', as *Truth* newspaper put it.

Furlong continued to career between the streets, low dives and the courts. There was no glamour around her or her crimes; she was simply a poor, homosexual woman who had to make her way in a very unfriendly world controlled almost entirely by men. In a city notorious for its colourful identities, Furlong became a well-known figure, a defiant 'deviant', as she was described in the language of the time; her courtroom antics and visibility as a street performer drew newspaper headlines right up to the time of her death of diabetes and cancer in 1953.

In many ways, the Iris Webber-Furlong story is the darker underbelly of the seemingly brighter and glamorous reputations of Tilly Devine and Kate Leigh. While Iris Shingles-Webber-Furlong fought fiercely to preserve herself and her lovers against all comers, police or criminal, she never controlled violent males. Devine and Leigh were able to manipulate the harsh realities of the underworld they inhabited for their own purposes and to profit from their enterprise and skill. Both women ran gangs of male gunmen, slashers and standover merchants who, mostly, did what they were told by the queens of crime. Iris just tried to look after herself and the people she loved.

GONE TO GOWINGS

One of the many colourful Australian idioms is 'as cunning as a shithouse rat'. This crude but evocative saying is a fitting description for the life and crimes of Antonio Martini. Remarkable only for the thuggish banality of his lengthy criminal career, his ability to escape from custody and an especially spectacular shoot-out with police in North Sydney, Martini is justly forgotten today, though a little mystery still lingers.

Although a product of the Melbourne underworld, Martini flitted from state to state, developing a reputation as a dangerous customer, a stylish dresser in the mode of the Hollywood gangster and as a persistent but rarely successful escape artist. Short, slight and swarthy, bullet-scarred and tattooed, he claimed to be of Italian ancestry, though also claimed that Martini was not his real surname. What that might have been, nobody seems to have ever discovered. He was arrested and gaoled several times under this name and it is the one with which he gained his greatest notoriety.

Martini made an early splash in the Sydney press in 1937 when he pleaded guilty to two charges of armed robbery and another of demanding money with menaces. He was said to be nineteen years old then and was sent to spend the next four years of his life in prison.

By February 1946 Martini was again in custody in Long Bay Gaol after his arrest for burglary. Taken to face the charge at the Darlinghurst Court, he was thoroughly searched a number of times before being locked in a holding cell with a few others awaiting trial that day. After an hour or so, the guard heard the unmistakeable grinding of metal on metal coming from the cell. Looking through the grille on the cell door, he found Martini busily sawing through a window bar surrounded by an expectant ring of prisoners. By the time reinforcements arrived, Martini was simply chatting with his fellow prisoners. The guards found the steel bar had been nearly cut through and the blade hidden behind the toilet cistern. It had almost been a win for Martini but he had to settle for pleading not guilty and was remanded in custody.

At this time, the burglar, gunman and would-be escape artist was already in prison serving a two-year stretch for an earlier pistol charge. But there were some legal doubts about the conviction and Martini was able to appeal, his case being heard just a few months after his previous visit to court. While waiting in the holding cells, Martini again magically produced a hacksaw blade and this time successfully sawed through the window bars. When guards next visited the cell, they found only the two other prisoners who had been waiting there with him. Answering the guards' puzzled questions, one of them said that Martini had 'gone to Gowings', an old Sydney expression referring to someone who has left in haste and does not want to be found.

And he wasn't, not for a very long while. When Martini was next sighted, it wasn't long before he reached the pinnacle of his nefarious career.

After the stunning escape, police forces across the country had been on high alert. They chased hundreds of anonymous and other tips about the gangster's whereabouts. They searched St Mary's Cathedral, several ships, private residences and kept watch on ports and railway stations. They found nothing. Apart from useless tip-offs, the underworld kept its collective mouth shut and Martini remained at large. An inquiry into the mystifying breakout produced little more than further mystification and no further action.

But Martini had been busy plotting. Towards midnight on 21 September 1946, there was a gunfight between police and criminals trying to blow the safe of the Crown Street Post Office in Surry Hills. A constable was lucky to escape with his life and the villains sped away in a waiting car. It turned out that one of the thieves was Antonio Martini, recently returned from Melbourne where he had been successfully lying low for months.

Immediately after this incident, police received a rare reliable tip-off that Martini and his accomplices planned to rob the Taronga Park Zoo strongroom. On the night of 22 September, armed police staked out the zoo's administration building. After hours of cramps and boredom, they were rewarded: two shadows suddenly appeared at midnight, creeping towards the building. The police stiffened. As well as pistols they were armed with a light machine rifle known as a 'Tommy gun'. They were taking no chances.

Suddenly, Martini and his accomplice, a crim named Ted Garland, sensed that they had walked into the trap set for them. 'Look out, Ted!' Martini yelled to his mate as police flashed on their torches and called on the men to surrender. Garland fired into the blinding torchlight, slightly wounding the sergeant carrying the Tommy gun. The injured policeman squeezed the trigger and sprayed bullets at the robbers. Garland fled but Martini was hit in the chest with a bullet from another policeman's pistol. Amazingly, he was only winded, saved by the thickness of his clothing. He staggered up and, with Garland, managed to reach their getaway car and disappear.

But not for long. Martini, Garland and the getaway driver, Garland's brother, were soon located in Little Arthur Street, North Sydney. They were quickly surrounded by police who had now added automatic rifles and tear gas to their arsenal. They urged the crooks to give up. The Garlands replied with a barrage of pistol shots. Called on again to surrender, the Garlands were promised that they would not be shot. They wisely took the police at their word and threw down their guns.

Once again, the wily ringleader had 'gone to Gowings'. Martini had managed to slip out of the building and through the police cordon. He dumped the suitcase full of gelignite the robbers had planned to use on the zoo safe and climbed through an open window of a nearby house. Inside were a mother with two children and a boarder. The quick-witted smooth-talking gunman spun them a yarn about being involved in a sly-grog raid, helped himself to a drink and then forced the boarder to open the front door of the house. Standing directly outside was Detective Crowley. Martini fired, as did Crowley. Both missed and Martini fled, shooting as he went.

Martini now displayed the agile speed that served him so well during his escapes. Police fired at him from all directions as he dodged into another house where he was soon cornered at the top of the stairs. In Wild Colonial Boy style, he defiantly refused to give up at first but then seemed to reconsider and threw out a pistol. It was a ruse. As police advanced cautiously up the stairs, he stuck his head round the corner and fired from another pistol. In a burst of Tommy gun bullets, Martini went down screaming in a pool of blood.

Police dragged the body upright, astonished to see that the gunman had disguised himself with bleached hair and white powder to lighten his appearance. Another trick. And he had one more up his sleeve. Although a bullet had hit Martini in the forehead it only stunned him. While he was being taken to hospital police found a small arsenal of pistols, a bandolier of bullets and other ammunition. During the action more than a hundred shots had been fired, fortunately with only two men slightly wounded.

Martini recovered and was tried together with the Garlands. With henchman Ted Garland, he was found guilty of attempted murder and sentenced to death, while Garland's wheel-man brother received fourteen years. The death sentences were later commuted to life imprisonment, and Martini and Garland were sent to Parramatta Gaol for life. But the wily gangster had no intention of spending the rest of his earthly existence there.

In 1953 Martini, Garland and some other inmates from the prison tailor shop where they were all employed locked staff up in the shop and went to the engineer's office. They secured him there, took a tall ladder and smashed their way through a locked door to the outside wall of the prison. Martini went up first and reached the top of the 10-metre-(35-foot)-high wall just as the guards began firing. He jumped into the grounds of the mental hospital adjoining the prison but landed badly and broke his right foot. Dragging himself up he hobbled painfully away as bullets thumped into the ground all around him but, again, did not hit him.

It was not long before large numbers of police and warders began to search for the fugitive. They found him unable to move or offer resistance and apparently trundled him back to gaol in a wheelbarrow. The determined escapee had been at liberty for about twenty minutes.

That was not Antonio Martini's last bid for freedom. He was sent to Grafton Gaol, at that time holding the most intractable prisoners, to serve the remainder of his sentence. Less than six months after arriving at Grafton, he was involved in an attempted breakout with a large group of prisoners, including Darcy Dugan. The men were charged, among other things, with mutiny and punished with months in various forms of solitary confinement. Darcy Dugan would later continue a chequered career that often saw him in the press, but the pages of the nation's newspapers fell silent on Antonio Martini. What happened to him after serving his time?

In 1999 an Antonio Martini, born in 1918, was buried at Springvale Botanical Cemetery, Victoria. The commemorative plaque reads in part:

> In Loving memory of
> ANTONIO MARTINI
> Beloved Husband of Edit
> Dear Father of
> Mario and Beatriz
> You Made Our Lives
> Interesting

THE GREAT BOOKIE ROBBERY

Intriguingly, nobody knows how much was stolen from the bookies after Melbourne's 1976 Easter race meetings. The official figure was only around a million dollars (around $7 million today) but those in the know thought it was more likely to be in the vicinity of $14 million to $16 million—or around a tidy $100 million now. The bookmakers were reluctant to divulge the true amount for reasons related to their tax returns.

The proceeds of the racecourse betting were gathered together at the Victoria Club in Queen Street, Melbourne. Such a large amount of money was a magnet for six of the state's underworld figures. Led by Raymond 'Chuck' Bennett, Norman Lee, Ian Carroll and Laurence Prendergast formed a gang to plan and carry out the heist. They prepared well.

Weeks before the robbery, the thieves took bolts from the fire escape door of the Queen Street building, cut them in half and glued them together again. The bolts were then replaced in the door. All they had to do on the day of the heist was to give the door a good push and it would open. They also managed to hack the elevator system, ensuring the lifts would be stuck between floors as they carried out the raid, making it difficult for anyone to escape or come to the rescue of the hostages they would take.

An armoured truck was due to deliver the money on 21 April. Inside the building, the heavily armed thieves hid and waited. And waited. The truck had a flat tyre and was fifteen minutes behind schedule. When it finally came and offloaded the notes, the bandits struck. Brandishing their weapons, which included M60 machine-guns and shotguns, they entered the floor yelling and swearing at the guards and the hundred or so people present.

'The bandits ordered everyone to lie face down on the floor,' one witness told the papers. 'They told us that if we didn't they would blow our bloody heads off.' After cutting through the security cage where the money was stacked, the thieves 'herded three office girls into a corner and told the men in the room to remain motionless or one of the girls "would end up dead"'. Then they began stuffing banknotes into bags they had brought with them. In ten minutes, they were gone, along with maybe $15 million, ripping out the telephones as they went.

Police blocked roads and other transport routes, describing the robbery as a 'commando style' raid and 'perfectly executed', suspecting it might have been an inside job. But bags full of bulky banknotes were difficult to move and even more difficult to conceal. They had various leads to follow and were optimistic that the thieves must soon be caught.

There are several different accounts of what the bandits did with the loot. One was that they had a laundry van waiting and drove the money to an unknown location. The other is that they were smarter than that and hired a room on another floor of the Victoria Club building and stashed the money, guns and balaclavas there. That allowed them to simply walk out of the building like everyone else during the confusion after the raid and return after the fuss died down to collect the loot.

Whichever story, or another, is true, almost none of the money has been seen since. Some notes were passed by Lee. He was arrested but police were unable to prove that he had any connection with the robbery and he was released. It was said that some gang members took their share and opened bars in the Philippines. Norm and Ray moved on to even bigger things, including trafficking drugs and more heists in America, South America, the Philippines and even China.

But that was not the end of it. Gangsters Leslie and Brian Kane were standing over the robbers for the loot. Ray Bennett was believed to have murdered Leslie Kane in 1978. Bennett went to trial but was found not guilty. He was shot dead the following year, probably by Leslie's brother, Brian. While enjoying a drink at his local pub, Brian Kane was murdered by two masked gunmen in 1982. The next year, Ian Carroll met a similar end, while Laurence Prendergast has been missing since 1985. Norman Lee was shot dead by police as he committed a robbery at Tullamarine airport in 1992.

No one was convicted for Ray Bennett's murder, nor has any more of the loot ever been recovered. According to the barrister who defended Lee, Philip Dunn QC, the robbery was one of the last old-school heists. Well planned, well executed and none of the gang ratted on the others. They might have killed each other, but they observed the old underworld code of silence.

The spectacular nature of the heist itself, the disappearance of the money and the fates of the robbers have made the Great Bookie Robbery one of Australia's most notorious thefts. It has been the subject of television shows, books and articles and has been drawn on for fictionalised movies.

Inevitably, this media attention throws an aura of romance over the Great Bookie Robbery bandits. In fact, they were some of the most vicious criminals of their era; several were associated with the notorious Toe-cutter Gang. These were standover men specialising in extorting the proceeds of other criminals' activities. Their victims were convinced to hand over the loot or have their toes removed with bolt cutters. Most complied. But not all. John Maloney was found dead in 1972, missing his toes. He was one of the casualties of the battle for control of crime on the waterfront involving the Federated Ship Painters and Dockers Union, known as the Painters and Dockers, a criminal confederacy responsible for fraud, drug trafficking, standover methods and more than a few murders.

THEY GOT THE LOT!

The night of 23 November 1978 was hot. The sleepy New South Wales Northern Rivers town of Murwillumbah was dark and quiet after the Imperial Hotel closed around 10.30. At some time after that, several robbers broke into the not-very-secure Bank of New South Wales. They silently made their way to the Chubb safe in which $1.7 million, possibly more, was stored, most of it in readiness for paying government employees.

A Chubb bank vault is a reinforced concrete box with a heavy steel door and sophisticated locks. To crack one requires great skill and, in this case, some high-tech equipment. The gang had a device known as a magnetic drill. It consisted of a circular electromagnet that was clamped to the metal door of the safe, allowing a diamond-tipped drill to make deep holes near the lock. Through the holes they passed a medical tube with a tiny camera, known as a cystoscope. This allowed them to see and manipulate the tumblers of the lock until they fell into place and unlocked the safe door. It was very delicate and demanding work that took hours to carry out. A few locals later recalled some suspicious activity around the bank; one even heard a banging sound in the early hours of the morning. Otherwise, no one heard or saw a thing, including staff in the police station with a clear view of the bank from only a hundred metres away.

At 7.30 the next morning, a security guard noticed the open back door of the bank. When officials and police got to the safe, they found the thieves had removed the dials of the combination locks and the door handles and closed the door. It was impossible to open the safe. Locksmiths, including Chubb specialists flown in for the job, were unable to free the door. In the end, council workers used sledgehammers, jackhammers and oxyacetylene tools to smash through the external wall of the bank and into the concrete vault. By then it was around 4.30 in the afternoon. Chief Inspector Frank Charleton was the first to get a look inside. 'They got the lot!' he exclaimed.

The thieves had cleared the vault and gotten clean away. A massive police search was mounted and a reward of $250,000 (over $1.45 million today) offered for information. But although a few people were detained, nothing ever came of the investigation and the money, worth around $10 million today, has never been recovered.

This was not the first heist by the Magnetic Drill Gang, as they came to be known. The crims had used their useful tool on numerous other robberies in the previous few years. They knew what they were doing and how to do it properly, but even then, they would need to have known the exact layout of the bank building and the best way in and out. Did they have inside help? Perhaps a bank employee or even a policeman recently arrived in town? These possibilities were investigated but came to nothing. Even when the same gang used the same method to lift millions in gold and jewellery from the Westpac Bank in Rose Bay, New South Wales in 1983, authorities were unable to track them down.

Who were these master criminals who seemed to rob at will, invulnerable to capture? It depends on whom you ask. The police have long suspected Melbourne crim and 'tank man', Graham 'the Munster' Kinniburgh. Once a member of the notorious Painters and Dockers, Kinniburgh was an expert safecracker and prominent Melbourne crime figure who was shot dead in 2003 during the Melbourne gangland killings era.

But another professional criminal has claimed to be the mastermind behind the Murwillumbah robbery. Bertie Kidd is a career robber and safecracker, said by some to be the 'most complete criminal' in Australian history though he is little known outside underworld and police circles. He claims to have meticulously planned the heist and the getaway plan, and that Kinniburgh, although invited to be part of the gang, had refused the job, believing that it was impossible. Kidd features in a trilogy of stories about his life and crimes that began publication in 2019. A larger-than-life character, his colourful career in and out of gaol veers between low-rent crimes, suspected murders and some impressively planned heists—like the Murwillumbah job.

Whoever was involved in the gang, they had a long-term strategy. In 1976 an odd robbery took place in Melbourne. The only thing stolen was the door of a Chubb safe. Some time later, a string of heists began involving the widely used Chubb safes. Police soon put two and two together when they found the distinctive evidence of the magnetic drill in the doors of the cracked safes. The thieves had plenty of practice and had already netted millions before they pulled off the theft in sleepy Murwillumbah.

As things stand today, although some of the Murwillumbah money is said to have turned up in Hong Kong, the loot is still missing and nobody has been held accountable for the crime, though the case remains open. The magnetic drill itself also remains a mystery. Who designed and built such a criminally clever device and where is it now?

The magnetic drill job is still remembered in Murwillumbah, of course. The town was so pleased to have been the scene of Australia's largest bank heist that local entrepreneurs printed T-shirts and other souvenirs emblazoned with the phrase 'They Got the Lot'. They say that English Great Train Robber Ronnie Biggs, then still an international fugitive, ordered several of the T-shirts for himself.

SWINDLING THE MINT

It's not called 'the golden west' for nothing. The gold rush that began during the 1890s with finds in the desert at what are now Coolgardie and Kalgoorlie has never stopped. Western Australia has a boom-and-bust economy that owes much of its continuing mineral prosperity to the glinting metal. The western third of the country was still a self-governing colony when it received permission from the British government to establish a mint in the 1890s. The operation prospered and ownership was transferred to the state government in 1970 and has continued as an exceedingly successful enterprise.

Among the various forms of gold and other precious metals refined and stored by the mint are bullion bars of almost complete purity. They are heavy, glowing and very tempting. In 1982, forty-nine of them were cleverly stolen. Then they vanished. What happened then and in the years since is a twisting tale of swindle, police corruption, legal proceedings and ongoing mystery.

In April 1982 a number of blank Western Australian Building Society cheques were stolen. On their way out, the robbers torched the building. This seemingly unnecessarily dramatic crime was followed five weeks later by another oddity. This time, it was the Perth Building Society cheques that were stolen and the building in which they were housed was again burned down. What this was all about would only become clear over the following months and years.

While the building society thefts and arson were under investigation, the Perth Mint was receiving regular telephone calls from potential buyers calling themselves 'Fryer' and 'Blackwood'. When three armed couriers arrived at the mint on 22 June with three cheques, no one was surprised. Staff apparently took the cheques without validating them and handed over bars of gold worth $650,000. The couriers transported the boxes of bullion to an office staffed by a temp rented for the day. Not too long after, another courier, hired anonymously via CB radio, arrived at the office, picked up the very heavy boxes and drove them to the small airport in the Perth suburb of Jandakot. The boxes were unloaded onto the ground outside an aircraft hangar. The courier left and so did the gold. Who took it and where it went is a mystery to this day.

Suspicion fell on three brothers: Brian, Raymond and Peter Mickelberg. Just how and why police concluded that these men were the villains were early puzzles in a lengthy series of courtroom dramas, forensic reports and corruption claims. The Mickelbergs had once fashioned a fake gold nugget that entrepreneur Alan Bond purchased for twice its imputed value. Ray and an accomplice served time for this separate matter.

Apart from this circumstantial evidence, the case against the brothers appeared frail.

The case came to court in 1983 and, based on police evidence, Raymond then 37 and Peter, then 23, were found guilty on eight counts of conspiracy to defraud, burglary, arson and fraud. Brian Mickelberg, then 35, was found guilty of only some charges and was later successful with an appeal. Raymond and Peter soon commenced a series of appeals in various courts. These mostly revolved around the police evidence that had been used to convict them. This consisted mainly of a fingerprint police allegedly discovered on one of the blank cheques used to steal the gold and a damning record of a police interview with Peter Mickelberg that he claimed had been doctored.

Tony Lewandowski and Don Hancock were the detectives in charge of the investigation. They repeated their sworn evidence at the various appeals. Forensic experts from Britain testified that the record of interview with Peter Mickelberg had been doctored. The claim that police had placed Mickelberg's fingerprint on the cheque was tested by experts from Scotland Yard, the FBI, as well as state and federal Australian police. Ultimately, not one was prepared to swear that the print was a forgery.

Despite the early acceptance by the courts that Peter Mickelberg's interview had been tampered with, the police continued to insist it had not. The two brothers remained in gaol on the basis of the fingerprint evidence.

As the appeals came and went, Hancock and Lewandowski continued their police careers, Hancock retiring as head of the CIB. He was later killed in a car bomb planted by a vengeful bikie over an unrelated issue. Despite growing unease with the soundness of the Mickelberg convictions, Lewandowski continued to claim that neither he nor Hancock had falsified the evidence. It was not until a Royal Commission into the case in 2002 that he finally confessed that he and Hancock had fitted up the Mickelbergs. In his statement he said:

> I have never copped a penny for this, I have had 20 years of hell. I have basically had enough of it. I lost my business, I have lost my wife, I have lost my son. I have gained nothing from this. I am now telling the truth. I have told lies and I am not proud of it.

Lewandowski, who had left the police force, disappeared overseas. He killed himself in May 2004 while awaiting trial for perverting the course of justice and related offences. In 2004, the Mickelbergs were finally successful with their eighth appeal and their convictions were quashed. There followed a series of actions for defamation and compensation that were partially successful. The Western Australian Police made a public apology in 2007 and since then the family has sought to have the records expunged. In 2016 the state government moved to claim Ray Mickelberg's home to pay for the legal aid that finally led to his release. This action was eventually dropped.

Despite the exoneration of the Mickelbergs, the mint swindle remains an uncomfortable issue for the government, the police and the legal profession. Newspaper articles, books and television programs about the case have appeared in the years since the original crime was committed, churning through the many conundrums of the case and its seemingly never-ending afterlife. Apart from 55 kilograms of the stolen gold that turned up at a

Perth television station in 1989 together with a note claiming that a well-known Perth businessman carried out the swindle, the loot is still missing. Closure, resolution and even revelation about the great mint swindle remain as elusive as ever.

In 2022 the mint was again in the news over allegations that it was being used to launder money. The Australian Transaction Reports and Analysis Centre (AUSTRAC) ordered a review of the business and its records, saying there were 'reasonable grounds to suspect' criminal activity in relation to the mint's compliance with financial transaction reporting laws. The government, which owns the mint, was taking this matter very seriously, said the then premier. Since then, the mint has also been accused of surreptitiously diluting the value of its gold bars, and in 2023 it became the subject of a federal parliamentary inquiry.

*Notorious con artist Amy Bock dressed in men's clothing
as Percy Redwood in 1909.*

4

FAKES, FRAUDS AND FORGERIES

ARTISTS OF NOTES

As economies moved towards more paper-based methods of financial transaction during the eighteenth century, new opportunities for forgery appeared. Highly developed skills of drawing, engraving, papermaking and printing were needed to fake banknotes and other documents. Artists, famously insolvent, were among those sometimes drawn in to counterfeiting. Of all the artists who arrived in Australia as part of the First Fleet, more than half were convicted of forgery. And they kept coming.

Knud Bull was one of a sizeable number of painters transported for applying their skills to forgery of one kind or another. After studying art in his native Norway, Bull embarked on another career. He became a counterfeiter. As the story emerged during his and an accomplice's trial at London's Old Bailey, Bull took a ship for England in 1845, planning to execute a forgery on the Norwegian banking system.

The thinking—if that was what it was—behind this seemingly roundabout plot was presumably that it would be easier to avoid discovery if the fake notes were printed in another country. Bull's motivations did not emerge at the trial, but as an emerging young painter he might have needed the money even though he came from a middle-class family. Throughout the proceedings there was also a suggestion that the crime was masterminded by another, possibly a 'foreign gentleman'. Even at that time, a high degree of organisation and funding was necessary to pull off an international job of this kind.

On the ship, by accident or design, Bull made the acquaintance of an employee of the English Mint. As the man recalled at the trial, the young artist quizzed him about papermaking in England, not an unreasonable topic of conversation for a painter. When Bull reached London he began searching for papermakers, engravers and printers. He had with him some samples of high-value Norwegian banknotes which he needed to accurately re-create. His rather thin cover story was that the paper was to be used to print tickets for an unnamed lottery. He needed engravers to forge the complex design of the notes and contracted out different sections of the design to several businesses to avoid suspicion. Together with the paper, these were to be brought together and taken to a compliant printer for the production of the fake notes.

The novice counterfeiter ran into difficulties straightaway. There were quality-control problems with reproducing the paper and the designs to the high quality needed. It wasn't long before suspicions were raised about the odd Norwegian circulating the papermaking and engraving premises of the city. Someone informed the authorities and a watch was set on Bull and his accomplice. The pair was not very careful about security, being observed in public holding up pieces of paper to the light to determine their quality. Finally, the police struck. Bull and his accomplice were caught with the papers and the plates. A series of witnesses gave damning evidence at the Old Bailey and the two were transported for fourteen years.

On the ship taking him to a convict's life at Norfolk Island the counterfeiter put his skills to more constructive ends and painted a number of maritime scenes. After Norfolk Island he was sent to Van Diemen's Land where Bull continued his career as the only professional landscape painter in Hobart, later teaching art there.

Despite enjoying career success, Bull was not a completely reformed character. He once tried to escape to Melbourne using poorly forged papers, only to be recognised and returned to servitude. His punishment was surprisingly light for what was usually a flogging offence—just twenty days solitary confinement after a few months in prison awaiting trial. As *The Hobarton Guardian* snidely observed: 'It is a fortunate circumstance for Mr. Bull that he is not an Irish State Prisoner,' a reference to the mistreatment that Irish political prisoners frequently suffered.

Bull seems to have learned his lesson at last and received a ticket of leave in 1852, marrying Mary Anne Bryen shortly after. He gained a conditional pardon in 1853, by which time the first of what would be five sons had been born. The family later moved to Sydney where Bull continued to paint works now considered important examples of colonial art and social history. How he and his family fared is not known but he died more or less in obscurity of typhoid fever in 1889.

Other artist forgers also had troubled times in colonial Australia.

Joseph Lycett was transported a generation earlier than Knud Bull, though his crime was the same and so was his sentence. A chronic alcoholic, Lycett again perverted his talents shortly after arrival in the colony. Hundreds of five-shilling bills were presented to the post office in May 1815. Too many to avoid detection. The expertly forged bills were traced back to Lycett who was found in possession of a small printing press.

Lycett was convicted and sent to the coalmines in Newcastle, New South Wales, an especially unpleasant experience for a fifty-year-old man. Fortunately, he was treated favourably for most of his sentence and painted a surviving church altarpiece while there. By 1819 he was taking private commissions and gained the favour of Governor Macquarie, who is thought to have arranged his full pardon in 1821. Now with a wife and two daughters, Lycett wasted no time returning to England where he published a series of aquatints of colonial views from 1824. Then he disappeared.

Based on a handwritten note in a copy of his *Views of Australia* held by the New South Wales State Library, the story goes that the artist was once again caught forging banknotes in 1828. Arrested, he slashed his throat, though was saved from death and left to recover in hospital. While there, he is said to have torn the wound in his neck open and bled to death.

Other artist forgers had less dramatic but still troubled careers. Scotsman Thomas Watling was transported for fourteen years in 1791 after a forgery charge in his native Dumfries. He was assigned to sympathetic masters and good use was made of his artistic abilities, which earned him an early pardon. He left a few years later and lived in Calcutta (now Kolkata) before returning to Scotland where he was again charged with forgery. He was freed when the charge was 'not proven' and seems to have then lived precariously on charity. The date and circumstances of his death are unknown.

English architect Francis Greenway arrived in Sydney in 1814 with a fourteen-year sentence, commuted from the death penalty. His architectural and artistic talents saw him quickly granted a ticket of leave and he went into business. He had an initially fruitful relationship with Governor Macquarie, though by 1822 his arrogance and generally unpleasant personality led to his dismissal from his official post. Greenway spent the rest of his life complaining of his treatment and died in 1837. Francis Greenway is recognised as one of the finest designers of colonial architecture and as a noted artist of his era. He is buried in an unmarked grave in the Hunter Valley.

THE LADY SWINDLER

In 1914 an 'In Memoriam' notice appeared in *The Sydney Morning Herald* newspaper:

ASKEW—In loving memory of our dear mother, Alexandrina Askew, who departed this life July 6, 1913.

In these ears as long as hearing hears
A low-set bell seems to toll
The passing of the dearest mother

That ever walked on earth.
Inserted by her loving son and daughter.

This conventional piece of Edwardian funereal sentiment belied the extraordinary life and crimes of the woman known as Alexandrina Askew, the 'Lady Swindler'.

Transported from her native Scotland in 1845, eighteen-year-old Alexandrina Grant, as she was then known, had several convictions before obtaining clothes by 'falsehoods, fraud and wilful imposition' earned her seven years in Van Diemen's Land. Clever deceptions would be the pattern she would follow for most of her life.

In Australia, Grant began her frauds by inventing a family who did not exist. She had been born to unmarried convict parents in a prison, a seemingly inevitable beginning to her long criminal career.

The tall, well-spoken young woman did not take to the constraints and drudgery of convict life. She frequently absconded from her assigned places and from the 'female factories' where she was often confined. Not that this stopped her going absent for nocturnal meetings with men. In 1849 she gave birth to an illegitimate child in the Cascades female factory in Hobart.

Grant later married a free man, William Askew. They moved to the Victorian goldfields where the now Alexandrina Askew continued her swindles at a dizzying rate, as partly described in newspaper accounts of her activities during the late 1860s.

A very clever series of depredations have recently been perpetrated by a lady swindler as she is termed by the victims. It appears that for a length of time the lady has been in the habit of visiting lodging houses and inquiring for apartments. Having satisfied herself of the respectability of the house, she proceeds to inquire into the character of the neighborhood and having obtained the fullest information of the next door neighbor, she takes her leave with a promise to call again.

Her next procedure is to call at one of the houses near, if they are lodging houses, stating that she has been recommended by the person she first visited. She describes herself as the wife of a squatter whose station is situated near Piggoreet, and that she requires the apartments for herself and husband. Having agreed to take the lodgings she proceeds to pay a deposit, when, lo! on feeling in her pocket, she cries, 'I've lost my purse; they have stolen my purse,' and forthwith commences to lament and bemoan her loss, exclaiming 'What shall I do; what will my husband say?'

The landlady naturally takes compassion on her forlorn condition, and promptly offers her the loan of a few pounds to alleviate her distress until, she has time to communicate with her husband. The offer is accepted after many refusals, and the would-be lodger goes on her way rejoicing never to return again . . .

The lady is always accompanied by a little boy, dressed in Highland costume, whose tears mingled with the sobs of his mother, are the secret of the facility with which she accomplishes her schemes.

This was Askew's conning technique for which she was up on at least a dozen charges in November 1867.

Askew was again in court in December, this time appearing at the Buninyong Police Court where she answered to several charges of obtaining money under false pretences. Alexandrina was discharged on the first count but remanded to Melbourne for the remaining case to proceed on bail of £100 (about $12,000 today).

The following January Askew was charged with being 'a rogue and a vagabond' at the Central Police Court and, as often happened, was again remanded. Askew was a clever con woman, always careful that her victims offered or lent her money, making it difficult for prosecutors to raise a provable charge against her. At Bacchus Marsh Police Court in January 1868, Askew's method of 'borrowing' rather than stealing money again stood her in good stead as 'the prosecution failed because the Bench held that the money had been freely lent to the prisoner'.

When her serial deceptions became too well known in one area, Askew and her family simply moved on to various locations in Victoria, South Australia and New South Wales. Despite these forced resettlements, her frequent court appearances, and occasional sentences, Askew seems to have maintained a reasonably stable marriage and family life. She had ten children and also brought up an illegitimate child of one of her daughters. Her death notice appeared in a Sydney newspaper because she had been living there for some years, running cheap lodging houses in the suburb of Redfern. She was in her late eighties when she died and, seemingly, still in the affections of at least some of her children.

As Askew's biographer, historian Janet McCalman revealed, the lady swindler's admittedly chequered life was nevertheless a rare success story for a female transport. Despite earlier misadventures, she married wisely, brought up a large family and did not fall prey to alcohol or other vices: 'Few of the 1636 Scottish women transported to Van Diemen's Land achieved anything like this ordinary triumph over poverty, stigma and marginalisation.'

A Strange Life

The strangeness began early in Amy Bock's life. Born in Tasmania in 1859, she and her family later moved to Sale, Victoria. Her father was a photographer and her mother a troubled woman whose difficulties included the delusion that she was Lady Macbeth. She died in an asylum when Bock was around sixteen. Possibly inheriting her mother's illness, Bock had an early tendency to make up stories and to use other people's names to buy goods, which she then gave away to others. Bright at school, a musician and horsewoman, young Amy was also an excellent actor, a skill she would use throughout her life, eventually with some very unusual consequences.

Bock spent two years in a Melbourne boarding school, then her father organised a post for the then nineteen-year-old as the teacher in a bush school. For the next ten years Bock taught around Gippsland and honed her ability to deceive and manipulate. She inflated attendance numbers to increase her salary and claimed expenses for broken windows that were intact. She also continued buying things and passing them on to others with no benefit to herself. Bizarrely, she once ordered coffins and had them delivered to a local family. On more than one occasion she wrote to her creditors, of which there were many, impersonating her sister and conveying the sad news that Amy Bock had died.

Eventually, Bock was arrested for fraud. People were aware of her mother's sad death and speculated on some sort of hereditary madness compelling the young woman to her inexplicable acts. The judge gave her the benefit of the doubt and she escaped a conviction.

In the mid-1880s Bock moved to New Zealand and began a life of even more intense fraud and fakery. Her first court appearance was shortly after her arrival. Again, she escaped conviction due to what the court considered her poor health and inability to be responsible for what she did. And she did an awful lot, most of it illegal and involving multiple impersonations, false pretences, stealing and the creation of fantasy roles, including a rich patron of the arts and promoter of a scheme to start a chicken farm.

Bock often gave away the proceeds of her crimes to those she considered to be in need, a peculiarity that attracted the attention of the press and the grudging respect of the police who frequently arrested her and came to know her *modus operandi* very well. The courts were not so accommodating, though, and Bock was regularly sentenced to imprisonment and hard labour for her crimes. Inside, with little opportunity to practise her deceptions, she behaved herself and usually managed to gain early release.

In 1909, after more than twenty years of serial offending and frequent bouts of prison, Bock mounted the most astonishing ruse of her, and perhaps of any other con artist's, career. Her scams were usually complicated, often involving sometimes multiple false identities for which she produced the appropriate supporting documents—all forged by her, of course. In this case, Bock adopted the identity of a man, a rich sheep farmer named Percival Leonard Carol Redwood. Employing her standard tricks for supporting herself, fleecing others and obtaining money from all and sundry, Bock established the friendly and popular persona of Percy Redwood in several high-class guesthouses, firstly in Dunedin, then in Port Molyneux in South Otago. 'Redwood' there met Nessie (Agnes) Ottaway, young daughter of a local guesthouse keeper. He courted her and won her hand in marriage, as they used to say in those days. The couple were married in April 1909 at a large and expensive wedding suited to a groom of Percy Redwood's wealth and standing. It had all been paid for—or rather, not paid for—through false pretences.

Although these facts did not come out at the time, there were already strong suspicions about 'Redwood' in the local community and the Ottaway family. After the ceremony, Nessie's father gave 'Redwood' a week to pay off his debts, otherwise he would not allow Nessie to be taken on the honeymoon. Others made discreet inquiries and soon discovered that there was no such wealthy sheep farmer as Percy Redwood. The police were informed and a detective familiar with Bock's previous scams recognised her style. 'Redwood' was arrested a few days after the wedding. As usual, Bock confessed her guilt as soon as the police confronted her and was taken to the Dunedin Supreme Court where she was described as looking like 'a diminutive man, well dressed, neat of limb, with neater feet, and rather good-looking'.

The trial was a sensation, of course, widely reported throughout New Zealand and Australia. Pleading guilty, Bock was sentenced to two years hard labour and declared an habitual criminal, meaning that she could be held in prison indefinitely at the governor's pleasure. As usual, Bock was a model prisoner and was out by early 1912, working as a teacher and housemaid in the New Plymouth area. In 1914 she began a brief marriage, this time to a man named Charles Christofferson. This arrangement lasted long enough for Bock to receive a discharge from her habitual criminal status.

It wasn't long before Bock was back in court, up to her usual tricks of obtaining goods by false pretences, in this case a piano. With the aid of a barrister who argued for her good character since release from prison, Bock got off with a fine. She remained around New Plymouth until moving to Hamilton in the mid-1920s. In 1931, then aged 71, she again appeared in court for obtaining money by false pretences. The 'faded old lady', as one newspaper described her, pleaded guilty and received two years probation. According to her biographer, Jenny Coleman, Bock was not heard of again until she died in Auckland in 1943, where she was buried in an unmarked grave.

But what of the bride Amy had duped in the masquerade of 'Percy Redwood'? Poor Nessie Ottaway was 'pale and worried' when she appeared at Bock's trial. What was she to do with herself in those days when young women were expected to be respectably married off? Could she ever find another suitor after such a debacle? She found not one, but two. In the year following Bock's trial, she married a widower twenty years older than herself. When he died a few years later, she married a man she had known as a child. She passed away in 1936.

Amy Bock's story was strange and sad. She played on her probably inherited affliction, once saying: 'The malady I suffer from now has been upon me from childhood, and no one but God and myself know the fearful horror I have had to face year after year in the knowledge that, instead of my being able to fight successfully against it (as I have prayed so often to do), it has rather overpowered me more and more.'

After her last conviction, Bock reportedly told police that she was 'tired of defrauding men; they are too soft and easy to work on'.

THE MAGICIAN OF MINES

One of this country's most colourful fraudsters never set foot in Australia. Horatio Bottomley was born in London in 1860. He had a stellar career in English finance and press publishing that included founding the respected *Financial Times*. His public profile as 'the people's friend' saw him elected to parliament several times. He was also a crook who set up many fraudulent businesses during his tumultuous life. In Australia, he made a fortune promoting a long series of dodgy mining enterprises, beginning in the 1890s.

The circumstances of Bottomley's birth were uncertain and his childhood years precarious. At the age of nine he was placed in an orphanage that he left at the age of fourteen and he then began to make his way in the world. After a number of false starts, he found employment in legal offices, gaining a knowledge of the law that would serve him well in his future business endeavours. He formed a publishing company at the age of twenty-four and later tried to float it on the stock market. He was prosecuted for fraud in 1893 but was acquitted. Soon after, he began promoting goldmines in faraway Western Australia, then at the beginning of a massive gold rush.

As with many of his English business dealings, Bottomley set up seemingly legitimate mining companies within which he obfuscated financial transactions through tricky share deals and internal reconstructions. There were holes in the ground that formed the basic assets of these enterprises and investors' money was spent on machinery and structural improvements that were duly reported. But strangely, no gold ever came out of the mines and investors were frequently convinced by Bottomley's considerable rhetorical skills to fork out yet more money. Much of it went straight into his pocket.

In the Northern Territory, Bottomley used a variation of this scam, setting up the Northern Territory Goldfields Company in London. He raised £300,000 (around $50 million in today's terms), mostly from hopeful investors, and used agents to purchase existing mines that were worked out of payable gold. The silver-tongued entrepreneur touted his mines as 'the richest goldfield yet discovered in the world'. They would pay fat dividends from the vast bodies of ore within them once the necessary upgrades and improvements to the shafts, pumps and crushing batteries were operating. Bottomley did upgrade most of the mines as promised, even equipping several with the then new-fangled electric lighting.

One of the operations, the Zapopan at Brock's Creek, did actually strike gold but it wasn't long before Bottomley was back to his long-suffering investors for further funds that would lead to returns 'beyond the dreams of avarice'. He needed another £100,000. A year later, in 1899, it was another £60,000. By 1901 the company's assets were valued at a whopping £4 million—or the nearly $700 million today. It all looked pretty rosy from London but on the ground it was a different story altogether.

There was already trouble at the company board when the 1899 capital raising was proposed. At a noisy board meeting Bottomley was called on to speak about the prospects of the company, which included the Big Howley mine, considered the jewel in the crown of the company's string of properties: 'Mr. Bottomley responded with alacrity, and said that, in the presence of the board, he would repeat that, for all practical purpose there was, in the Howley mine, gold of the value of £4,000,000 in sight. Unless there has been a foul conspiracy to deceive everyone all round, the mines were of immense value.'

By 1901 alarm bells were ringing in Australia and in London. Bottomley was openly derided in the financial press:

> As a conjuror he beats his confronters into fits . . . Why, however, we place the noble Horatio at the top of the pedestal is because he conjures without the aid of a confederate. There may be minor accessories in his play—humble dummies and scene-shifters, mimes and choristers of various sorts—but he handles the magic devised for his assemblies of the faithful alone, and charms away wrath by his own unaided eloquence.

It was reported that the company did not have cash to pay its workers in the mines and that money was being squandered in return for nothing at all. There was a shareholder revolt and creditors moved in on the mines in 1902. By this time, although remaining chair of the company board, Bottomley had secretly sold his shares and suffered little financial damage when the company was wound up.

Ever the smooth operator, Bottomley simply pivoted to another Australian mining dodge. Amazingly, he was able to convince investors to fund his new Northern Territory Mining and Smelting Company, which rode a rise in the price of copper. When the price of that commodity dropped in 1907, the company was wound up. Once again, Bottomley faced the courts, this time for conspiracy to defraud. Once again, he slipped out of the legal net.

While these schemes and their consequences were playing out, Bottomley was pursuing other interests. He was now a rich man who could enjoy a lavish lifestyle, and he did. There were luxurious houses and apartments, mistresses, unwise plunges on racehorses. He also returned to his publishing interests. He pursued these with the same lack of attention to details and the usual principles of accountancy and while his publications flourished for a while, they eventually lapsed into the mire of financial mystification that surrounded most of Bottomley's enterprises.

Bottomley also promoted various schemes, including a joint stock trust that failed during one of his several terms as a member of parliament. He was subsequently sued successfully by one of the enraged investors, a rare loss for the audacious entrepreneur whose true financial situation was revealed. Drowning in debt, Bottomley could not pay and was declared bankrupt. This automatically disqualified him from holding a seat in the House of Commons where he had been responsible for some useful social reforms.

Bottomley continued his publishing interests, ran dodgy sweepstakes and lotteries, and managed to keep up his excessive lifestyle until World War I. A golden opportunity! He reinvented himself as a jingoistic public speaker with considerable success at home and at the front. After the war he managed to have his bankruptcy discharged and was again elected to parliament. He also set up another scheme involving bonds, which, as usual, he rorted. After several legal encounters Bottomley was at last convicted of a serious fraud charge in 1922 and given a sentence of seven years hard labour. Released in 1927, he made efforts to revive his business career that came to nothing and he was bankrupt once more by 1930. He died in reduced circumstances three years later.

Horatio Bottomley's obituaries lamented the waste of his undoubted talents. An Australian newspaper headed an article on his life and death with the question 'Hero or villain?' and quoted what Bottomley had to say shortly before his death: 'when I am dead the papers will print things about me they would not have dared to write while I was alive. Well, I suppose the vultures must have their feast.' The article concluded that 'Horatio Bottomley had all the gifts except character and principle, and lacking them his life was ruined.' So were the lives and finances of many of those foolish enough to invest in him.

Clairvoyant Crimes

Although sitting at the less serious end of the wrongdoing spectrum, obtaining money by telling fortunes has a long criminal history. In Britain it was associated with witchcraft and vagrancy, and treated in a similar way in the Australian colonies, which later became states and territories. From early in the twentieth century, the commonplace 'gypsy' fortune tellers at the showground, astrologers and amateur readers of tea-leaves and cards began to be seen in a harsher light.

Fortune tellers were linked to social paranoias about white slavery and abortions. The rise of Spiritualism and its claims to connect the living and the dead also contributed to the growing perception that fortune telling was a form of fraud. Those who provided divination services, often women looking to provide for their children, were increasingly arrested and prosecuted. One of those making a very good living from clients anxious to know their fates was Mary Scales, said by one newspaper to be 'one of the most remarkable figures in the legal history of the state'.

Born in Tasmania, Mary Scales had few advantages in her early life. She was illiterate and worked in menial positions until she began faith healing and seeing the future in company with her husband, George. He welcomed the clients into their business premises, a massage shop, and took their money. They were then ushered into a darkened back room where Mary read their fortunes, usually after providing a massage. It was a nice little business.

Husband and wife were at the Darlinghurst Quarter Sessions in 1903, charged with telling the fortune of George Hamilton the previous December. A reporter from the *Evening News* published the inside story, noting that the prosecutor soft-pedalled the charges, arguing that anyone foolish enough to believe that the future might be foretold 'deserved to lose their half-crowns [2 shillings and 6 pence], or whatever they paid for the privilege of being fooled'. He went on to say, 'But fools should be protected sometimes, and for that reason these prosecutions had been taken.'

As the case proceeded, George Hamilton—actually Constable Hamilton working undercover in an operation to entrap Mary and George—gave evidence of his session with Mary. He had to give George three shillings before going into the room where Mary sat with the secrets of his fate at her fingertips. He was beckoned to sit at a round table opposite Mary and to place his palms downwards. Then, as readers of the *Evening News* were informed, the seer began:

> 'You were born under the sixty planet, and are very unlucky' . . .
> 'I was born under the same planet,' was the next information.
> 'Your planet has been reigning for the past 11 years.' The constable was told that there was a change in store for him, and that he would never do any good until he took a water journey. He was also told that two women had entered his life about seven years ago, and that one of them was between colours. That was explained to mean a half-caste.

As the case went on the court was enlightened with 'amusing evidence' when Hamilton was called to give evidence in support of the Crown case. The prosecutor asked Hamilton if any of Mary's predictions had come true: '"Specifically, have you had promotion?"—"No". (Laughter.)' The judge picked up on the fun:

> HIS HONOUR: 'Have you been going down?'
> HAMILTON: 'No.'
> HIS HONOUR: 'I don't like asking these questions; but has any half-caste woman come into your life?'
> HAMILTON: 'Not that I am aware of.'

Then Mary and George's solicitor joined in:

SOLICITOR: 'Were you going about with a woman policeman to-day?'
HAMILTON: 'I don't think she's a Policeman.'
SOLICITOR: 'But she is attached to the police somehow?'
HAMILTON: 'At Redfern.'

Hamilton then went on to recount, 'she said my mind was very much muddled, and I should have ruled under Government'.

'Muddled. Yes,' replied the fortune teller's defence, 'that's the sort they want.' (Laughter.)

After this farce, the defence argued there was no case to answer. His Honour disagreed and Mary Scales was called to the witness box. She said she carried on her business of 'planet reading' at the massage shop she ran with George in a posh Sydney arcade. Mary defended her good character and said she had 'treated' many people. His Honour wanted to know if the massage had any connection with the planets.

Yes, it's the same. I find out from the planets if people have been ill. Suppose a doctor sent a patient for massage treatment.—I should have to 'sit' with him to see what I had to massage him for. I cannot write or read, and I 'go under the influence' and sit. So that I can do that person good.

In Hamilton's case, she had sensed his health was 'going down' and 'That means . . . that a person is getting near the death planet.' Mary's solicitor commented that 'He has hung out so far.' (Laughter). The judge responded 'Do you want much more about this case? Because it is becoming uncomfortable. She may say something about our death planet.' (Laughter.)

The only one to maintain some sort of decorum in this shambles was Mary. She said to the prosecutor, 'I am gifted with double sight.' After more banter in which Mary complained that her business had dropped off because of the charges against her and George, the prosecutor asked:

'Do you know anything about astronomy?'

'No,' Mary replied. 'I go into a trance. I don't read these stars that you can see, I am taken away beyond them sir. I am shown what to do.'

'Any idea how far you go?' the prosecutor queried sarcastically.

'I am taken to fine worlds, something like this.'

The reporter covering the case wrapped up this account of the absurd proceedings with the observation that 'Witness was understood to say she had never seen either heaven or hell.'

Mary and George were found guilty, bound over for twelve months and released. They were soon back to business, eventually amassing a substantial fortune from Mary's 'double sight' and the desperate gullibility of their clients.

This was far from Mary's only encounter with the legal systems of both Australia and Britain. She was again arrested in 1907 but this time appealed against the verdict in the Supreme Court of New South Wales and, finally, in the High Court of Australia. She won her case on the legal argument that the fortune-telling legislation brought to Australia was not part of the colony's legal system when it gained a court system independent of Britain in 1828. Of course, new laws against fortune telling were soon passed to cover this gap and the cat-and-mouse game between prophets and police continued as before.

By the time Mary and George Scales retired, they were worth a very great deal of money, mostly derived from Mary's work. When George died in 1920, Mary had a reasonable expectation of receiving her share of their joint estate. But George had changed his will to leave the money in trust, providing Mary only with an allowance. Dissatisfied with this, she contested the will but was unsuccessful. She then went all the way to the legal body of last resort, the Privy Council in England. There, she won back her right to the money in 1926.

Did Mary Scales really believe she had the ability to tell fortunes? Many others clearly did and were willing to pay generously for the opportunity to hear her foresights. Having one's fortune told was a form of entertainment and, for many perhaps, a form of therapy for their troubles. Reformed fortune tellers often claim this is the case. They also admit that they were duping their clients with claims of extra-normal powers.

Mary died in 1928. Her will bequeathed funds to her female descendants only to pay for education, health-care and clothing. All the things that she had lacked before she began telling people about themselves and their future.

The Age of Con

As the story goes, Detective Chief Inspector Harry (Henry) Mann of the Western Australian Police was wined and dined at London's swanky Cafe Monaco in the early years of the twentieth century. His genial hosts were from a group of Australian con men with records longer than the arms of everyone at the table. The cafe was their London hangout and distribution centre for the proceeds of crime. Cop and crims were obviously well known to each other and this strange moment says a lot about the relationship between the police and the Down Under Dupers who dominated Britain's confidence games for decades.

In the years directly before the Great War of 1914–18, right through to the end of World War II in 1945, there were more Australian con men on British police registers than those of any other nationality—by a long shot. They were recognised as highly skilled exponents of their nefarious schemes and were very successful. When caught, many had what amounted to small fortunes in their bank accounts and stuffed into the upholstery of their expensive furniture and cars—and they were just the stashes the police found. No self-respecting trickster would be without a secret hidey-hole or two for the inevitable emergencies. Bags of cash were essential to set up the bigger cons and to fund the lavish lifestyles needed to impress rich marks.

And there were plenty of them. Especially after World War I, Britain, Europe and the United States were awash with money flowing through newly opened international financial channels and connections. Business deals and schemes were being rolled out around the world in oil, minerals and a hundred other lucrative enterprises. A lot of people made a lot of money—and often spent it lavishly and ostentatiously. Perfect pigeons for gangs like London's Hanley Mob, among others working the same rackets.

Sometimes the wealthy individuals suckered in were themselves con men of a kind, wheeling and dealing in the white-collar areas of finance and investment. But they were rarely found out and, if they were, could usually buy their way out of trouble. Eventually, their activities would play a part in the great stock market crash of 1929 and the deep depression that followed. But, for now, it was not only an era of excess and indulgence, it was also the golden age of the con.

Just how and why Australians became the main exponents of the con in Britain, and sometimes Europe, is a mystery. Operators like Bludger Bill Warren, Dictionary Harry (Harry Harrison) and Dave the Liar (David John Lewis) excelled in new and clever versions of classic cons. These included the infallible betting system (and its variant known as 'the brass'), 'the pay-off' (and an adaptation known as 'the rag'), and other scams large and small also perfected by the cons from Oz. In one celebrated operation, Bludger Bill and some accomplices took down the immensely wealthy English shipping magnate, Sir Walter Cockerline, for more than £20,000—just under $2 million today—in 1923.

At the time, for—let's say—professional reasons, Bill was sojourning on the continent. He'd fleeced a businessman in Portugal of £15,000 and found it necessary to fade away, turning up on the French Riviera. Here, the normally foul-mouthed Bill with his strong Australian accent became the owner of a South African diamond mine or three. Employing his practised skills, Bill checked into the same expensive hotel as Sir Walter, and soon made a good friend of him. Only a day or two later, Bill introduced Sir Walter to an acquaintance who was, quite coincidentally, a guest at the same hotel. The acquaintance was an American oil king.

After getting to know each other a little more, the convivial trio visited Monte Carlo for some wagering at the tables. As they refreshed themselves with a coffee, the oil king noticed a man he described as 'the biggest bookmaker in the United States'. The bookmaker, whose betting limit was said to be 'the blue sky', was invited to the table and was soon a member of the affable group.

The fix was in.

It wasn't long before the conversation was about betting on the gee-gees. Bill and the oil king placed big bets through the bookmaker and invited Sir Walter to join the fun. By day's end, the bookmaker was pleased to tell the informal syndicate that they had netted £170,000 in winnings.

It was time for the sting.

When settlement of the bets was due, Bill, very annoyed, informed Sir Walter that the bookmaker's club through which he had laid their bets would only pay up when the punters proved they could show they were men of substance. 'But,' said Bill, flashing a large wad of cash, 'I'll put up the "cover",' as it was called. Being gentlemen, of course, the others couldn't allow Bill to pony up the full amount of their joint obligation so they each wrote personal cheques for £25,000.

Sir Walter then had to return to England before the group's winnings were drawn. Soon after he arrived, he received a wire from France. Bill was embarrassed, naturally, but he'd had a spot of bad luck and was temporarily short of £12,000 of his share of the cover. Would Sir Walter possibly be so good as to advance him that sum until the winnings were available?

Completely conned, Sir Walter obligingly wired the money to Bill and never heard from the diamond magnate again.

Until the French police caught up with Bill and his wife in Paris. They had fled there in a newly purchased luxury car after another mark had complained to the authorities. When the police raided the con man's apartment they found stashes of banknotes in various European currencies, as well as share certificates and a lot of diamonds being worn by Bill's wife. The expensive car was also full of loot.

One of the advantages of being a confidence trickster was that the risk of being caught was very low compared with most other forms of crime. Victims were often too embarrassed to admit they had been so easily fooled and often reluctant to report their loss to police. Even when they did, it was often difficult for prosecutors to make winnable cases because the nature of the transactions could often be represented as commercial business deals, gambling wins and losses, or gifts. There was rarely a paper trail documenting what happened, whatever that had been. In the case of Bludger Bill, the French court in which he was brought to book was at first reluctant to admit the case at all, as the prosecution failed to establish Bill's true identity, even with help from Scotland Yard. The wily fraudster also maintained that his arrangement with Sir Walter had been a commercial matter.

This and the odd loophole in the laws of the various countries in which the Aussies operated meant that they often escaped conviction. The only recourse available was to prosecute them for fraud under civil law, a course taken by several victims who had the financial resources required. Not that this made much difference to their finances. Bill and his accomplices were tried and convicted, spending some more years in a French prison. It's unlikely any of their victims ever saw their money again.

Confidence tricksters are a special type of criminal. They depend on their wits, powers of persuasion and the gullibility and greed of their 'marks', or victims. They have been fleecing the foolish forever and will never stop. Their wiles and ploys are complex and clever, as well as despicable. As one writer on the subject put it in 1935: 'in its higher reaches, the art of the confidence trick is a subtle science demanding more than common qualities of nerve and brain—or, if you like, a front of brass and a fertile cunning. Steal a fiver and you get thrust into gaol; steal a million and they build you a monument. That is the creed of the master of craft.'

Con artists are generally considered to be elite criminals who avoid violence in favour of elaborately researched and constructed frauds usually perpetrated against those whom most people think are too wealthy for their own good. That includes the averagely paid police officers tasked with tracking con artists down. Chief Inspector Mann was in London to visit colleagues at Scotland Yard and swap intelligence on the roots and scams of the con men well known to them all. They were few enough in number to be recognised by police who often had an ambivalent relationship with them. The hunters and the hunted shared a bond of common interest in crime, even if from different perspectives. The diners at Cafe Monaco were all aware of their roles that night but suspended hostilities for a few convivial hours, each no doubt hoping to learn something to his advantage from the event.

Confidence tricksters also need to keep up with changing times. The Australians were at the forefront of the new, twentieth-century breed of operators. A few gentlemen thieves and suave manipulators of an earlier age were still around but had largely been succeeded by a brasher, often more proletarian crim, better suited to the world of self-made millionaires, often with colonial connections. The same skills of deceit and manipulation were used to rob the rich and had evolved, from the lowliest short con to the most sophisticated long con, into finely staged performances in which the star was also the mark.

The con men, and some women, weren't exactly benefitting the poor but they did not batten onto everyday mugs. Not worth the trouble, of course. Since that time, scams and cons have increasingly targeted you and me through the internet and mobile phones. We're not filthy rich but there are an awful lot more of us and it's all too easy to play the Nigerian money scam: simply the modern form of an ancient con known as 'the Spanish prisoner'. These tawdry rorts employ the tricks of deception, diversion and persuasion used by the earlier fraudsters, but they are crude echoes of a much cleverer and more artistic form of criminality. The old-time operators weren't known as 'con artists' for no reason.

HOW TO BE A CON ARTIST

The term 'confidence man' seems to have taken its modern form from an article in the *New York Herald* in 1849. A man named William Thompson was arrested for a short street con in which he walked up to a stranger and engaged them in conversation. After a while he asked, 'Have you confidence in me to trust me with your watch until to-morrow?' In what was obviously a much more trusting age, the surprised mark usually handed over their expensive timepiece. Williams simply made off, laughing as he went. He was dubbed 'the Confidence Man' and so the name has stuck. In Australia we also use the typically shortened form of 'con man' and also 'con artist'. There was also some older slang, including 'illywacker', derived from 'whacking the illy', meaning to perpetrate a con.

Conning, of course, has been around forever, probably since the ancient Greek figure of myth, Hermes, is said to have invented lying. In Elizabethan English someone gulled by a confidence trickster of the time was known as a 'coney', a rabbit or, as we might say today, a bunny. Those who carried out these crimes were coney catchers, and they were as numerous and successful as they have been ever since.

The number of English terms for those who do practise the con is revealing of how prevalent it is. They include swindler, cheat, imposter, charlatan, huckster, shyster, fraudster, flimflammer, sharper, bilker and fleecer, among others. As well as these widely used terms, different countries have more specialised references, such as the American 'bunco man' and 'grifter'.

Australia has not been wanting in producing its own crime-speak. In its earliest form this was the slang of British, mainly London, criminals. It arrived fully-fledged with the First Fleet and continued to evolve in a form usually known as the 'flash language' and was a prominent feature of everyday conversation in the colonial years. A correspondent to Tasmania's *Cornwall Chronicle* in 1852 provided a few choice phrases from the underworld vocabulary of the time, including 'mawleys', for fingers dipping into a 'cly', or pocket; 'blowens' (prostitute); 'magsmen' (confidence tricksters); 'dummy hunters' (wallet thieves) and 'buzgloaks' (pickpockets). This colonial history of flash talk and the crimes that went with it continued to breed new generations of Australian confidence tricksters into the twentieth century.

The years between the two world wars, 1918 to 1939, were golden ones for confidence tricksters. Squadrons of card sharps, magsmen, spielers and fake toffs haunted hotels, railway stations, shipping terminals and anywhere else where large numbers of people were in motion and not as secure as they might be at home. For the con artists of whatever kind, and there were many, these individuals were all potential 'marks'—likely victims of some of the venerable but amazingly successful tricks.

In the era before portable radios, one of these was associated with betting on racehorses and usually known as 'the brass'. It required a mark who was not very knowledgeable about the turf and whom carefully observant swindlers had identified as a likely victim. A seemingly chance encounter with the mark was easily engineered at the bar or gaming tables by a personable member of the gang. After a drink or two and flattery about what a man of the world the mark must be, he was introduced to a couple of other like-minded fellows. They were all well dressed, charming and, apparently, well off. More drinks and the conversation came round to the horses running that after-noon. The mark's new friends were very keen on a sure thing and intend to bet big. One gets up to go to the telephone, the only way to lay an off-track bet at the time. As he gets up, he has a thought. Would the mark like to be in on the flutter? Why not!

The bets are duly laid and the convivial group of wagerers settle down to a few more drinks while they await the outcome of the race. One of the men later makes another call and brings back the news that they have won. Why not go again? And they do, but this time they lose. They have one last chance to recoup their losses on a certainty in the last race of the day. They all place large bets. Of course, the horse does not win and the chummy atmosphere evaporates. The mark is suddenly confronted with a demand for a cheque to cover his share of the large amount seemingly lost. Or else.

There were endless variations on this basic confidence trick. It was a relatively safe one for the swindlers because victims were often too embarrassed to report their folly, though sufficient numbers did to justify police across the country investing resources in detecting crimes of this sort. A special addendum to the *New South Wales Police Gazette* was developed. Known as 'Supplement C', it detailed 'pickpockets, confidence men, cardsharpers, etc. who operate throughout the Commonwealth' and aimed to identify as many con artists as possible, along with the tricks they inflicted on the unsuspecting and the gullible.

A favourite of the time was one of the most ancient scams of all. Played especially at country shows and race meetings and on long distance trains, the 'three card trick' or 'find the lady' is a version of the even older 'shell game', also known as 'thimblerigging' or the 'pea and thimble game'. In the version played with cards, the swindler has three playing cards, two aces and a queen, the 'lady'. The cards are placed face down on a flat surface with the queen in the middle. The dealer then rotates the cards and those watching are invited to pick where the queen ends up. Would anyone like to make a small wager?

About now someone in the crowd loudly places a bet—and wins. It seems easy. He wins again and the cardsharp is handing over pound notes. Another person in the crowd, known as a 'buttoner', suggests to the chosen mark he has carefully stood beside that this is easy money. Let's have a go. They do and have several wins.

It's a fast game. The two betters win some, then lose a couple of rounds, then win some more. All the time the buttoner is urging the mark on, diverting his attention from the fact that he is actually losing money. The card sharp and the buttoner keep this up until the mug has done his dough.

The dealer needs to be something of a magician for this trick to work. The classic sleight of hand involves picking up one card in one hand and two in the other. This allows the skilled conjuror to make it appear that the lower card is being dealt, fooling the mark into thinking that is the 'lady' while the dealer has actually already switched the cards. Another of the many techniques used is to bend or crimp one of the cards, making sure the mark sees this being done. Thinking that makes the money card easy to spot, the mark picks it only to be disappointed. The dealer has secretly unbent the card while moving it around. A skilled operator can do this imperceptibly.

Again, there were many variations on this basic scam, but its portable equipment made it a favourite of those who lived much of their lives on the run for one reason or another. It was also easy to ditch the cards if a policeman should happen to turn up during the game.

More sophisticated confidence tricks, sometimes known as 'long cons', were carried out by well-practised gangs of spielers. A case in Sydney during 1930 involved three crims setting up a fake business known as the Climax Agency. They sought out suburban shops as agents for a potato peeler they were marketing. Shopkeepers could purchase the product from the agency at fourteen shillings a dozen and could sell them to customers for whatever mark-up they liked. After the agreement was made, two of the crims would make a bulk order from the shopkeepers who would then pay a third member of the Climax Agency the fourteen shillings for the ordered potato peelers. The two men who had ordered the products never returned, leaving the shopkeeper fourteen shillings poorer and the crims that much richer.

This con was eventually revealed and the Climax Agency shut down by the police. The scammers were tried, found guilty and placed on a bond that required them to pay back £30 to the agents they had defrauded. It is likely that they made a lot more money out of this low-key but deviously clever operation. Just another trick of an eternal trade.

Also Known As . . . ?

Globetrotting Ethel Livesy arrived in Australia to great fanfare in September 1945. She told the breathless newspaper journalists that she was visiting to catch up with her sons, both serving officers, now living in Adelaide. During the recently ended war, the widowed Mrs Livesy had entertained 'hundreds of Australian servicemen' in her sumptuous homes in Wales and on the Isle of Man and generally done her bit as a woman of substance and position might be expected to do. The newspaper added that Livesy, known as a Manchester cotton heiress, also had homes in Monte Carlo and on the English Riviera of Torquay.

Barely three months later, Livesy was in Sydney to wed public servant James Rex Beech in exclusive Darling Point. Hundreds of guests had been invited. There was to be a full choir, a release of doves and a 32-carat diamond ring to seal the matrimonial bliss. Imported French champagne would elevate all present to the same euphoric state. A Parisian 'Molyneux frock' and an elaborate bouquet completed the lavish crowd-stopper. 'About 200 guests assembled for a sumptuous breakfast in the flower-decked ballroom at the Hotel Australia on Saturday evening. Crowds blocked the pavement and road outside the hotel waiting to get a glimpse of the bride in her special Paris model frock . . .'

But the guests, the choir and the doves waited in vain. The wedding was mysteriously cancelled when the groom was given 'certain information'. In company with his solicitor, Beech had earlier arrived at Livesy's flat in the fashionable suburb of Edgecliff where she was dressing for the event. What passed between the intended groom and bride was not known. As her housekeeper told the detectives who arrived at the flat next morning: 'In the early hours, she went to bed, and a little while later she got up, packed a few things, including her wedding ring set with 75 diamonds—which she told me cost her £150 [$12,000] and left the flat alone . . . I do not know where she has gone, but I believe that she has left the flat for good. The wedding presents were left.' She also told them that she had helped Livesy take off the expensive dress she had already donned for the event, discovering in the process that it was one she had worn before.

Police caught up with Livesy and she was remanded on £200 bail at the Central Police Court on a charge of false pretences under the name of Florence Elizabeth Ethel Gardiner. She arrived 'in a big sedan' and 'wearing a long black coat over a brown flowered frock, with a black hat and veil'. The case could not proceed as certain documents from South Australia had not yet arrived and the defendant was remanded until after Christmas.

In January Livesy flew to Adelaide after jurisdictional difficulties with her legal representations. She was to appear at the Adelaide Criminal Sessions with her Sydney solicitors on a twelve-year-old charge of false pretences. Then she conveniently fell ill and it was thought unlikely she would attend the court.

Eventually, she was convicted by a jury on two counts of false pretences. The judge said he was not sure what her real name was and an unknown man in the court called out 'Anderson is her name'. The judge ordered the man removed, then released the multi-identity woman on a three-year bond.

But Livesy—or Gardiner or Anderson—was not taking these setbacks lying down. Next month she filed a writ against poor James Beech for breach of promise. She wanted £10,000 (around $750,000 today) compensation. While this claim was pending, 'Mrs Livesy' was declared bankrupt. She had failed to pay the bill for the alcohol to be consumed at the wedding reception. It was said that the groom and guests drank it anyway. Who could blame them?

Once again, Livesy was too ill to appear at her bankruptcy proceedings and by July that year her location was 'unknown'. In October her breach of promise suit was abandoned, with costs awarded against her.

Never shy of publicity, Livesy made a filmed interview in 1946 telling a self-justifying version of her life story. The Pathé movie news clip shows a plump, middle-aged woman with what many Australians would consider a 'posh' English accent confidently delivering a pre-written script directly to camera. She made a couple of minor slips but was quite convincing.

Displaying a string of pearls around her neck, the shrewd fraudster claimed to have been an air raid warden in the London Blitz and to have carried out the maimed bodies of victims. She was, she said, someone who had suffered a few hard knocks in life but had come out on top. All these things that people were saying were untrue and only her real friends had stood by her. She seemed particularly unhappy with Sydney 'society'. There was no mention of a Manchester cotton fortune or homes in Monte Carlo and Torquay.

With her face in cinemas across the country, it didn't take long for the bold fraudster's creditors to catch up with her. In February 1947, Livesy finally had to turn up and face the music, this time before the Registrar in Bankruptcy. Explaining her situation, she claimed that she 'would never have been bankrupt if she had heeded a friend's warning that her legal adviser's charges were excessive'. The registrar wanted to know about various sums of money she had borrowed. Livesy said she had fully expected to be able to pay them back when she received a sum she was due from England. She also claimed that she had never said to anyone that she had an income of £5000 or £8000 ($380,000 to $610,000 today) a year. The final statement of her assets 'showed liabilities of £3.700 and assets of £1.270'.

Livesy was not heard of again until December 1950. She was back in Adelaide where she was given two months in gaol for a four-year-old charge of stealing crystal glasses and rubber boots. It was noted that she had previous convictions for false pretences in South Australia and Victoria, as well as in England and New South Wales. She was said to be 53 years of age and to be employed in 'domestic duties'. After this sentence, she performed another of her vanishing acts. She may have then attempted to stage her death but in any case, was later operating a real estate scam in Western Australia.

What was the truth about this great imposter? There were a few faint wisps of honesty floating through her many personas.

She was born Ethel Swindells into a solidly respectable Manchester family in 1897 and did have some connection to the Isle of Man. She did indeed receive money from her family in England, most of it swindled from her father. This, and her other frauds along the way, allowed her to travel the world in some style, establishing an image as a woman of substance.

Swindells' criminal career began in World War I when she received a portion of the pay of several active service soldiers while being married to only one of them. When these handy income streams dried up she abandoned the child she had with one of the men and took to further false pretences and serial marriages. One of her unlucky later grooms was an Australian, facilitating her connection with the country where she would conduct many of her impostures.

By the time of her death in 1972, Ethel Swindells had married at least eight times, often bigamously, and birthed four children. She is thought to have used more than forty aliases during her long career of delusion and deception.

TAR AND FEATHERS

Grant Hervey had one of the more unusual career descriptions— poet, swindler and forger. This colourful character was all these things, and more, in the 53 years of an eventful life. The talented but wayward Hervey was also a journalist, aspiring politician, impersonator and probable bigamist who carried out some intriguing scams, including the attempted secession of an entire region of New South Wales.

Hervey began life unremarkably in rural Casterton, Victoria in 1880. He was named George Henry Cochrane, later changed to the more imposing Grant Madison Hervey, perhaps an early indication of what was to come. After starting working life as a blacksmith and foundry worker, his talent as a versifier led him into journalism in Western Australia, New South Wales and Victoria. Contemporaries admired his work though thought he was a little too fond of drink and romance. In 1905 he was attacked by the angry husband of a woman he was squiring along Melbourne's Bourke Street. Hervey pulled out a pistol and fired at the man, later escaping a charge of attempted murder.

An accomplished public speaker, Hervey was hired by various interests to spruik their political and social agendas. This brought him into contact with power brokers, including John Norton, the proprietor of the *Truth* newspaper and a notorious Melbourne political and business identity. It was now that Hervey's addled criminality fully emerged. He conceived a bizarre scheme that involved telling Norton that he was having an affair with his wife and offering, for a fee, to provide the salacious details. Not surprisingly, Norton was sceptical and contacted the police. They set up a 'sting' operation in which police concealed themselves in an adjoining room while Norton met Hervey. Incriminating evidence was gathered like this over several meetings, eventually leading to Hervey being charged with attempting to obtain money by false pretences.

During the same period, another of the chancer's harebrained schemes backfired badly. He had a telegram sent to the editor of his hometown newspaper falsely claiming that Grant Hervey had been made bankrupt. Hervey hoped that the newspaper would publish this falsehood, allowing him to sue for defamation. The paper did publish and Hervey duly sued. But his plot was uncovered and he was also charged with forging and uttering as well as the John Norton deception. Altogether, he was sentenced to four years hard labour.

After his release in 1919, Hervey embarked on another odd adventure. This time he became an American journalist: 'Last week Mr Grant Hervey, a bright but unballasted young Australian writer, posing as Mr. G. Madison Harvey, American journalist and man of big ideas, struck Mildura with a fine scheme for the general advance of the Mid-Murray-Darling section of the Commonwealth and the making of a Greater Mildura.' The plan 'Harvey' proposed was for the Mildura region to form a 'soldiers' memorial state' and develop independently of New South Wales and Victoria. The irrigation and land settlement schemes of the Murray–Darling depended heavily on soldier settlers after World War I and his proposal had a degree of local support. But, at the large public meeting where Hervey enthusiastically promoted his plan, his real identity was unmasked by Clement—usually Jack—De Garis, the promotional mastermind behind the creation of the 'Sunraysia' brand and region.

De Garis was employed by local interests at a very high salary to promote the region and its produce and it was clear to him that Hervey was after his job. He had waited to respond until this public meeting gave him the opportunity to confront the challenger. De Garis asked 'Harvey' to answer questions about whom he was representing, who he really was and what he had been doing over the previous few years. Knowing the game was up, the poseur tried to tough it out. He threw off his overcoat:

[and] declared in impassioned tones that he had spent a good deal of the time mentioned in prison. He was sent to gaol on the 19th August 1915 (after eight months of trial) and he was released on the 19th June, 1919. His real name was Grant Madison Hervey. John Norton and he were in business together on the paper 'Truth' and Norton swindled him. He swung the man a double-cross which broke him up but which incidentally led to his own imprisonment. It was while in prison that he evolved the scheme of a Greater Mildura. He was an Australian not an American as he had represented. Knowing Australia as he did, he felt that the people would pay more attention to 'a man from abroad' than they would to an Australian. He believed in his scheme and had hoped to get it accepted.

Not surprisingly, this went down very badly with the 2000-strong crowd. The chairman said he personally resented Hervey's actions and declared the meeting closed. But that was far from the end of the affair.

Hervey persisted with his 'Greater Mildura' proposal. He became the editor of a local newspaper through which he promoted his ideas and attacked De Garis. He also started an intensive rumour campaign that his rival was on the verge of bankruptcy. When De Garis, then pursuing other ventures in Western Australia, heard about the posters that suddenly appeared in Melbourne carrying this falsehood he offered a large reward for the names of whoever was behind the slurs. No one had much doubt who it was.

By now, local feeling against Hervey was running high. When he arrived by train from Melbourne in October 1921 a 'local vigilance committee' was waiting for him. Hervey's house was surrounded and threats were made against him. Police came and broke up the riot but the next day Hervey attempted to escape in a car and was captured by the vigilantes. They took him to a nearby airfield and tarred and feathered him (probably with kapok) and ejected him from the community.

> The news of the incident spread about the town, and a large number of people soon assembled. Cheer after cheer went up as they heard of Hervey's treatment. One of the crowd announced from the top of the fire tower that Hervey, who, he said, had been doing much harm to Mildura, had been tarred and feathered. There was tumultuous cheering, and the town was alive with excitement, all night.

This rough justice ended in a trial at which the assailants were convicted, though in summing up the judge called Hervey 'despicable' and his journalism 'foul and filthy'.

Hervey continued his public speaking, journalism and other activities, including forging and uttering cheques for which he received a two-year sentence in 1923. According to one account, he was back in Melbourne again in 1929, posing once again as an American under the assumed name of G. Madison MacGlashon of New York. In 1931 he was committed for trial in Sydney, charged with signing someone else's name to a telegram. Two years later Grant Madison Hervey, together with his aliases, was dead from diabetes at the age of fifty-three. His obituaries noted his wayward genius and regretted the squandering of his talents.

The charlatan and fraudster did have one win. The slurs he made against the solvency of Jack De Garis stuck in the minds of potential investors. The ambitious land development scheme he promoted in Western Australia failed for lack of investment. His financial troubles drove him to commit suicide in 1926.

A MAN OF FACES

Just who was Anthony Vincent Duerden, if that was even his name? Nobody seems to have known during his criminal career and nobody knows today. Efforts to track down the elusive imposter and con artist have turned up very little.

During the 1930s, Duerden—we'll call him that for convenience—turned up in South Australia under various aliases that included Anthony Rothesay, Stuart Worthley (Wortley) and Ronald Palmer. There, he was arrested, tried, imprisoned and eventually discharged.

The charges against him were all for the small-time, run-of-the-mill crimes of another chancer. But in 1940 Duerden hit the big time, for a crim anyway. He became the first person to be charged under what were then new national security regulations. The *National Security Act* and its provisions of 1939–40 gave the federal government powers to use sections of the *Defence Act* for compulsory orders across the country. Citizens could be ordered to work in certain industries and occupations, food and petrol rationing was introduced and electricity supplies restricted through blackouts and brownouts. The media industries of the time were to be subjected to censorship and authorities gained wide powers to regulate most areas of civil and military life.

In December 1939, a Lieutenant Dreyer of the Royal Navy visited the New South Wales coastal town of Woy Woy. He said he was on board a British destroyer taking on coal further north at Newcastle in preparation for transporting Australian troops across the seas. Dreyer struck up an acquaintance with a man named Charles Redford. He was the proud father of a son serving as a rating on HMAS *Canberra* where, sadly for the father, he would be on duty during the Christmas period and so unable to join his family for the festivities.

Dreyer told Redford that he was in touch with the authorities at Sydney's Garden Island naval base and that he would use his influence to have his son furloughed for Christmas. A grateful Redford was happy to travel to Sydney with Dreyer on Christmas Day, looking forward to seeing his son. At some point during the day, Dreyer asked Redford for money and the penny dropped.

As the details were reported from the trial, Dreyer was in fact Anthony Duerden. He had come into possession of some papers that allowed him to pose as a naval officer, assisted by a merchant navy uniform he had obtained to provide a nautical veneer to his imposture. Police investigations revealed that Duerden had never been in the Royal Navy or the Australian Navy, though his occupation was given as a 'ship's engineer' which, if true, probably meant he worked in cargo freighters.

The prisoner claimed from the dock that he was on the Royal Navy reserve list, in which capacity he was 'on loan at Jervis Bay'. He also stated that 'what I did did not harm the Commonwealth', which was probably true but irrelevant. He also claimed to be the son of a rear-admiral in the Royal Navy, a claim seriously doubted by police and never verified. It was also shown that there was no destroyer anywhere near Newcastle and the authorities denied that the imposter had ever been on loan to them from the Royal Navy.

The prosecution stated that Dreyer/Duerden had caused a good deal of trouble while they were trying to fight a war and so took a very serious view of his behaviour. The false navy officer was lucky, though. Police withdrew the charge of obtaining money by false pretences and he was given a prison sentence of just six months for impersonating an officer. Duerden was no threat to national security, but his activities were obviously an irritation to the naval authorities. In the atmosphere of wartime concerns, he was fortunate to get off with such a light sentence.

After that, the man of faces seems to have vanished altogether. Who was he and where did he go? Verifiable facts are thin on the ground. He was aged 40 when sentenced. Born in England, his accent probably helped his subterfuges in the very Anglicised Australia of the time. He was clearly a smooth talker and a practised con artist. Perhaps he carried on his criminal career under other aliases. Or perhaps he was a ship's engineer and sailed away forever after serving his time, plying his tricks in other parts of the world. We'll probably never know.

Glorified Jam Labels

Counterfeiting did not end with the forgeries of the colonial era. Fake money continued to be a problem after Federation in

1901, leading to the responsibility for issuing banknotes being transferred from the states to the Commonwealth Treasury in 1910. Ten years later the forerunner of today's Reserve Bank took over the issuing of all banknotes. But that didn't stop the crims for long.

In 1921 a stack of forged one- and ten-pound notes were discovered circulating around the country. The notes were very crude, prompting the official Note and Stamp printer of the time, Thomas S. Harrison, to observe that they were 'nothing more than what might be termed glorified jam labels'. Harrison urged the government to incorporate engravings in the design of new banknotes as a way to make them difficult to forge. Future notes usually did include engraved portraits, though the crooks soon found ways around that security device. Mostly, they got caught, but not always.

A large number of phony five-pound notes appeared in Sydney in 1940. Pubs seem to have been the favoured distribution points for these fakes and many hotels suffered serious losses as a result of the notes being passed across the bar in the hurly-burly of drinking sessions. Despite the damage done and the apprehension of quite a few people caught carrying forged notes, it seems that nobody was ever prosecuted for the crime. A police officer thought that 'The plant that produced them is probably at the bottom of the harbour by now'.

After another flood of faked fivers in the mid-1950s, the decimal era that began in 1966 brought new banknotes with gee-whiz anti-counterfeiting technologies. The year was not yet out before the crims had figured out how to get around that little problem. More than $100,000 worth of dodgy $10 notes floated around the country. The culprits, an extended family, were caught when one of them unwittingly passed a forged note at a local bakery. An astute shopkeeper took down her car number plate and telephoned the cops. Seven people went to prison for the crime.

This incident led to the main burden of investigating fake money moving mainly to the organisation that is now the Australian Federal Police, in partnership with the Reserve Bank. The current, supposedly forge-proof polymer banknotes we use were also motivated by this case. They worked well for a while. But from the early 2000s there has been a rise in the number of counterfeits detected. As with almost everything in today's world, the counterfeiting game is now high tech. Law enforcement successes in cracking several large-scale forgery operations saw a drop in the detection rate of this crime from around 2015.

The most popular denominations for faking are the $50 notes. The high penalties for counterfeiting—up to $75,000 in fines and up to fourteen years in prison—motivate those so inclined to maximise their criminal investment. High-quality forgeries of polymer notes are now fairly common as the fakers find ways to forge or obtain the special substrate material on which the genuine notes are printed.

Compared with the high rates of counterfeiting in the United Kingdom and some other countries, Australia is fairly lucky, so the chances of being caught with a dud note are relatively low. But, if you're still using cash in the era of digital money, you may feel an urge to reach for your wallet, just in case. Look for these features.

Notes issued between 1995 and 2018 include microprinting, and a raised print—called intaglio—that is easy to feel with your fingers. If you hold the note at a certain angle its value changes direction. And beneath an ultraviolet light, the serial numbers will glow and also reveal the value of the note.

Banknotes issued since 2018 have some additional security features similar to video games. There are two pictures of black swans that either ripple or change colour and another one that can be seen in green, accompanied by an orange-pink wattle branch, as well as a number of other moving images and clever tricks to foil counterfeiters. One of these is a see-through seven-pointed star within a circle, made up of three points on one side of the note and merging seamlessly with four points on the reverse. All Australian banknotes should be difficult to rip and should also reopen after being scrunched up. There is even more wizardry revealed on the Reserve Bank's website.

These inventive banknotes, together with alert law enforcement, aim to protect the country against counterfeiters. While forgery is often thought of as a relatively mild form of criminal activity, it can have serious financial consequences for individuals and businesses. If the public loses confidence in its physical currency there may also be social and economic costs.

That's the good news. The bad news is that the Reserve Bank no longer reimburses businesses and individuals if they have inadvertently accepted bogus notes. If you have, you've been done.

*The Black Widow of Richmond, Martha Needle, in September 1894,
a month before her execution. Needle was convicted of the callous
poisoning of her three children, her husband and her future brother-in-law.*

5

MURDERS AND MYSTERIES

DEATH OF A CONSTABLE

In 1803, Sydney was a scatter of stone and timber buildings hugging the shores of the harbour. Narrow streets and lanes separated the dwellings. Many of the streets faded into bushland and there was almost no public lighting at night. Around daylight on 27 August, someone made a grisly discovery on the side of Farm Cove Road. It was 'a breathless Corpse, shockingly mangled, and with the guard of his cutlass buried in his brain; the sheath lay near the body, and his hat more than 20 yards [18 metres] distant'.

The body was Joseph Luker (Looker), an ex-convict constable. He had been watching a house in Back Row where there was reason to believe thieves had taken a stolen desk filled with cash. The New South Wales Corps was ordered to blockade the town and a number of likely suspects were soon rounded up. They were taken to the Coroner's Inquest held the next morning, where the wounds on the body were examined:

> On the head of the deceased were counted Sixteen Stabs and Contusions; the left ear was nearly divided; on the left side of the head were four wounds, and several others on the back of it. The wretch who buried the iron guard of the cutlass in the head of the unfortunate man had seized the weapon by the blade, and levelled the dreadful blow with such fatal force, as to rivet the plate in the Skull, to a depth of more than an inch and a half [4 cm].

The inquest concluded that William Bladders, alias Hambridge, was the murderer, together with a person or persons unknown. He was found guilty of wilful murder and detained in custody while efforts were made to find his accomplice or accomplices.

In the meantime, Joseph Luker was laid to rest in a ceremony featuring his fellow constables. Four of them lowered his wooden coffin into the grave. As the report put it, 'The deceased was a man of very fair character throughout the Colony, and was a free man a length of time previous to his assassination.' Later, a gravestone was erected; the inscription read:

Sacred to the Memory of
JOSEPH LUKER, Constable;
Assassinated
Aug. 19, 1803, Aged 35 Years.

The authorities continued to investigate the murder. As well as the brutality of the crime, Luker had been a representative of whatever law and order could be made to prevail in early

Sydney town, so it was important to bring his killers to justice. It was finally concluded that one of the dead man's colleagues, Constable Isaac Simmonds, known to some as Hikey Bull, was one of the murderers. In a touch of the grotesque, he had also been one of the pallbearers at Luker's funeral. Together with William Bladders and three others, Simmonds was tried for murder. Remarkably, he was found not guilty of the crime, as were the others who were mostly found guilty of the robbery only. One of the accused, Joseph Samuels, was sentenced to death for his part in the robbery. The man who had died upholding the law was let down by the legal system, receiving no posthumous justice other than the hanging of a robber, and even that was to have an astonishing outcome.

When Samuels was taken to the gallows he had a lot to say before meeting his maker. Wishing to unburden his soul of whatever might interfere with salvation, he claimed that while they shared a cell, Simmonds had confessed to him that he was the murderer. He said that Luker had surprised him with the stolen desk and then he had 'knocked him down, and given him a topper for luck!' He claimed Simmonds had also said 'that he would hang 500 Christians to save himself'.

In the crowd witnessing this final testament was Simmonds himself, brought from confinement to see what happened to malefactors. He tried to stop Samuels from further incriminating him but Samuels was not to be denied his last words. They confirmed what most people thought anyway, as the newspaper put it:

Odium and suspicion were attached to Simmonds from the very day on which the dreadful crime was perpetrated, and every eye was fixed in doubt upon his countenance when he assiduously assisted to lower the mangled corpse into the grave: Although from the want of that full and sufficient evidence which the Law requires he had escaped Condemnation, yet he had been arraigned at the arbitrary tribunal of Public Opinion, and most of the spectators had pronounced judgement against him in their hearts. It is not to be wondered then that testimony like the present, proceeding from the lips of a dying man, whose only probable concern it was to ease his burthened conscience in the hour of death, should at once remove all doubt, if such remained, and the feelings of the multitude burst forth into invective.

After this, Samuels uttered a fervent last prayer and got into the cart that would shortly be pulled away, leaving him strangling in the air, then 'at length the signal was given, and the cart drove from under him; but by the concussion the suspending cord was separated about the center, and the culprit fell to the ground, on which he remained motionless, with his face downwards'.

They picked him up. The cart was brought back to position and he was manhandled onto it. A new rope was strung from the gallows and Samuels 'was again launched off'. This time, the rope unravelled and 'continued to slip until the legs of the sufferer trailed along the ground, the body being only half suspended'. The crowd was horrified, some calling out that providence had intervened because Samuels had revealed the identity of the killer.

Regardless, the law had to take its course. The seemingly lifeless body of the condemned man was lifted up onto the shoulders of a few men while the executioner prepared yet another rope. Then, incredibly, 'The body was gently lowered, but when left alone, again fell prostrate to the earth, this rope having also snapped short, close to the neck.' At this pathetic sight, 'Compassion could no longer bear restraint' and the crowd demanded a reprieve. The provost-marshal in charge of the hanging sped to the governor's quarters and returned with one. Samuels had by now lost control of his faculties and even when restored babbled incoherently, completely unaware of what had just happened to him.

Returned to sanity, more or less, Samuels was sent to the coalmines at Newcastle. He disappeared a few years later during an attempt to escape by sea. A troublesome Simmonds was flogged and later sent to Newcastle where he served fifteen years. He died in Sydney in 1833.

Was Samuels saved by divine intervention, as many believed? When one of the ropes was later tested it was found to be defective at the exact point where it broke, sparing the fortunate convict from an early arrival in the hereafter. No other faults were reported in the other two ropes.

From Beyond the Grave

Stories of voices from beyond the grave feature in folklore around the world. Usually, the voice belongs to someone who has been murdered but whose grave is unknown and whose killer has escaped detection. Someone, or ones, among the living report a dream in which the victim tells or shows them where the body lies. In one South Australian murder case of 1875, folklore and fact are said to have worked together to reveal the truth of a brutal murder.

Mary Buchan was a nineteen-year-old Mount Gambier woman and church-goer who was 'keeping company' with 22-year-old William Page, also known as William Walker. He had arrived in town from Adelaide and was working mainly as a coachman and groom. The relationship progressed to the point where marriage was envisaged. Buchan and her suitor met at Hedley Park, a substantial dwelling and estate on the edge of the town, after Buchan left church on the evening of Sunday, 11 July 1875. There was a conversation that ended with the young woman's screams as William Page savagely murdered the woman he had so assiduously courted.

Mr Moules, a bank manager, was returning from church about eight in the evening when he heard 'an unearthly scream'. He thought it came from the haystacks in a nearby paddock. His wife and several others also heard the screams. All thought that there was something unusual about the awful sounds but did not report them. It was not until Moules heard that Mary Buchan was missing that he made a connection and mentioned the incident to police.

Buchan's mother had reported her daughter missing when she did not return from church. It was not like her to have simply taken off without telling anyone, as Page maintained she had done. He claimed that Buchan had gone to Victoria in search of her father who had recently gone there for business reasons. Mrs Buchan was having none of it but the police received a report of a woman dressed in black and answering Buchan's description riding through Casterton, Victoria, on a bay horse. Although they were suspicious that Page was a probably unsavoury character, they were initially inclined to believe his story. Mrs Buchan insisted that the mysterious rider was not her missing daughter. But where was she?

At this point the supernatural aspects of the case appeared. It was reported that on the night of Buchan's murder her mother had dreamed that 'a resident in Ferres-street [sic] invited her into her house to show her a wonderful sight. On going in she thought she saw a white calf without its head. She remarked, "What a strange sight!" and awoke with a deep impression that some great calamity was impending over herself or her family.' There would be further revelations of the supernatural long after this incident but, for now, cold hard facts began to emerge.

A police inspector had eventually arrived from Adelaide and, after 'inquiries', located Buchan's body in a shallow grave not far from the haystacks. It was a grisly sight. Decomposition had begun and Mary had been terribly beaten around the head and upper body with a blunt object. She had then been strangled to death. Police found parts of a stockwhip weighted with lead near the haystack. It did not take long to confirm that the whip belonged to Page.

Already in prison for wife desertion, Page was charged with the murder and tried amidst great public revulsion. It was held that Mary had pushed him to commit to marriage but he demanded sex instead. When she refused, he savagely attacked her.

The evidence against him was damning. He had been seen later in the evening of Mary's death with bloodstains on his shirt. The weapon used to bludgeon Mary was his stockwhip. Page had later borrowed a spade which he took to the field, saying he needed to cover up some empty bottles before the reapers came at harvest time.

Page pleaded guilty to the charge of wilful murder. He was asked by the judge if he was aware of the import of his plea. He replied that he was and that he had nothing to say before sentence was passed. The judge told the prisoner to hold out no hope of mercy and that 'The sentence of the Court is that you be taken to the place from whence you came, and there be hanged by the neck until you are dead; and may God have mercy on your immortal soul.' At this, the court erupted in applause, though 'the prisoner maintained the same air of dogged indifference which had characterised him throughout, not once evincing the slightest emotion'.

Mary Buchan's murder and her killer's trial and punishment were extensively covered by the Australian press, and in New Zealand. Sermons were preached on the tragedy at Mount Gambier churches and there was great unrest in the community at the senseless and brutal nature of her death, with its overtones of sexual menace. A large memorial headstone was erected over her grave, paid for by public subscription.

William Page, alias Walker, was hanged around eight in the morning at Mount Gambier Gaol on 27 October 1875. He made a confession at the gallows and also left a three-page written confession, claiming in both that he had not planned to kill Mary Buchan and that he had not molested her. Then the hangman 'Placed a white cap over the felon's eyes, and secured his legs with a handkerchief. A few seconds subsequently the signal was given, the bolt withdrawn, and the prisoner died apparently instantaneously. The body swung round for a few seconds, and twitched convulsively.'

There ended the history of a sad tragedy, but not its memory. In an early example of dark tourism, MP Hugh Fraser told newspaper readers of his country trip in 1882 during which he 'saw the place where poor Mary Buchan, another victim to murderous purpose was ruthlessly laid low. Even this sparsely peopled country has had its history of terrible crime.' He made no mention of dreams. Similarly, Mary Buchan's great-aunt wrote to a local newspaper about the murder in 1915 without referring to a dream although well acquainted with the family version of events and acknowledging that 'As my grandmother said the only comfort her people had was the knowledge the doctors gave them that Page had not accomplished his purpose.'

It was not until 1929 that a descendant told a newspaper that Mary Buchan's distraught father had dreamed that Buchan appeared and placed her hand on his shoulder, asking him to get up and find her remains, which lay in a ploughed field amidst a triangle of trees. The wife of police Inspector Hunt of Penola, who was confined to bed with her newborn baby, was also reported to have recounted a very similar dream in which Mr Buchan went out to look for the burial site. He was unable to enter the grounds of Hedley Park until the police, including Inspector Hunt, gained access. On entering the grounds Hunt immediately recognised the field and 'drew a deep breath and gasped, "My God! My wife's dream."'

As often happens, newspapers picked up on this ghost story, as well as Mrs Buchan's earlier premonition, and recycled them well into the 1950s. Interest, invariably referring to the spooky aspects of the case, continues today on the internet, a modern Australian example of an ancient tradition.

FRED THE RIPPER

Could he have been 'Jack the Ripper? The remarkably evil life of Frederick Deeming is one of the most chilling stories of Australian, and global, crime. Even if he did not commit the Whitechapel murders of 1888, his known slayings make him one of the worst serial killers of the nineteenth century.

Beaten by his unstable father and imbued with fear of damnation by his God-obsessed mother, Frederick Bailey Deeming got off to a bad start in life almost as soon as he was born in Leicestershire, England, in 1853. He was already known as 'Mad Fred' when he went to sea around the age of sixteen and soon became a cunning criminal. Fraud and false pretences were his favoured offences, though he also thieved from time to time.

With an ability to turn on the charm and a persuasive way with words, the ruggedly handsome young sailor with blue eyes, fair hair and a ginger moustache had little trouble forming serious relationships with respectable women. In 1881 he married Marie James in England. By the middle of the next year he was in Sydney where he had jumped ship and started work as a plumber and gas fitter. By the time his wife arrived to join him, Deeming had already served a six-week sentence for stealing gas-burners. The couple would have four children over the next few years, during which Deeming briefly ran his own plumbing business until he was declared bankrupt and served two weeks for committing perjury. In January 1888 he turned up, alone, in Cape Town, South Africa where, using the alias Henry Lawson, he conducted several successful swindles.

Back in England in 1890, and still calling himself Henry Lawson, Deeming bigamously married Helen Matheson, using the proceeds of a fraud to pay for the wedding. Soon after, he had to quickly leave the country and escaped to Uruguay, South America. He was later arrested there, returned to England and given nine months in prison for fraud, though he avoided any charge of bigamy.

After his release in 1891, Deeming took another alias, Albert Williams, and rented a house in Rainhill, Lancashire. By this time, his (first) deserted wife and children had tracked him down and Marie revealed her husband's bigamy to Helen. Apparently too embarrassed at the social stigma this would bring upon her, the second Mrs Deeming did not inform the authorities. Deeming, now fearing what else Marie might reveal about him, made an elaborate pretence of reconciliation and convinced her and the children to join him at Rainhill. It was a fatal error.

Shortly after the reconciliation 'Williams', now posing as an army officer, married for a third time. The unlucky woman was Emily Mather who, after the expensive wedding, sailed with her new husband to India where he said he had a posting. But Deeming changed the arrangements and the newlyweds went to Melbourne instead. Here they rented a house in Windsor. Always ostentatious, even if mostly with other peoples' money, the outwardly charming 'Druin', as Deeming was now styling himself, soon became well known in the suburb. But in January 1892, he and his third wife disappeared.

Now a chain of events began that would lead to Deeming's eventual downfall. The next tenant in the Windsor house complained of a foul smell in the premises. A hearthstone in the bedroom was pulled up to reveal Emily's badly decomposed remains. She had been beaten around the head and her throat had been slashed. In the house police also found a copy of the invitation to the wedding banquet of A.O. Williams and Helen Matheson.

In a little over a week, the police tracked Deeming down to the Western Australian mining town of Southern Cross, where he was calling himself Baron Swanston and posing as an engineer. After murdering Emily, he had committed some further frauds and sailed to Sydney. There the apparently personable murderer soon convinced another young woman to become his fiancée. He then left for Western Australia, arranging with her to follow him when he was settled.

Deeming's arrest ignited what would become a national and international press sensation. An English journalist used details from Australian sources to backtrack Deeming to his previous rented premises in Lancashire. The authorities there were prompted to investigate. Under the kitchen floor they found the bodies of Marie and the four children, all with their throats cut. The enormity of Deeming's crimes was now apparent.

The press certainly thought so and went into one of the regular 'feeding frenzies' that have become all too familiar since. A kind of mass public hysteria arose, known as 'Deemania'. The accused was called 'a human tiger' and his actions dubbed 'the crime of the century'. He would also be described, inaccurately, as 'ape-like' and a forensic expert would later claim that his skull was similar to that of a gorilla.

Although entitled to the presumption of innocence, Deeming was effectively tried and found guilty in the newspapers of the English-speaking world. He was tried for the murder of Emily under the name of 'Williams'. His defence team, which included Alfred Deakin, destined to be an early Australian prime minister, argued that the accused had been denied a fair trial, which was probably true. Deeming was almost certainly an epileptic, having suffered from fits for much of his life. He may also have been a schizophrenic fantasist who actually became the identities he invented as he committed his crimes. But after an unwise address to the jury from the dock and some unconvincing psychiatric testimony, he was quickly found guilty and sentenced to death.

After being refused leave to appeal by the Privy Council, Edward Bailey Deeming, alias Albert Williams and at least four other pseudonyms, was hanged on 23 May 1892. Always a poser, he walked to the gallows smoking a cigar. His last words were reportedly 'Lord, receive my spirit.' Outside the prison wall, 12,000 people assembled to await the news that the monster was dead.

Deeming's death was celebrated in an English children's street rhyme based on the then-popular belief that Deeming was Jack the Ripper. The London kids got the date of execution wrong but the meaning is clear:

> On the twenty-first of May,
> Frederick Deeming passed away;
> On the scaffold he did say—
> Ta-ra-da-boom-di-ay
> Ta-ra-da-boom-di-ay!
> This is a happy day,

An East End holiday,
The Ripper's gone away.

Deeming was undoubtedly guilty of the horrendous murders of his children and two wives, with the likely intent to kill another. But could he have been Jack the Ripper?

In the overheated press speculations on the case, the fact that Deeming's movements in 1888 were murky, together with the grisly nature of his crimes, led to speculation that he might have been the Whitechapel killer. Some credibility was attached to the claim when Deeming told fellow prisoners that he was the Ripper and also expressed a murderous dislike of women. This was based on his venereal infection, probably syphilis, contracted from a prostitute during his extensive travels. When directly questioned about this on the eve of his execution, Deeming refused to confirm or deny the possibility.

But the theory has so many flaws that it is taken seriously by very few. A major problem is that Deeming's murders bore little resemblance to the butchery of most of the Whitechapel victims. Nor were the women he killed prostitutes. Unlike the Whitechapel murderer, Deeming was not known to have taken trophies of his victims. Finally, wherever Deeming was during those bloody months of 1888—probably South Africa—there is no evidence that he was anywhere near London, let alone the East End.

But there is no doubt that Deeming slew Emily, the crime for which he eventually hanged, and that he also killed Marie and his children. He never confessed to any of these murders but, while in prison during the lead-up to his trial and as he awaited execution, Deeming wrote his autobiography, later destroyed, as well as some poetry, which included the lines:

> The Jury listened well to the yarn I had to tell,
> But they sent me straight to hell.

THE BLACK WIDOW OF RICHMOND

'I have nothing to say, thank you sir' were the last words of Martha Needle, executed in 1894 for poisoning her lover. She had previously dispatched her three children, her husband and a prospective brother-in-law, and attempted to kill a sixth person by the same means. While Needle collected hundreds of pounds in insurance money for some of her victims, she spent most of it on their headstones. She never revealed why she committed the terrible crimes against those around her and speculation about her motives continues to this day.

Martha Charles was born into a poor family in South Australia in 1863. She was sexually assaulted by her stepfather and left home at the age of thirteen to begin domestic work, a common career for working-class women of that era. Martha was said to be violent towards her alcoholic mother 'who feared her exceedingly'. She married carpenter Henry Needle when she was eighteen and they had three daughters together. The family moved to the Melbourne suburb of Richmond in 1885 and from that point relations between Henry and Martha deteriorated and he frequently and brutally abused her. The killings began that same year.

Martha and Henry's three-year-old daughter, Mabel, suffered a brief illness and died in February. Her life was insured for

£100, duly collected by Martha. It was not until 1889 that Henry Needle died, again from mysterious causes. His insurance was worth £200. The surviving daughters, six-year-old Elsie and almost five-year-old May, passed away from unexplained causes the following year. The children and their father were buried together in Kew cemetery. Martha composed a touching verse for the metal plaque that marked their final resting place:

Little lips that murmured mamma, still and silent now
    are they;
Tiny feet no longer patter, Hushed forever 'neath the clay.

Now without a family, the good-looking and well-dressed Needle began to take in lodgers. In 1893 she began an affair with one, an Adelaide man named Otto Juncken. Otto's brother, Louis, at first supportive of the relationship, came to oppose its further development. While staying in the Needle house in 1894, Louis became ill. He improved a little, but after another of Martha's meals he died.

A third Juncken brother, Herman, travelled to Melbourne to settle his brother's affairs. After eating meals prepared by Needle on several occasions, he became ill. A doctor who treated his symptoms suspected poisoning and had a sample of Herman's vomit analysed. It contained arsenic.

The police were informed and Herman Juncken agreed to entrap Martha Needle. He asked her to prepare lunch for him and while holding a cup of tea she had made him, summoned the waiting police. Martha tried to spill the contents of the cup but was prevented. Analysis showed enough arsenic in the tea to kill five people. The mass poisoner was caught at last. After exhuming the bodies of Henry, Mabel, Elsie and May Needle, the body of Louis Juncken was also exhumed. All showed traces of arsenic, mostly at fatal levels. Needle was charged with Louis's murder and the chilling tale of her murderous career emerged.

The 'Black widow of Richmond', as the press dubbed her, was a bundle of suppressed rage. Since her early family life, she had shown a vengeful aspect of her personality in relations with her mother who was known to have beaten the child. She was said to have been troubled with 'fits' and developed delusions about her parentage. Letters she had written during her affair with Otto Juncken contained death threats and hints of suicide. When Louis Juncken continued to oppose Otto and Needle's marriage plans, she had purchased some bait known as Rough on Rats and used it to permanently settle the disagreement.

Martha pleaded not guilty but the case against her was convincing. It only took the jury three-quarters of an hour to return a guilty verdict. Martha responded in a low but firm voice, 'I am not guilty. It is undeserved, I am not guilty of this charge.' The judge then said 'Martha Needle, it is not my intention to keep you one moment in suspense. If conscience is not already doing its work nothing I can say will have any effect. It is my duty only to pronounce the sentence of the court.' He then condemned her to death.

Lovelorn and loyal Otto Juncken gallantly pretended to agree with Martha's plea of innocence to help her state of mind as she awaited execution. But the gaol chaplain found that this was interfering with his ministrations. After failing to convince Juncken to change his mind, the chaplain took it on himself to inform Needle that her beloved was in no doubt that she had murdered his brother:

> This communication roused Mrs. Needle from her habitual lethargic state, and in a perfect storm of passion, which lasted about five minute she denounced the clergyman's statement as a fabrication designed to wring a confession from her. When that passionate outbreak had subsided Mrs. Needle resumed her former calm demeanour, and would pay no more heed than she did before to anything Mr. Scott had to say.

At 10 am on 22 October 1894, Martha Needle stood on the scaffold at Melbourne Gaol. The condemned poisoner listened respectfully to the words of her spiritual comforters. She 'maintained her impenetrable demeanor to the last' and 'asserted her complete innocence of the crime for which she was about to suffer up to within a few minutes of her execution'. After politely refusing to say anything further:

> She then walked to the centre of the drop, apparently without need of assistance; the executioner quickly adjusted the rope, and in less than two seconds the lever was pulled, the drop fell, and the last penalty of the law had been enacted. Death must have been instantaneous, for with the exception of a momentary clenching of the hands there was no movement of the body after it had fallen the length of the rope.

If Martha Needle did finally confess to one or more of her crimes shortly before her execution, it seems that her words were not recorded or reported. She went to her death without explanation or expiation.

Was she mad or just seriously bad? Opinions vary but perhaps the author of a study of Needle's life and crimes is closest to the mark. Dr Samantha Battams undertook an exhaustive investigation of Martha Needle and concluded that she was probably suffering from a dissociative order and the syndrome known as Munchausen by proxy, in which the sufferer secretly harms someone in order to bask in sympathy and the attention of others.

Whatever drove Martha Needle to poisoning, her story has an odd twist. Her nephew, Alexander Newland Lee, was hanged in 1920 for callously murdering his wife and three of his seven children with strychnine, then widely used as rat poison.

THE BABY FARMERS

'A hangman commits suicide' ran the headline in the Sydney *Truth* newspaper of 7 January 1894. Thomas Jones, also known as William Perrins, led an eventful life in Europe and America under the name of Porter before turning up in Australia where he eventually became the Victorian hangman. There were rumours that he was not happy with his role and when it became his duty to hang a woman he refused. 'I'd far sooner kill myself' people heard him say.

Jones tried unsuccessfully to find a substitute willing to undertake the execution. He informed the sheriff of Victoria, effectively his boss, that he could not do it and his wife reportedly threatened to leave him if he hanged a woman condemned for murdering babies left in her care. Unable to bear the internal and external pressure, Jones hit the bottle and a few days before the execution was due, he 'became hysterical, marched direct to his quarters in the Melbourne Gaol, locked the door, stooped over the bath and deliberately cut his throat'.

Before the era of organised foster caring and childcare institutions, those with children who were unwanted, or whom they were unable to care for, had few options. One was to seek out a 'baby farmer'. These were people who, for a fee, undertook to raise orphaned, illegitimate or otherwise unwanted children in their own homes. This arrangement often worked out as well as it could, but in several notorious cases, baby farmers became serial killers.

When Frances Knorr's husband went to prison in 1892, she was left pregnant and without support. She moved from Adelaide, where the family had been living, to Melbourne where she began to take in unwanted children. Knorr moved house frequently and, in the garden of one place she had recently vacated, the next tenant dug up the remains of a child in September 1893.

By now, Knorr and her released husband had moved to Sydney where she was arrested after Melbourne police found two more bodies in premises she had rented. She was charged, initially with her husband, and tried in November 1893. Despite her story that the babies had died of natural causes and that she had only buried the bodies, she was found guilty and condemned to hang. Rudolph Knorr, her husband, was discharged.

The trial generated intense public interest. The prosecution depicted Knorr as a promiscuous woman and a bad mother. When the verdict was brought down, public opinion was divided. Many, including Thomas Jones's wife, thought that Frances Knorr should be granted clemency as there was evidence that she suffered epileptic fits and her desperate circumstances were mitigating factors. A petition claiming to come from 'the women of Victoria' argued that 'the killing of any woman by any body of men does not accord with the moral sense of the community'.

Frances Knorr was hanged on 15 January 1894 in Pentridge Prison. She wrote several letters before her execution. One was advice on how to regulate the baby-farming industry. The other was her confession that she had strangled two of the babies to death.

The circumstances of Francis Knorr's trial and execution have continued to attract disquiet. As the petition from 'the women of Victoria' implied, there has always been a suspicion that Knorr was the victim of social perceptions and stereotypes. During the 1890s some women's organisations and medical professionals espoused the notion of 'ideal mothers'. This received legislative support in the form of the *Infant Life Protection Act* of 1890 reflecting the idea that women's proper role was as mothers. Women who did not fit this idealised view were considered deviant, especially if, like Frances Knorr, they were lower class. The power of society, the police and the judiciary combined to make Knorr appear as a criminal mother for whom there could be no judicial mercy.

Similar issues had played out differently a year or so before in New South Wales. The colony had passed a *Children's Protection Act* in 1892 that aimed to regulate the cottage childcare industry through registration of those providing such services and banning lump-sum payments to carers. The ineffectiveness of this legislation was quickly highlighted by another horrific baby-farming case.

John and Sarah Jane Makin went into the baby-farming business in early 1892. By the time they were arrested in October that year they had disposed of thirteen and possibly more children left in their care. The remains were found in and near premises the Makins had rented in the inner western suburbs of Sydney. The couple were eventually tried for the murder of one boy and found guilty. Both were sentenced to death, with a strong jury recommendation of mercy for Sarah Makin.

There were appeals, including one to the Privy Council in England. Sarah Makin's sentence was commuted to life imprisonment but John Makin was confirmed for execution. He was hanged in Darlinghurst Gaol on 15 August 1893. He denied his guilt to the end. His wife served eighteen years of her life sentence. After campaigns by her family, 'Mother Makin' as she became known, was released without fanfare in 1911 and died in 1918.

Confronting though these cases were, and remain so today, the worst revelations were yet to come.

Western Australia had a licensing system for those who took unwanted children into care. The arrangement seemed to be working well, until 1907. Alice Mitchell, 52 years old, had been in the business of looking after children for some years when one child in her care died. It would turn out that she was probably responsible for the deaths of at least thirty-six others. Already under suspicion, this case led to a coronial inquiry that determined Mitchell should go to trial for manslaughter. It came out that Mitchell had been getting away with her deadly practice due to the incompetence of the medical and inspecting authorities and a loophole in the law that allowed her to send the dead children directly to the undertakers without the need of an inquest. This also made it difficult to prosecute her to the full extent her crimes deserved. She was sentenced to a relatively light sentence of five years with hard labour.

Although Mitchell was only found guilty of one fatality, it seems very probable that she also caused the deaths of thirty-five other children, probably by malnutrition. That would make her Australia's worst known serial killer.

The Man–Woman Murderer

In 1920, the press couldn't decide whether Eugenia Falleni was a man or a woman; to hedge their bets, they came up with the label 'man–woman'. Whatever the confusion about gender, Falleni was definitely a murderer.

Assigned female at birth in Italy around 1875, Falleni was taken to New Zealand when her parents emigrated there a few years later. From an early age, she preferred men's clothing and as a teenager shipped as a stoker on a ship bound for Sydney. At some point in the late 1890s, she became pregnant and gave birth to a daughter. Placing the child in care, Falleni took on the identity of 'Harry Leo Crawford'.

Working as a man in a range of jobs in Sydney, by 1912 Crawford was a yardman and driver for a Wahroonga doctor. In this occupation, he met the widow Annie Birkett and her nine-year-old son. In 1913 Crawford married Annie and the money she had managed to save. The couple opened a confectionery shop in Balmain and later moved to Drummoyne. By all accounts, it was a troubled relationship. Whether this was because Annie Crawford discovered her husband was transgender is one of the many mysteries of this story. Crawford's grown-up daughter had by this time rejoined her mother and was living in the family home, reportedly placing a strain on domestic relations.

On Eight Hour Day, 1 October 1917, Crawford and his wife celebrated together with a picnic at Chatswood, then a much bushier area than it is today. Annie Crawford never came home. Harry Crawford made no missing person report and told his stepson and anyone else who asked that his wife had left him. Later, Crawford and his missing wife's son moved house and continued living together. In 1919 Harry Crawford married again, apparently maintaining a convincing presentation as male. But the masquerade was about to end.

The day after Crawford returned from the Chatswood picnic without his wife, a beaten and burned body had been discovered in the area. Police were unable to identify the remains until 1920 when dental evidence confirmed that it was Annie Crawford, and the body was buried. Harry Crawford was found and arrested in July 1920, asking to be held in the female rather than the male cells. When Crawford appeared at the preliminary hearing, he was dressed as a man.

A salivating press pounced on this confusing but sensational situation and followed the case obsessively, transmitting every detail to an avid readership. Crawford was described as 'very pale. She is of slight build, with small brown eyes and black hair and on a finger of her left hand she wore a gold ring. She was dressed in a dark grey suit of men's clothes, a white turn-down collar, Broadway tie, soft tennis shirt, patent leather lace-up boots, and carried in her hand a soft grey felt hat.'

Police believed that Crawford's daughter, who had left the home after the family left Drummoyne, possessed important information about the case. For five days they tracked her through various temporary addresses and located her in Pyrmont. She was described as 'a slight, pleasantly-spoken, and good-looking young woman'. At Crawford's trial she would testify that Crawford, her mother, always dressed in male clothes.

An application to exhume the burned body of the 'Chatswood Tragedy' victim was granted. There was so little left of it that nothing new was discovered, other than the grisly likelihood that Annie Crawford had still been alive when she was set alight. The remains were returned to relatives and reburied.

Still dressed as a man, Crawford was remanded while police pursued further inquiries. He was committed for murder in August and went to trial in October. Fanned by press speculation, the case had generated intense interest around the country. The court was packed, including many female spectators. This time, Crawford sat in the dock dressed as a woman. The prisoner's defence argued that the prosecution had not proven that the burned body was that of Annie Crawford and had not established a motive for Harry Crawford to kill her. The Crown relied on her son's identification of items found near the body as belonging to Annie. The jury took only two hours to find the accused guilty and Harry Crawford was sentenced to death.

An appeal was rejected. But in November the death sentence was, without explanation, commuted by State Cabinet and the murderer went to Long Bay Gaol and served the time as a woman. Falleni was suddenly released in 1931, aged and said to be 'looking extremely careworn and feeble'. It seems that—despite the guilty verdict at the trial and police suspicions that Falleni had murdered before and also plotted to throw Annie's son over Sydney's notorious 'Gap'—some influential people had their doubts about the soundness of the case. The prison doctor and governor were among those recommending release based on doubts aired by a noted criminologist. The Minister for Justice authorised the release after visiting Falleni in gaol but refused to provide any details about the reasons for the decision.

Falleni was taken to the home of wealthy supporters to prepare for re-entry into the world, a fact that predictably sent *Truth* newspaper into a journalistic rage: 'There are many more deserving cases in gaol than that of Falleni, whose crime, which brought to light all her monstrous sex perversion, revealed her as a menace to the community,' and so on.

Eventually, Falleni assumed a new female name and became an apparently successful operator of rented accommodation. She died after a motor vehicle struck her as she walked along Oxford Street in June 1938, carrying £100 (just over $10,000 in today's money) that she had recently received from the sale of 'a residential' in Paddington.

This unusual case has continued to interest many. The seemingly bizarre nature of the several relationships and crime of the 'man–woman' were extensively recalled by the press at the news of Falleni's death, and the case was occasionally dredged up through the 1940s and '50s. Eventually, Eugenia Falleni began to be enlisted into the raising of non-binary gender awareness from the '50s, as sex-change operations began to be performed and publicised.

With all these enigmas, it's not surprising that writers, doctors, academics and musicians have engaged with the ambivalent story of the 'man–woman'. As one of Falleni's biographers put it:

> Doctors, psychiatrists, journalists, endocrinologists, feminists, playwrights, film makers and historians have tried to make sense of Falleni. They have labelled her variously as a sexual hermaphrodite, a homosexualist, a masquerader, a person with misplaced atoms, a sex pervert, a passing woman, a transgendered man, and as gender dysphoric. Falleni proclaimed her innocence of the murder but never explained what induced her to live as a man.

The Lolly Shop Murders

It was soon after ten o'clock on the night of Saturday, 30 June 1928. The lolly and fruit shop run by Esther Vaughan and her widowed sister, Sarah Falvey, in the Sydney suburb of Dulwich Hill had been busy and the till was full. Passers-by heard a man shout, 'Open that door!' He shouted the demand again. Then two gunshots rang out, followed by a woman's scream.

Neighbours rushed to the little store. One saw a man with a pistol walk quickly out of the shop followed by a staggering Sarah Falvey. The man threw a mask into the gutter, leapt onto a motorcycle with sidecar and roared away. Whoever the killer was, he left empty-handed. The shop's till was unopened.

When James M'Dowell, who lived next door to the two sisters, 'heard the sound of the two shots he rushed into the street and saw Mrs. Falvey lying on the ground. He picked her

up and she said, "She's shot—burglars"—and died in his arms.'
Mrs Falvey's sister, Esther, died later in hospital.

A morbid crowd gathered and detectives were quickly on
the scene. Sadly, about twenty minutes after the shootings 'a
woman pushed through the crowd in front of the shop and
cried, "My, mother My mother! She's not dead!"' It was Sarah
Falvey's daughter.

Witnesses were able to give police a good description of the
suspect. He was aged between twenty and twenty-five years,
around 1.78 metres (five feet ten inches), thin and well dressed
in a woollen overcoat and grey felt hat. He had come to the
robbery and, as it turned out, double murder, in a collar and
tie. But despite the number of witnesses to the crime and the
evidence of the discarded mask, police had difficulty tracking
down the killer.

They weren't helped by the more sensational elements of
the press. The shocking callousness of the murders over the
apparently trivial takings of a suburban lolly shop guaranteed
strong public interest in the case. Newspapers were only too
ready to sensationalise the case even further. The mask conjured
up stereotypical images of disguised villains. The killer became
a 'masked terror' who somehow eluded capture. Who was the
sinister figure with such a ready trigger finger? *Truth* newspaper
even speculated, despite the eyewitness accounts, police were
considering an odd theory that the murderer was a woman.
A *Smith's Weekly* writer concocted a complete fantasy of events
in the lolly shop on that fatal night, virtually admitting the
deception to readers: 'Time alone may tell if the story, as told
here, is a faithful recital of the facts of that fateful night. In

any case the theory that is the basis of the deductions is quite feasible. Read it—Reading time: 10 minutes.'

A reward of £500 (equivalent to $45,000 today) was quickly posted by the government. No one came forward to claim it and within a few days of the tragedy the impatient press was referring to failed efforts to solve the crime and claiming that police were 'baffled'. An inquest was opened but immediately adjourned for lack of evidence as journalists obsessed over the details of the murdered sisters' wills. Esther Vaughan's estate was valued at a modest £359 (or $32,659 today). But Falvey's very respectable legacy was over £3500 ($300,000 today). What these details contributed to the investigation of the murders was never made clear but the media of the day were adept at insinuating that they might.

One speculation arising from the investigation of the murders was that there was more to the crime than simply knocking over the lolly shop till. It was rumoured that the sisters were better off than their relatively humble business might suggest. Police did find more money stashed around the property, but even that only brought the total potential loot to £55 ($5000 today). Not worth the risk of an armed robbery, far less a double homicide.

Finally, almost two months after the murders, police arrested eighteen-year-old John Reynolds. Witnesses to the crime identified him from a police line-up. Reynolds was charged but later acquitted. He was sentenced to gaol time on unrelated charges of false pretences and the reconvened inquest delivered an open verdict on the murders. The identity of the killer remained a mystery.

Rumour, speculation and pure fantasy dragged on into the following year. A man walked into police headquarters in Sydney and made an elaborate confession to the lolly shop murders. He was dismissed as a crank. The press continued to run stories on the underworld's silence and the continued failure of police to crack the case. In 1940 another obsessive man falsely confessed to the murders and ten years later crime reporters were reminiscing about the still-unsolved case.

It was not until the modern era of internet and mostly amateur investigations of cold cases that the perplexing end of Sarah Falvey and Esther Vaughan returned to the spotlight. A number of podcasts have dealt with the story, which has, in turn, been picked up again in some sectors of the media. Only time will tell if this interest in heritage crime will throw any light on the callous killings that took place nearly a century ago.

A Nice Girl

One of Queensland's coldest cases could still bring a $50,000 reward to anyone with information leading to a conviction. But the likelihood of this happening is very slim because 22-year-old Betty Shanks was murdered in 1952.

Shanks was the kind of young woman everybody liked. Bright and personable, she had been educated at Brisbane Girls Grammar School and the University of Queensland and was working as a clerk in the Commonwealth public service. Why would anyone want to kill her, especially in such a brutal manner? Answers to that question have mostly eluded investigators for over seventy years but it seems that, nice girl though Shanks was, she had some secrets.

The known facts of the crime are very clear. Returning home from night classes on 19 December 1952, Betty Shanks left her tram at the Grange terminus at 9.32 pm and began walking the short distance to her home in Thomas Street. She got as far as Carberry Street, where she was pulled into the backyard of a house and beaten to death between 9.38 and 9.53 pm. It was a brutally violent attack that smashed out Shanks's front teeth and left boot-polish residue and impact marks across her body. Her bra strap was broken and her underwear removed, though there was no evidence of a sexual attack. Nor did it seem like a robbery. Shanks's purse and its contents were found strewn around but nothing was missing, not even her jewellery. The only other evidence was two bloody handprints on a fence.

It seems that nobody except the killer witnessed Shanks's murder, though seven people recalled hearing screams about the time the attack occurred. Oddly, none of these people bothered to investigate, though an off-duty policeman living next door to the scene of the crime looked out of his window. He didn't see what was happening just a few metres away in the neighbour's backyard because his view was obscured by the house. It was the police officer who found Shanks's body early the next morning when he went to collect his delivered newspaper. Ever since then, Queensland police have been searching for her killer.

A number of possible suspects were investigated. One was a local doctor who committed suicide shortly after Shanks's death. The only connection ever found between the doctor and the dead woman was a mutual friend who may or may not have been having an affair with Shanks. DNA testing in 2009 seemed to rule this man out as a suspect, though doubts over the reliability of this evidence have been raised by many. This man also had an alibi, seemingly not being in Brisbane on the night of the crime.

Another theory was that Shanks had been murdered by a soldier. An army tattoo rehearsal was being held at nearby grounds on the night of her death. It was thought that the marks imprinted in her face could have been made by the gaiters (ankle coverings) soldiers then wore over their boots.

Nothing ever came of official inquiries into these and several other unlikely possibilities, leaving the field open to amateur sleuths. Several books have dealt with the Betty Shanks mystery. One, *I Know Who Killed Betty Shanks* by Ted Duhs, suggests that she was in a passionate relationship with a man who was a member of the Communist Party of Australia. At that time, affiliation with communism was a matter for serious interest by the security services. The Cold War was producing espionage dramas around the world. Australia would soon have its own when Vladimir Petrov and his wife, Evdokia Petrova, defected just a few years after. Later in the 1950s a sting operation by the Australian Security Intelligence Organisation (ASIO) saw the first secretary of the Russian embassy, Ivan Skripov, outed as a spy and expelled from the country. According to Duhs' book, based on his access to ASIO files, Shanks had herself been identified by the organisation as a potential recruit.

It seems unlikely that Shanks's political connections were related to her death, but as well as revealing her ASIO connection, researcher Ted Duhs has provided strong evidence that the most likely killer was a man named Eric Sterry. He had done some handyman work at the Shanks family home and apparently struck up a relationship with the young woman. Sterry's own marriage was in decay and he was a violent psychotic. Years after the crime, his daughter claimed he had once made a night-time visit to a school near the scene of the crime and returned covered in blood.

On the night of the murder, witnesses saw a man wearing a brown suit loitering in the area. It is argued that he was there to meet Shanks near the tram terminus, probably with the intention of taking her to his car, presumably for sex. Although Shanks had apparently been happy to go with Sterry previously, on this night she rejected his advances. Enraged, he threw her over the backyard fence and, by now in an uncontrollable fit of rage, beat her to death. This scenario is the best fit for the known facts and has some support from a still-living witness who saw the man in the brown suit very near the murder scene on the night in question.

The mystery of Betty Shanks's life and death has disturbed the Queensland public and perturbed police since 1952. Speculations about her killer have often been published and calls for an inquest into the crime have been raised. These have, so far, not been answered, but there is still considerable public interest in having the mystery solved. The savage murder of Betty Shanks remains one of Australia's most perplexing cold cases.

THE ASSASSINS

When everyday people like you and me are deliberately slain, it is called 'murder'. When political figures or high-profile dignitaries are dispatched by foul means, it is called 'assassination'. Although political murders have been frequent in world history, in Australia we have had relatively few and most of these have not been political.

Radical politician Percy Brookfield was killed in 1921, though the motive of his killer was probably not political. The disturbed son of Ivens Francois 'Toon' Buffett, a Norfolk Island politician, shot his father dead in 2004. New South Wales politician Hyman Goldstein was believed murdered in 1928, but if so, his death was related to a business matter rather than political differences. Queensland Labor politician Albert Whitford was shot dead by a jealous husband in 1924.

One assassination probably did have political dimensions. New South Wales Labor Member of the Legislative Assembly, John Newman, was fatally shot at Cabramatta, New South Wales in 1994. His death was connected to the machinations of local criminals who also had aspirations to preselection for the Australian Labor Party.

A few political assassinations have been attempted. Prince Alfred, the second son of Queen Victoria, was the victim of an unbalanced Irish nationalist in 1868. He recovered from his wounds. Campaigning against conscription during the Vietnam War era, Arthur Calwell, then leader of the federal Australian Labor Party, was shot and wounded but quickly recovered.

These few homegrown incidents suggest the relative tranquillity of Australian politics compared with those of many other countries. Nevertheless, since 1970 there have been many terrorist attacks around the nation, some successful, most not. Some of these have targeted high-profile diplomats or other government officials. Many of the perpetrators remain unknown, but in two cases, arising from the fraught history of Turkey and Armenia, a shadowy militant group is thought to have been responsible.

The Armenians are a Christian people indigenous to western Asia who, after a long interrelationship with the Muslim Ottoman empire, were massacred in large numbers during the 1890s at the order of Sultan Abdul Hamid II. Relations between Armenians and the modern state of Turkey have been troubled ever since. Between 1915 and 1917 most of the Armenian population of Anatolia (Asia Minor) was deported or massacred by Turkish Ottoman forces. While the Armenian genocide has always been officially denied, some Australian soldiers serving at Gallipoli and in Palestine during World War I witnessed these events or came across other evidence of them and, in some cases, also rescued Armenian survivors.

After the war, the short-lived First Republic of Armenia was established and the modern Republic of Turkey was created in 1923. Throughout this period, Armenia's continued attempts to assert cultural and national identity were resisted and, despite intermittent attempts to stabilise relations, the two countries have mostly been bitter enemies.

Since the 1970s, Armenian nationalists have evolved secret militant organisations to attack Turkish activities and interests around the world. The Justice Commandos of the Armenian Genocide was an early name for this group, which is thought to have later transformed into the Armenian Revolutionary Army and other names. These entities are thought to be the armed element of the left-wing nationalist Armenian Revolutionary Federation and are said to have been responsible for more than seventy murders around the world. Under whatever banner, members of this network are believed to have been responsible for several assassinations and attempted assassinations in Australia.

On 17 December 1980, the Turkish Consul-General Sarik Ariyak and his bodyguard, Engin Sever, were leaving a house in Sydney's exclusive suburb of Dover Heights around 9.45 am. There had been threats on Ariyak's life and, as a precaution, he and his bodyguard had swapped cars. Two men on a motorcycle suddenly appeared and shot Ariyak and Sever at close range. Ariyak died instantly and Sever died later in hospital. The consul-general's wife and eight-year-old daughter both witnessed the killings.

Police later received a telephone call in which a woman claimed that the murders were carried out by the Justice Commandos of the Armenian Genocide. Investigations led nowhere and it was not until 2019 that the killings were reinvestigated and the original reward of $250,000 for information was increased to $1 million, said to be the highest ever made for a terrorist act in Australia. Some progress was made, with computer-generated images of the suspects being prepared and some possibly related items located in Sydney Harbour.

In August 2022, the New South Wales Joint Counter Terrorism Team (JCTT), an alliance of the NSW Police, the Australian Federal Police, the Australian Security Intelligence Organisation (ASIO) and the New South Wales Crime Commission, released further information about the case. The telephone call made to police shortly after the killings had been recorded. In the belief that there might still be people in the community with relevant information, police hoped that hearing the partly inaudible recording might jog someone's memory or produce some other relevant information to aid the ongoing investigation.

Six years after the deaths of Sarik Ariyak and Engin Sever, the Armenian militants struck again. At 2.16 am on 23 November 1986 a 4-kilogram bomb tore through the Turkish consulate in South Yarra, Victoria. The only fatality was one of the bombers, who was obliterated when the device exploded prematurely. His accomplice was caught and sentenced to 25 years in prison. He was released on appeal after ten years.

Armenians have been immigrating to Australia since the 1850s. Official estimates of the number of Armenians currently living here suggest up to 60,000. Turks did not immigrate here in significant numbers until the 1960s. Estimates of Turkish and Turkish-descended Australians suggest around 70,000, though some sources give much higher numbers. Australia has not recognised the Armenian genocide and pursues a policy of maintaining cordial relations with both Armenia and Turkey.

RACK MAN

A gambling man with a serious habit left his home in Newtown, Sydney, one day in January 1993. He was off to Queensland's Gold Coast, a favourite location for losing money. When he hadn't returned after a couple of days, his partner became concerned and reported him missing. The high roller was not found until 2018.

In that year, police were able to use DNA to identify a body that had lain in the Glebe Morgue since it was hauled up by horrified fishermen near Flint and Steel Beach close to the mouth of the Hawkesbury River at Broken Bay. A mystery had finally been solved after 25 years. But establishing the identity of the dead man only raised new questions yet to be answered.

The unknown male body was no ordinary John Doe. When the fishermen dragged the remains to the surface, they were lashed to a heavy steel frame, or rack. Descriptions of this contrivance differ but it seems to have been made of a vertical bar or sheet across which four more rods, one being L-shaped, were welded lengthwise. The body was tied to this structure at the neck, elbows, knees and ankles, giving the semblance of a crucifixion. A plastic bag that once covered the grisly array had mostly disintegrated and the body itself was also decomposing.

'It was inside big plastic bags but looked pretty much intact,' said the skipper of the fishing boat. 'There were a few tears in the plastic and you could see the bones . . . there didn't seem to be any flesh or anything on it.' Police confirmed that some bones were missing and that what remained of the clothing on the body was 'a black gluggy mess'.

This was the period before DNA could be used to establish identities and investigators had to rely on more traditional forensic techniques. 'Unknown Human Remains E48293', as the body was officially known, was a dark-haired male of European descent, aged between 21 and 46 and perhaps a little over 1.60 metres (five feet two inches) in height. Fingerprints had decayed in the salty water and there was nothing distinctive about the teeth to provide further clues.

Various experts looked at other evidence and a computerised facial reconstruction produced a slightly creepy image. When the portrait was published, many people came forward with information about criminal gangs and their grislier methods of victim disposal, but none of this led to identification of the remains. The state coroner concluded the remains of the body on the rack 'were those of a male Caucasian who died from the effects of blunt force head injuries inflicted by a person or persons unknown. But as to when and where the deceased person died and the identity of such deceased person, the evidence does not enable me to say.'

Over the next 25 years or so, theories about the crime abounded. The rack was a solid piece of work, seemingly welded together solely for the unpleasant purpose to which it had been put. What was left of the body tied to it looked to have suffered considerable violence before death. Such a bizarre murder led police and most observers to suspect the crime might have been committed as a warning of some kind. But of what, and how effective was a submerged warning? Had the man on the rack fallen foul of the mafia? Perhaps he had been a member of some shady mob? Was it some sort of satanic ritual killing? Nobody knew.

The mystery joined the 500 or so other cold cases and missing persons files held by the New South Wales Police. In those files were such names as Christopher Dale Flannery, a hit man—known as Mr Rent-a-Kill—who had himself gone missing, presumed the victim of a gangland reprisal. Drug dealer Joe Biviano was there, as was Peter Mitris, a disappeared Kings Cross businessman. There were plenty more missing under-world characters, but none seemed to match with the remains in the morgue.

As the use of DNA techniques improved, forensic scientists were able to gradually eliminate most of the possible names from the missing persons lists. In 2018 the New South Wales coroner's office announced that the remains had been identified as those of the gambler from Newtown. His name was Max Tancevski. At last, the rack man had an identity, essential for police investigation into the crime. But after such a long time it was difficult to establish much more. Tancevski was certainly a serious gambler and had some debts but, as far as could be discovered, nothing that would have led to such a gruesome end. Today, the reason for his murder remains a mystery, as does the identity of his killer or killers.

An Enduring Enigma

The man was propped up against a wall along the beach in Adelaide's Somerton Park. Passers-by on the night of 30 November 1948 thought he was a drunk but the tall, well-dressed man had been dead since around 2 am. An inquest determined that he had been poisoned, but with what substance and whether by his own hand or that of another, nobody was able to say. But who was he? The Somerton Man or 'Taman' Shud mystery has continued to baffle police, scientists and hosts of amateur sleuths ever since.

Examination of the dead man's clothing revealed that the usual labels had been deliberately removed. The tailoring of the clothing suggested that he might have been American or had at least spent some time there. Police later recovered a suitcase from the Adelaide Railway Station that they believed had been left there by the mystery man. Among the items in the case were some unusual objects, including a specialised knife, scissors and a screwdriver. There was also some other clothing, some of it labelled with variations of the name 'Keane'. Despite these clues, police were unable to identify the body and could only determine that the man was not a resident of Adelaide.

A death mask was made and the body was put into preservation mode pending further investigations.

The following year, a re-examination of the clothing uncovered a roll of paper hidden in a trouser pocket. The paper seemed to have been torn from a book of Persian poetry known as *The Rubáiyát of Omar Khayyám* and bore the words 'Tamam Shud', usually translated to mean 'the end' or 'it is finished'. A few months later a man came to police with a book that someone had thrown into his car around the time that Somerton Man was discovered. It was the *Rubáiyát* and a missing section exactly matched the fragment found in the dead man's pocket.

The book also had some handwriting in it that looked like a code of some sort. And it contained the telephone number of a local resident, a nurse named Jessica or 'Jo', Thomson. When police asked her to identify the death mask, she seemed deeply shocked but insisted that she did not know the dead man. Police did not follow up this lead any further and the puzzling body was buried in June 1949.

But the mystery lived on, eventually bringing together two investigators who were determined to discover the truth of Somerton Man's life and death. Ex-policeman Gerry Feltus and engineering academic Derek Abbott worked together and separately on the case for over two decades. They followed leads, dead ends and hunches of their own and other seekers of the truth. Was Somerton Man a spy? Russian maybe, or possibly even American? Did he have a relationship with Jo Thomson? If so, of what kind?

The trail eventually led to a DNA analysis of some of the hairs trapped on Somerton Man's death mask. Abbott worked with American forensic genealogist Colleen Fitzpatrick, who analysed the hairs and used the results in conjunction with a genealogical database, GEDmatch, to identify a distant relation. Through subsequent genealogical research of around 4000 people they came up with the name of a man who seemed to fit the few known facts of the case.

Carl Webb was born in Footscray, Victoria in 1905. He was an instrument maker when he married in 1941, though he left his wife six years later. Webb's sister was married to a man named Thomas Keane. These facts and some other circumstantial evidence led to an exhumation of the body of Somerton Man in 2022. At the time of writing, South Australian authorities are conducting their own tests on the remains to confirm or deny the identification of Somerton Man as Carl Webb.

If the man found on Somerton Beach in 1948 does turn out to be Carl Webb, this will be a major breakthrough in a cold case that has perplexed Australia and much of the world. But there remain many questions yet to be answered. What was he doing in Adelaide? Was he murdered or did he suicide? Why? How?

Ronald Ryan escorted by police back to Melbourne in 1966 after his escape from Pentridge Prison. During the escape, Ryan murdered a prison officer, for which he was hanged a year later, the last person in Australia to be legally executed by hanging.

6

BY HOOK OR BY CROOK

SOMETHING ABOUT THE HANGMAN

The first known hangings in what we now call Australia took place in 1629. The Dutch East India Company's ship, *Batavia*, was cast onto the Abrolhos Islands off Western Australia. In a small boat salvaged from the wreck, the captain and a few of the crew managed to reach company headquarters in Java and eventually return with a rescue party. In the meantime, there was a mutiny among the survivors on the islands and a murderous tyranny developed in which many were mindlessly slaughtered. When the rescuers arrived and discovered the horror of what had happened, they hanged seven of the mutineers.

In the penal colony of New South Wales, the first hanging was carried out in February 1788, barely a month after the arrival of Arthur Phillip's First Fleet. Food was scarce in the colony and stealing it from the stores was a major problem. The first to be condemned to death were sentenced for this crime. On the appointed day, convicts and marines all waited to observe the grim example Governor Phillip wanted made of food pilferers—but there was no executioner. No one had thought to appoint one. A reluctant convict was bullied into performing the act by marines unwilling to carry out the execution themselves.

Phillip's hope of making a terrifying example of food thieves was not realised. Convicts and soldiers continued to pillage food stores and many of the executions over the next few years were primarily for those caught and sentenced for these acts of desperation. Not that there was a shortage of malefactors hanged for other reasons, including robbery, bestiality, rape and murder.

Since those years, many hundreds of people have been hanged, especially in the first decades after European settlement. As the nineteenth century progressed, public executions were gradually phased out and more humane methods of dispatching the condemned were devised. Instead of simply strangling the doomed man or woman at the end of a rope strung from a tree or beam, the mechanical 'drop' was introduced. The weight of the body falling through the trapdoor fractured or dislocated the victim's neck, leading to instant death.

At least, that was the theory. Botched hangings using the new improved method were frequent, as it was easy for the hangman to mess up the fine calculations of body weight and height of the drop on which a quick death depended. Too short a drop and the victim was left strangling. Too long and there was a possibility of decapitation. Henry Tester struggled for over half an hour when hanged at Deniliquin, New South Wales, in 1882. William Liddiard's head was almost completely severed when he was hanged in Grafton, also in New South Wales, in 1886.

Capital punishment was phased out in each state at different times. The last person hanged in Australia was Ronald Ryan in 1967. He was controversially executed in Pentridge Prison for the murder of a warder during an escape attempt.

The men—no women—who sent these unfortunates to the hereafter were often intriguing characters in their own right. Many served for lengthy periods in the well-rewarded role, though they were shunned socially and seem to have had more than their fair share of problems.

Alexander Green, a Dutchman transported for stealing in 1824, was New South Wales hangman from the 1820s until 1855. He was removed from his position for drunkenness, mental fragility and insolence. By then he had executed almost 500 people, including bushrangers, convicts, women, First Nations people and the seven stockmen hanged for their part in the Myall Creek massacre. After his removal, Green was committed to an asylum.

'Nosey Bob' Howard was the New South Wales assistant hangman, and later principal hangman from the 1870s until his retirement in 1904 when he was in his early seventies. His nickname referred to a nose disfigured in an accident that left him unable to follow his occupation as a cab driver. With a large family, Howard signed on to the safe and well-paid public service posting. Over a lengthy career he would 'turn off' some of the most notorious criminals in New South Wales, including the bushrangers Jimmy Governor and Jacky Underwood, and Louisa Collins, the last woman executed in the colony.

Howard claimed he was happy in his job, though there was considerable public revulsion directed at him, especially when he bungled executions. He was a notorious drinker, though seemingly always sober when at work. Nosey Bob Howard died in 1906, only two years after his retirement. He was so well known that, as with England's Jack Ketch, 'Nosey Bob' became a general term for the executioner, immortalised in the colloquialism 'I'm that thirsty I'd drink with Nosey Bob.'

Queensland hangmen frequently tried to hide their identities and used disguises, so great was the social stigma associated with their occupation. Researchers have identified nine hangmen who worked in Moreton Bay, Brisbane and the colony, including Alexander Green who did the job while Queensland was still part of New South Wales. John Hutton was executioner for many years from 1862 to 1885, managing to become a wealthy property owner and brothel keeper with income earned from his position.

In Van Diemen's Land, later Tasmania, Solomon Blay was hangman from 1847 until 1887, with some time out for a return to England, from where he had been transported in 1837. Blay was still in his twenties when he took up the necessary but reviled position as hangman.

A superstitious man who turned his head away as he sent his victims to eternity, Blay also had a fear of being photographed. His tenure as hangman is said to have been the longest in the British empire and in the last years of his life he was well known as a spinner of yarns about his exploits to anyone who would listen.

'Old Sol', as Blay was familiarly known, was responsible for around one-third of the many hanging sentences handed down by Tasmanian courts, some of which were carried out on Norfolk Island. As observed by researchers in this area, 'Tasmania shares with New South Wales an ignominious history of capital punishment in the first half century of settlement'. When Solomon Blay died in 1897, his effects included the noose knots of the ropes he had used to hang some 200 condemned men and women.

THE BUSHRANGER AND THE LADY

Harry Power (aka Johnson) was an old-school bushranger. He was respectful to women, generally robbed only those who could afford to be robbed and, as far as anyone knew, was never a killer. At least, that was the image he worked hard to project as he lay dying in Pentridge Prison in 1877.

Power was residing in Pentridge, on this occasion, for fifteen years. After transportation from Ireland in 1840 he'd gained his freedom and come to the Port Phillip district in the late 1840s. Here, he plied his trade with humour and, for a bushranger, reasonable civility and a touch of style. According to one unlikely but revealing story, he once ran into three armed men who were out on his trail. Quick-witted Power asked them to protect him from the dreaded bushranger and accompanied them on the hunt. After winning their trust with this trick, Harry later held them up, took their guns, stripped them and made them walk home naked.

Power was sentenced to thirteen years hard labour in 1855. After seven years of servitude, he escaped, finding a congenial home in the mountains then known as the Wombat Ranges of the Ovens district. Here, he enjoyed the help of the local selectors, particularly the Quinn, Lloyd and Kelly families. He was in prison again in 1864 but escaped in 1869 and returned to the Ovens district and the fine life he'd been leading there, holding up travellers and coaches, sometimes with the help of one of the young Kelly boys. Power was kept safe from the police through a network of locals who, he claimed, were well paid for their service from the proceeds of the bushranger's many robberies. He claimed to have carried out more than 600 in this period.

It all came to a sudden end in 1870. Power's busy bushranging schedule and the failure of the police to catch him eventually brought down a large reward of £500 (around $66,000 today) on his head. He disappeared across the New South Wales border for a while but was soon back in his old haunts and still eluding capture. Whether Power antagonised the volatile Quinn, Lloyd and Kelly families or whether James Quinn simply decided he could do with the £500, nobody knows. Quinn had a word with the police and it wasn't long before they nabbed the sleeping bushranger. Back to Pentridge he went for another long stretch.

Now, seven years after beginning his sentence, Power had received the last rites and was keen to talk to the journalist Julian Thomas, better known by his pen name, 'Vagabond', then doing some social diving in Pentridge for his sensational newspaper stories. Not surprisingly, Power was bitter about his betrayal. He was even suspicious that the young boy who rode with him on one or two robberies might have had a hand in it. Power had not been impressed by his apprentice's bushranging talents but the boy, now grown up, was about to become the most notorious bushranger of them all. The following year, Ned Kelly and his gang would unleash Australia's most infamous bushranging outbreak.

Harry Power should have been dead by then. But 'Vagabond' had swallowed the personable but wily bushranger's sob story hook, line and sinker and spun it into newspaper gold—'Let no one think that I mean to make a hero of him. In his day he was a most dangerous ruffian but compared to many who are now in Pentridge he is a saint.' It seems that this tosh had an impact on many readers. Some were in a position to turn their sympathy into charity, chief among them Lady Janet Clarke.

Janet Snodgrass had worked as a governess for the children of wealthy grazier, William Clarke. She married him in 1873 and used her position and his money to develop a prominent role as a philanthropist, social worker and advocate for women's rights. After reading the article written by 'Vagabond', she and others successfully petitioned for Power's release. He made a near-miraculous recovery and went to work for Lady Clarke on the family's Sunbury property for the next fourteen years or so.

Over the years, the bushranger's legend had grown quite a bit. Some were telling this tale about him in 1890 . . .

On one occasion when making his way across country, Harry Power lost his reckoning, and learned about noon that he was evidently bushed and very hungry. Some sheep were feeding a little distance away, and riding across he shot a young wether, and cutting a chop from the quivering carcase, made a fire and grilled it. With a few Johnny cakes from his saddle bag, and a drink of water, he proposed to make a comfortable lunch when he was interrupted by a couple of men who rode up. 'Did you kill that sheep?' asked one of them.

'Yes, sir,' said Power humbly, 'I lost my way and was hungry, so I killed the sheep. But I'll pay for it.'

'Oh, that won't do me,' remarked the visitor, 'I want you to know that I am overseer of this station, and a magistrate. I intend to make an example of you, so saddle up and come in with me.'

Power asked once more to be let off but was rebuffed by the overseer. He then offered to give the overseer his name, but the man was not interested.

'Perhaps not, but I'd better tell you, I'm Harry Power.'

Two seconds later a frightened overseer was apologising to the notorious bushranger, and within half an hour after finishing his lunch, Power mounted on the best horse on the station and was making a beeline for his hut, in the Wombat Ranges.

The year after this whopper was printed, Power got a job as a caretaker and guide on the very hulk where he had once been imprisoned in the 1850s. The *Success* had been decommissioned after a long and eventful career as a merchant ship, emigrant ship and then a prison. The leaking vessel was sold to entrepreneurs and turned into a floating museum of convictism. Who better than a previous inmate to look after it and show the curious around the whips and chains liberally displayed throughout the ship?

But Power wasn't at this job for long. In the same year he started work on *Success* he drowned in the Murray River near Swan Hill at the age of 71, either by misadventure or suicide. The following year, *Success* sank at its moorings but was refloated to begin another phase of a long and eventful career. The ship travelled to Britain and America as a museum, went back into merchant service in 1918, sank again, but was again salvaged and used once more as a ship of convict horrors until the 1930s. In 1946, *Success* ended more than a century of service in flames.

Despite Harry Power's high profile as a more or less gentleman bushranger during his lifetime, he is mostly forgotten today. But the afterlife of his unsatisfactory apprentice continues to enthral and appal us in nearly equal measure.

PILFERED PEARLS

'Snide' is a slang term of uncertain origin, though long used in underworld parlance to mean something suspect or illegal. We might use the word 'dodgy' as a close substitute. In the Australian pearling business, the word meant a stolen pearl, or mother-of-pearl shell. This form of workplace pilfering was a major problem in the industry and is not unknown even today.

Australia's modern pearling industry began in the late nineteenth century, centred on the Northern Territory port of Darwin and the Torres Strait, as well as in Broome and Cossack, which were the main pearling ports in Western Australia. It was a labour-intensive industry with often-dangerous conditions and a usually poorly paid multicultural workforce. The incentives to easily make some fast money were hard for many to resist. By the 1930s sniding was a major problem, though little discussed outside pearling communities.

A rare public venting of the issue appeared in a 1937 newspaper article. The writer, identified only by the initials 'M F', pointed out that 'Easily the greatest source of dead loss to the Australian pearlers today is the iniquitous "sniding" of valuable pearls secured by the divers.' Over the previous ten years, the pearl traders who controlled the industry were losing large amounts of money through this form of thieving.

The technique was simple, safe and profitable for those involved. The long chains of the snide trade began with the workers who prised the shells apart to obtain the mother-of-pearl on the inside, prized both for its beauty and, for many decades, its practical use in making clothing buttons, furniture, combs and other decorative applications. If the opener was fortunate enough to discover one of the relatively few shells to contain a pearl, it could be instantly snatched and easily secreted. Even when the lugger owners raided their own boats as they returned after a diving voyage, they rarely found any pearls. And even if they did, things did not necessarily go well.

On one occasion an incoming lugger was boarded by the owner when it was still some way out to sea. He searched for a long time, and just when he was about to give up his quest he saw his Japanese head diver glance towards a tiny crevice between the wall of the cabin and the decking above. He went to the crevice, and found two pearls, each worth approximately £800 (around $80,000 today).

Success! No. The pearler had to stand on a box to reach the hidden pearls. Unfortunately, it broke under his weight and he dropped the two pearls back into the crevice. They rolled along a plank and through a hole in the side of the ship and back into the sea where they came from. If these stolen treasures had not been lost, they would have most likely been sold in the European or American markets 'at exceptionally high prices'.

According to one owner of a lugger fleet 'The channels along which a "snide" is passed are so long that about 40 "middlemen" get a profit out of a good "stone".' He claimed that more than half of the residents of Broome's Chinatown were living off the snides stolen from his fleet. True or not, by this time, the pearlers had given up counting on pearls as part of their annual profits and simply calculated the value of the shell. But even that could disappear.

After filling up with shell, a lugger could easily sail to a secluded inlet along the coast. There, under cover of darkness, the crew could unload half a ton, or even a ton, of the valuable cargo onto another vessel moored there according to a previous arrangement. The men would be paid off and the purloined pearl shell would be taken out of Australian waters, most likely to Japan.

In the morning the Australian lugger would be quietly drifting for shell, and the Japanese vessel, with probably half a ton of stolen pearl shell, would be far away. More often than not the rightful owner would never suspect that some of his shell had been stolen, as the hauls from the sea beds vary considerably.

The pearl masters tried to fight back but their efforts were foiled by the racism of the time. Falsely believing that 'white men' would not stoop to such thievery, a policy of hiring only European labour was instituted, but 'Unfortunately, with the European men on board the luggers the stealing of pearls did not diminish. Horrified at the thought that white men were partial to "get-rich-quick" schemes, pearlmasters decided to save the additional expense of the white man's wages.'

Twenty years earlier, a case in the Western Australian Supreme Court revealed that sniding was commonplace among shell openers: 'everybody did it'. Evidence was given of 'A man buying a stolen pearl from a Malay for £50 and selling it next day for £450'. One shell opener was reported to have only been active for a year and was supposedly living on only thirty shillings a week yet already owned a lugger worth £850.

Even in recent times, the allure of purloined pearls remained strong. Nowadays, the prize is not wild pearls or mother of pearl but cultivated pearls. Since the 1950s, the cultured pearl has been the mainstay of the industry. In 2005 almost 300 of these valuable gems were stolen from a farm at Quandong Point, about 50 kilometres north of Broome.

As well as their monetary value, pearls have a romantic aura of tropical seas, dangerous occupations and folklore. But even here crime has a role. The legend of the Roseate Pearl is based on theft.

The story goes that a diver found the fabulously lustred pearl but it was stolen from him by another diver. Underworld figures then stole the pearl from him and sold it to a buyer who then died of a heart attack. This began the chain of ill luck attributed to the stone and a succession of owners, mostly dodgy, who all suffered untimely ends. The pearl was then considered to be cursed. Eventually, in 1912, a passenger took the pearl, said by then to be worth over £12,000 (or over $1.5 million today), aboard the steamship *Koombana*. She was lost in a cyclone with all passengers and crew. The Roseate Pearl is said to be lying somewhere on the sea floor in the lost wreck of the ship.

This yarn arose from the singular circumstances of pearling and the lives of those who worked to bring the lustrous treasure of the seas to the waiting markets of the world, legally or otherwise.

CONFESSIONS OF A THIEF

It was the usual busy Monday at Sydney's Central Police Court on 16 November 1863. Among the twenty-six accused brought before the court was a fourteen-year-old boy named Joseph Bragg. He was charged with stealing a loaf of bread from William Pritchard, who had caught him in the act. Pritchard asked the boy why he had not simply asked for the bread if he was hungry, rather than stealing it. Bragg replied 'that he would not ask for bread if he could take it'.

This defiant response led Pritchard to turn the boy in to custody, not for him to be punished 'but that he might see whether something could not be done to rescue him from the wretched course upon which he appears to have entered'. The good-hearted Pritchard had even gone to the trouble of finding work for the young Bragg 'which he decidedly refuses to take'. It would not be Joe Bragg's last encounter with people who wanted to help him but for now, while 'Their Worships said that it was distressing to see so young a person in such circumstances—circumstances to which he had been brought through the neglect of abandoned and profligate parents; but as he has been before convicted of larceny, they have no alternative but to send him to gaol for three months.'

Joe Bragg was already well on the way to that wasted life from which William Pritchard had tried to save him. Just a few months earlier he had been charged with rolling a drunk at Redfern. A few months after the stolen loaf incident he was charged with stealing the cash box from a shop. It was the beginning of a long career of crime, prison, lost opportunity and faded hopes.

At the age of seventeen Bragg pleaded guilty in Brisbane's Central Police Court to a charge of assaulting a police officer and was given the alternatives of a fine of £3 or fourteen days in prison. Three years later he graduated to an appearance in the New South Wales Supreme Court before Chief Justice Sir Alfred Stephen on a charge of wounding with intent to do serious bodily harm. The judge read out Joseph Orton Bragg's unenviable record of fifteen convictions and imprisonments, including a stint in the Tarban Creek Lunatic Asylum. Privately, Stephen believed that Bragg was a criminal who 'clearly required permanent restraint'. Officially, he sentenced him to five years hard labour on the roads.

After his release, Bragg returned to his criminal ways, frequently associating with the Sydney street gang known as the Forty Thieves. He had a relationship with a woman named Mary Moore and in 1880 was tried with her for assault and robbery involving a particularly unpleasant method known as garrotting. The assailant slipped a wire or thin cord around the victim's throat and tightened the restraint against the windpipe, immediately cutting off breath. Garrotting could easily be fatal, either accidentally or by intention. Fortunately for Bragg, his victim lived. The garrotter received another five-year sentence and twenty-five lashes.

Bragg served much of his time in Berrima Gaol, where he underwent a seemingly marvellous transformation. The violent, thieving, alcoholic thug discovered books. He 'first experienced the deliciousness of thought', as he put it in his memoir, during the frequent periods his intransigence earned him in solitary confinement. While this cruel form of incarceration broke many prisoners, Bragg actively sought it out, even pretending to be insane so he would be locked up alone with his books. Once he cut his own throat, fearing that the prison authorities were trying to keep him away from the books he devoured.

During his time at Berrima, Bragg not only resisted prison authority but actively protested against it. He testified to a parliamentary inquiry in 1878 about the brutality routinely employed in the prison. The commission heard of prisoners being gagged and repeatedly placed in darkened cells. One cell was fitted with two metal rings to which prisoners were handcuffed for punishment.

Upon his release, Bragg came into contact with George Ardill, a Baptist social reformer who ran what would today be called halfway houses for ex-prisoners. Ardill encouraged Bragg to give up crime and grog and to put his abilities to good use. Bragg spoke at Temperance halls and the Sydney Domain about his life of crime and his redemption, a role that suited the high opinion he held of himself. He also wrote his life story, *Confessions of a Thief*, published by Ardill as part of his social campaigning.

Joe Bragg's tale of his rough beginnings and even rougher life followed by reformation was a testament to the possibility of salvation for even the most hardened criminal. Ardill sent a copy to the English criminologist Havelock Ellis, who was greatly impressed by Bragg's story. Ellis, who had spent some time in Australia, was interested in the social and psychological roots of crime and in reforming the penal system to use more rational forms of punishment. Ellis used Bragg's biography in his published works as evidence that recidivism was not an inevitable consequence of criminal life.

Unfortunately, Joe Bragg's stint of going straight was a short one. In 1889 he was back in court for beating and neglecting one of his sons—both named after him. Three years later Bragg was sent to prison once again, this time receiving a seven-year sentence for robbery with violent assault. He appeared in court under the name Joseph Orton but, as several reports noted, on his arms 'the familiar name of Joseph Bragg is indelibly tattooed'. The litany of Bragg's record was read out in court and one newspaper stated that he 'was well known at one period as professing to have been converted'.

From this time, the name Joseph Orton Bragg no longer features in the pages of Australian newspapers. Unless the report of a court appearance by a 'Joseph Orton Braggs' published in 1910 refers to him. On that occasion, the accused was fined five shillings and costs for driving in Bankstown, New South Wales, without carrying a light. A Joseph O. Bragg was buried in an unmarked grave at Sydney's Rookwood Cemetery in November 1917.

TOMMY THE AMBLER AND BOGAN BILLY

The annals of Australian crime are full of clever and daring escapes, often followed by epic stories of the pursuit and recapture, or death, of the escapee. Many of these stories are little known though can sometimes be recovered from the pages of old bush newspapers.

This account of the capture of bushranger Tommy the Ambler (real name, Jones, maybe), is one of these.

Tommy the Ambler seems to have made no other impact on history and folklore, which is a shame. He displays proper bushranger style—he escapes from gaol, eludes the cops (for a while), rides a fine horse, has sympathisers and confederates prepared to help him, and carries a serious weapon.

As the story goes, the Ambler was banged up in the Bourke Gaol in 1882 on a charge of horse stealing when, probably with the help of 'his many friends in the district', he staged a breakout and went bush. It was only a couple of years after Ned Kelly was hanged and the authorities were still nervous about another bushranging outbreak. So was everyone else. It wasn't long before 'Rumour after rumour succeeded each other in quick succession that five or six men had been seen in the scrub all armed to the teeth, and that "Wild Wright" was among their number.' Isaiah 'Wild' Wright was a prominent sympathiser of the Kelly gang and bushranging was still a sensitive issue in the region, in the 1860s, long after Ben Hall, John Gilbert and the rest had been dealt with. The activities of this small-time crim could still be seen as threatening the community and all available police resources were mobilised to track the Ambler and his associates down.

Senior Constable Piggott led the chases, assisted by three constables and two trackers. They had their work cut out. Rain barely ceased from the time the police began the chase. Unable to light fires for fear of alerting their quarry, the police travelled wet, cold and half-starved. The Ambler's sympathisers fed them false leads and they were eventually forced to turn back to their starting point at Canonba to resupply. After just a few hours rest, Piggott rallied his men and they again headed into the unwelcoming bush in search of the Ambler's muddy tracks.

At the end of three days their provisions began to run short, and for the two following days the men were reduced to the greatest extremities. The rain obliterated the tracks for the most part, but where they were discernable [sic] they appeared to be getting more distinct. Senior-constable Piggott, encouraged by this, determined to push on. The trackers now began to proceed with more caution. Constables Chaseling, Cameron, and Atkinson (the latter said to be a splendid shot) kept their rifles in readiness to prevent a surprise.

Then Bogan Billy, one of the trackers, pointed ahead. There was Tommy. He saw the police at the same moment.

Tommy the Ambler was alone, there being no Wild Wright or other desperadoes, who had been spoken of as comprising the gang—only the one contemptible, small, but squarely-built individual, Jones. Contemptible, however, though he looked, he is said to be a very fine horseman and bushman, unequalled in the colonies for daring. On catching sight of the police, the offender took the bush for it.

The Ambler immediately disappeared into the thick scrub.

Constable Cameron fired his piece, but the bushranger was not to be intimidated by that, and when the echo of the rifle was dying out, could be heard the laugh and chuckle of the bushranger, as if mocking his pursuers. There was a heavy fence between them, and it was the work of more than a moment to remove it; but with a strong pull altogether, the obstacle was soon removed. The police remounted, and were soon again in pursuit.

Another fence line and boggy ground slowed the pursuers down again but after another half an hour or so of jumping fences and struggling through the bush, Piggott caught sight of their quarry. He spurred his horse towards the bushranger and when he got into range, raised his rifle and 'called upon him to stand'.

> At this moment Jones looked around, and seeing that he was covered jumped off his horse. For a moment he seemed as if meditating as to whether he should fire or not, but dropped his weapon and held up his hands. Piggott was now alongside of him, and in a moment had him secured, and was in a few moments afterwards joined by his comrades.

The gallant Piggott and his men had their man. He turned out to be someone Piggott had arrested four years earlier after chasing him for almost 1800 kilometres. The bushranger's friends and associates were rounded up and arrested and he was escorted to Bathurst to face the music. The country breathed a sigh of relief to be spared a feared bushranging outbreak and life returned to normal. Tommy the Ambler was no doubt gaoled again and then we hear no more of him.

But we know a fair bit about the chequered career of tracker, Bogan Billy, a man who moved easily across the borders between the legal and the illegal. He was born in Wiradjuri country, through which flows the Bogan River, in the 1860s and was working on a pastoral property near Cowra, New South Wales, by the age of ten. He was also getting into trouble with the law, mainly stealing horses.

These minor infractions did not stand in the way of his later employment as a police tracker, in which capacity he met

Senior Constable Piggott. In the same year he helped track down Tommy the Ambler, Bogan survived an attempt on his life when he was the principal witness for the prosecution in a case brought against a European. He resigned from the force and returned to a life of wandering and crime around western New South Wales.

In 1895 he escaped from a train carrying him to Bathurst for trial under police custody with another prisoner, named Albert Katz. The two overpowered their guard and made a dramatic leap from the train. Katz was soon recaptured, but Bogan Billy then led police on a year-long pursuit. He was finally taken in Charleville, Queensland, and trained—more securely this time—back to Bathurst where he faced a charge of intent to commit murder, a capital offence.

Bogan Billy was found guilty of the lesser charge of malicious wounding with intent to do grievous bodily harm and sentenced to seven years in prison. While serving out his time in Parramatta Gaol, he sickened and died of lung disease, probably tuberculosis, in 1900. He had no known family or descendants.

TIN-POT CRIMES

Even the most seemingly trivial events can become crime scenes. The lost folk custom of 'tin kettling' welcomed many newly married couples into rural communities during the nineteenth and early twentieth centuries. More or less harmless though it was, sometimes things could turn nasty.

Tin kettling, or sometimes 'tin tattling', is the name by which this widespread marriage custom was known in Australia. It usually took place after the bride and groom had retired to wherever they were going to spend their first night of wedded bliss. Allowing them enough time to settle down, the rowdier youths and younger men of the area gathered near the premises equipped with kerosene tins, pots, pans, maybe even a concertina or anything else that made a lot of noise. At the agreed moment they began beating on their noise-makers, catcalling and often throwing stones onto the roof of the marital residence.

With variations, this animated custom was practised in western Europe, Britain and America. In Germany and in the Barossa Valley it was known as 'polterabend', in America as a 'tin kettle band' or a 'Dutch band' and sometimes as a 'shivaree'. It seems to have been mostly observed in rural communities and can best be thought of as a humorous welcoming of the newlyweds into what were usually small communities. A more recent, though now probably defunct, custom of tying tin cans and other decorations to the newlyweds' car as they leave for their honeymoon may be an echo of the earlier tradition.

Reactions to the tin kettling experience varied. In some places, particularly but not exclusively where German people had settled, it was an honour to be tin kettled at your wedding and considered a mark of respect for the bride and groom as well as a sign of community approval for the union. Sometimes, the couple subjected to this rough music were expected to invite the noisy revellers into the house for a cup of tea, or perhaps something stronger. Not that the tin kettlers were likely to need much more alcohol after the earlier wedding festivities.

But not everyone enjoyed the attention. According to one writer on the subject 'performance invariably gives dire offence to the parties, whom it is intended to honour'. It could also easily become a public as well as a personal nuisance if it were kept up for a long time, as it sometimes was. But usually, there was little point in complaining as "'Tis a custom of the country, and therefore to be winked at by the police,' according to one observer.

While the ceremony had its cosier aspects, it could also become a scene of crime, as frequently reported in newspapers from the 1850s.

> Yesterday several charges of assault were brought before the bench. The two first were Sarah Bailey v. Samuel Clift, and Sarah Bailey v. Thomas Wise. These charges arose out of the fact that a number of young men assembled opposite Mr. Bailey's house on the 10th instant, to keep up the ancient but disagreeable practice of ushering in a wedding by unmusical noises, beating tin kettles, smacking stockwhips, etc.; Mrs. Bailey not approving this, went out and tried to disperse them, and words proving ineffectual, she tried a whip, but was obliged to give it up, and as she retreated, she stated she was struck by some bones on the back, thrown by the young men, and by a stockwhip lash curling round her . . .

Clift was able to provide witnesses who testified that Mrs Bailey gave at least as good as she got with her whip. He got off. His mate, Wise, was charged with throwing the bones, probably marrow bones as these were often part of the custom. He was not so lucky and had to pay two shillings and sixpence in costs or go to prison for a month.

A few years later in Avoca, Victoria: 'Complaints having been made to the Inspector of Police, that several persons have been insulted on the occasion of their marriage—by a number of people calling at their dwellings, and hooting, shouting, and playing on tin kettles &c, before the said persons dwellings, very much to the annoyance of those persons and other inhabitants of the township . . .'

Local police wasted no time in issuing a stern warning: 'This is to give notice that this is insulting behaviour, whereby a breach of the peace may be occasioned, and is punishable under the 16th of Victoria, No. 22, clause 5. The Inspector has given instructions to the constables of this district to arrest all such persona who may be found so offending. —Hugh Ross Barclay, Inspector Police Department, Avoca, 26th September, 1859.'

Some reports from South Australia detail more serious law-breaking. At Marrabel in 1871 four local youths set up a tin kettling of some newlyweds in the traditional manner. But things soon got out of hand. They took to breaking windows and began destroying the window frames. The groom reported the incident and three of the offenders were brought to court. They escaped conviction with a published apology, legal expenses and £20 compensation to the complainant.

At Baker's Swamp, New South Wales, tin kettlers made such a nuisance of themselves in 1903 that an enraged relative of the newlyweds sent them reeling with a shotgun blast. The same year a man was stabbed at a tin kettling near Bethany, South Australia, where 'The gathering of tinkettler's [sic] was an extremely noisy and rowdy one, and much larrikinism was in evidence.' That event saw no fewer than thirty-one 'persons' charged with disturbing the peace.

There are frequent references to these mock serenades in newspapers right around the country from the mid-nineteenth century. If caught, perpetrators were usually charged with disturbing the peace and given relatively small fines, as at Casterton, Victoria, in 1903 where six young boys were each fined two shillings and sixpence in default of six hours imprisonment.

It is likely that tin kettling was disrupted by World War I when many young men went away to fight and weddings became less frequent. In some areas it continued into the 1940s then faded away. A late incident in 1953 at Wattle Flats, New South Wales, again involved a shotgun and led to a charge of malicious wounding.

That seems to have been the last report of the custom, though there are signs of a recent revival of sorts. Recalling her German grandparents' tales of raucous revelling on the Darling Downs during the 1930s and '40s, 'Jo' and a few mates tin kettled a friend on her birthday. It was during a COVID-19 lockdown but everyone had a great socially distanced time out on the grass in front of the birthday girl's house. She was 'very surprised and quite touched as well'.

No shotguns required.

Dumb Luck

Crime runs the full spectrum of human experience. Clever, careful, predetermined, accidental: the list could be very long. Crime can also be stupid.

The bloke who broke into a pharmacy in the Sydney suburb of Redfern one early morning in December 2006 was stupid and unlucky. He managed to force his way through the glass doors at the front of the shop but was then confronted with an iron grille. As he tried to get through this serious obstruction, clearly visible from the street, the glass doors slid closed behind him and locked tight. The robber was penned between the grille and the doors, displayed for anyone to see. A local publican did and called the cops.

They were greatly amused to find their quarry neatly trapped and awaiting release into their caring custody. The laughs grew even louder when it was discovered that the thief had actually managed to purloin some goods—rolls of toilet paper.

Even dumber was a Queensland Gold Coast drug dealer. In 2015, the would-be gangster videoed himself making tough-guy moves in his bathroom. This might have been just a little macho vanity except for the fact that he was holding some marijuana buds at the time. And, in plain sight just behind him, was a very large bag of the drug, much more than anyone would require for personal use.

The police who arrested the dealer couldn't believe their luck when they found the incriminating video on his phone. And they couldn't stop laughing either, much to the deep embarrassment of the crim who later faced major drug charges after having obligingly provided the police with all the evidence needed to charge him.

At another pharmacy, this one in Melbourne, a crim attempting a break-in managed to get himself stuck in the chimney. It was only a few weeks before Christmas 2018 and the luckless burglar was, of course, compared with Santa in the headline 'Claus for Concern'.

Yet another contender for Australia's dumbest crime had lethal consequences for the wrong victim of a murder's bullet. This fatal farce played out in the Sydney street gang underworld of the 1920s and '30s.

It was the era of early closing and the 'six o-clock swill' when pubs closed at that time, causing an inevitable rush of thirsty drinkers. Railways painter and family man, Jack (John) Thornton, and his brother Charlie hurried off to the Camelia Grove Hotel in the suburb of Alexandria for a quick couple before closing on Boxing Day evening, 1930. They were joined by a few friends and another brother.

Before long, an argument broke out between Charlie Thornton and a twenty-year-old crim named Tibby Bell. He was a product of the rough-and-tough Waterloo gangs and there was bad blood between him and the Alexandria Thornton. These suburbs were among those parts of Sydney considered to be 'hotbeds of crime', as they were usually dubbed by the press. As well as their criminal elements, though, they were also tight-knit working-class communities where residents mostly knew each other and often stuck together despite the stigmas attached to their areas.

Accounts differ, but Bell and Thornton either had a fight in the backyard of the pub or were only with difficulty prevented from physically settling their differences. Whatever did or did not happen and whatever their disagreement was about, it ended when Bell took off in a very bad mood.

With their last drinks in hand, the Thorntons and a small group then gathered outside the pub to finish off the session. Suddenly, Bell returned carrying a revolver. He pointed it at the group of drinkers, squeezed the trigger and shot Jack Thornton in the stomach.

Thornton dropped to the ground, blood pouring from the wound. Someone cried out that Bell had shot the wrong man as the gunman menaced the shocked group with the pistol. Then he ran off as the remaining Thornton brothers and their mates gave furious chase. He fired two more shots as he went but hit no one else. Then he burst into a nearby house, tried unsuccessfully to make a telephone call to someone, and disappeared.

Jack Thornton was rushed to hospital but fell into a coma and died. He left behind a grieving mother, brothers, a widow and two young children.

Police soon caught Bell who, unsuccessfully, pleaded self-defence. He was sentenced to death, though this was commuted to life imprisonment, a sentence of which he served only ten years before receiving a commutation. He died in 1977, known forever as the crim who shot the wrong man.

BODGIE BEAT-UPS

Sex, drugs . . . but not rock'n'roll. The bodgies were a youth group before Bill Haley and the Comets brought the back beat to popular music in 1955. Bodgies listened mostly to American jazz. They also spoke American slang, dressed like mostly black American hipsters of the era and sported distinctive haircuts, said to derive from the style of Cornel Wilde, a popular Hollywood actor of the 1940s and early '50s. These influences had reached Australian youth during World War II when large numbers of American troops, many African American, passed through the country, bringing sharp dressing, music and dance.

Together with their girlfriends, the 'widgies', bodgies were Australia's first teenagers. They dressed in clothes seemingly designed to provoke their elders. The males usually wore drape jackets, pegged trousers and thick crepe-soled shoes. The widgies emulated the dress styles of Hollywood starlets. Like all teenage groups since, they were the focus of parental, moral and official alarm. According to some, it was all about sex, as a Launceston magistrate argued: 'I do not associate them with the accepted forms of juvenile delinquency at all. They indulge in sex orgies. All they are interested in is sex . . . they are not gangsters; they do not break into homes or steal cars, but they must be regarded as serious because their whole cult is based on sex.'

This magistrate was only one of many who feared that lack of parental control had produced these strange and dangerous creatures in the midst of Australia's then grey, conservative society. A prominent churchman claimed that 'The cult resembled the insane existentialist cult in Paris, which has led to murder and other crimes, and to complete civic irresponsibility,' making a highly unlikely connection with the alienated philosophy espoused by French intellectual Jean-Paul Sartre and the Beatniks.

As well as the outrages of sex, the lustful black music of jazz and blues, and their hair and clothes, the bodgies were also, according to some, raging drug addicts. Marijuana had been available in Australia for many years, though it was generally restricted to underworld users, bohemians and affluent nightclubbers rather than the working class from which bodgies and widgies arose. The 'Yanks' gave the drug a powerful boost in the 1940s and some bodgies undoubtedly took up the habit, as would many more young people in the 1960s. But even if they weren't smoking 'reefers', the bodgies and widgies were said to be indulging in alcohol-fuelled orgies, as newspapers like *Truth* enthusiastically detailed at every opportunity.

All these confronting behaviours quickly produced what most historians of the topic have seen as a moral panic. Respectable citizens were scandalised. These strange, drug-addled perverts were likely to murder them in their beds and were perceived as a threat to the fabric of Australian society. Pressure was soon exerted on the police to clean up the bodgies. A Bodgie Squad was formed in Melbourne and specialised in breaking up groups of youths, beating them up in the process. Brisbane police formed a similar squad in 1957 and elsewhere in the country, authorities kept a close eye on the youths and their activities.

As a rule, the bodgies were rarely serious criminals. Like other modern youth trends, including sharpies, rockers, surfies, mods, punks and so on, they were a fashion or style group rather than a gang. Their interests centred on dress, dance, music and probably much the same amount of sex as any other generation. Their infractions were mainly public brawling or in the minor league of crime, like the seventeen-year-old of no fixed address known as 'Big Shoulder S' who was convicted of larceny and placed on a £10 two-year good behaviour bond in 1952: 'Big "Shoulders' Sims'" black hair was worn long and oiled, and he was dressed in a long draped coat, with massive shoulders, tight trousers, and crepe-soled shoes.'

But even if they were not gangsters, bodgies and widgies were effectively criminalised by the conventional attitudes of the time and sensationalist press beat-ups. In 1958, Brisbane bodgies were blamed for 'an orgy of wanton destruction' at the Royal Show. Although there was no evidence to connect bodgies with this event, the sensationalist *Sunday Truth* tried and convicted them anyway, linking the bodgies with the long-gone larrikins: 'Irresponsible larrikins are responsible for thousands of pounds worth of damage to valuable agricultural machinery equipment on display at this year's Royal Show. In an orgy of wanton destruction, the bodgie-type hoodlums slashed tyres and rubber hoses, scratched equipment and ripped away loose parts . . . because of the louts [sic] system of operation in "packs", complete with "lookouts", no bodgie arrests were made during the week.'

However many bodgies and widgies might still have been around by the 1960s, the new trends in popular music, clothes and entertainment soon put them well past their use-by date. Like all youth groups, they faded into jobs, marriage and respectability. But the memory lingered on.

The late Bob Hawke was Labor Prime Minister from 1983 to 1991. 'Hawkie' had several nicknames, including the 'boudoir bandicoot', a reference to his reputed love life and 'the Mild Colonial Boy', a put-down by his political opponents. But he was more widely known as 'the Silver Bodgie'. His distinctive silver hair, worn in a bodgie-like style, together with the legendary drinking of his younger days and down-to-earth personality endowed him with the larrikin image that did him no harm at all in the polls.

Skyjack

Captain John Benton was preparing to land Trans Australia Airlines (TAA) flight 408 at Brisbane airport on the evening of 19 July 1960. It had been a routine journey out of Sydney with the usual crew complement of six and forty-three passengers. Around ten minutes before touchdown was expected, flight attendant Janeene Christie came into the cockpit and told the captain and his first officer that a man with a sawn-off rifle and a gelignite bomb was threatening to blow up the plane.

It was Australia's first mid-air hijacking, or skyjacking, though planes around the world had been commandeered for various reasons since the earliest years of commercial aviation. Usually, the hijackers demanded to be taken somewhere other than the listed destination. And that was what Alex Hildebrandt wanted Captain John Benton to do: fly him and everyone else on board the *John Gilbert*, as the plane was named, to Singapore, Darwin or anywhere north of Brisbane.

Benton turned the aircraft out to sea and told First Officer Thomas Bennett to alert another TAA flight captain travelling on the plane, a man named Dennis Lawrence. He was already moving towards the hijacker with the emergency escape axe and sat down in the seat behind Hildebrandt. Assisted by two flight attendants, Lawrence and Bennett struggled to subdue the hijacker who fired a shot into the cabin roof, almost hitting Bennett. Lawrence then smashed the flat edge of the fire axe into the side of Hildebrandt's head and tore the bare wires of the bomb out of the stunned man's hands.

Another passenger, charter pilot Warren Penny, joined the struggle and was asked to stand guard over Hildebrandt. Penny described his experience to a journalist:

'That began the diciest seven minutes of my 32 years of flying,' Mr. Penny said. 'When I heard the shot I thought a fuse had blown in the galley and there might be a fire. I unsnapped my seat belt and raced forward to grab an extinguisher. As I raced up I saw one of the pilots had a man pinned in his seat, holding him down. The pilot shoved the hatchet at me and said, 'If he moves smash him across the skull.' I said, 'Right,' and I meant it too. If he'd batted an eyelid I'd have let him have it.'

Despite the scuffle, it seems that many of the passengers remained unaware of the dangerous situation that had been unfolding, fortunately averted by the actions of passengers and crew, as further described by Penny:

> The man was still pretty stunned from the crack he'd had across the head from the pilot and blood was dribbling from one side of his mouth. He did not start to get his senses back until a couple of minutes before we came down. The pilot [Lawrence] stood next to me, pinning the man to his seat while I stood over him with the hatchet. He yelled through to the crew members in the cockpit, 'Get her down as fast as you can'.

Captain Benton did exactly that and Hildebrandt was taken away by police after the aircraft landed safely in Brisbane.

The son of post–World War II Russian displaced persons, Hildebrandt was charged with attempted murder and firearms and explosives crimes committed aboard an aircraft in flight. His motive was unclear. Psychiatrists diagnosed paranoia and a persecution complex based on his childhood ill treatment by his father. He was unemployed at the time of the hijack attempt and his behaviour in court reflected his sad story. Hildebrandt appeared without legal representation. When asked if he wished to question Captain Benton, he gesticulated wildly towards the TAA crew in court and cried 'They are nothing but a bunch of idiots.'

He was found guilty and sentenced to two years prison on the explosives charge, three years for attempted murder and ten years for the attack on the aircraft and its passengers and crew.

An appeal succeeded on the grounds that the aircraft was over New South Wales at the time Hildebrandt had armed his crude bomb and so not subject to Queensland jurisdiction on that charge. He served only the three-year attempted murder charge in Queensland and was arrested by New South Wales detectives on release. He went to trial in New South Wales and was convicted on the threat to the aircraft charge and served another seven years in that state.

We can only hope that Hildebrandt received help and treatment during his years of incarceration. His intended victims were traumatised and his actions led to the enactment of new Commonwealth legislation from 1963 specifically designed to deal with the new crime of skyjacking.

The next Australian skyjacking was in 1972 when an Ansett aircraft flying from Adelaide to Alice Springs was taken over by a disturbed man in similar circumstances. The incident ended with a brave policeman being gravely wounded and the hijacker suiciding.

In 2003 a Qantas flight from Melbourne to Launceston was saved from an attack by another unbalanced individual who wounded several crew members with a sharpened wooden stake. He was subdued by passengers and was later found not guilty of hijacking, attempted murder and grievous bodily harm and ordered to take psychiatric treatment. His stated aim in attempting the skyjack was to crash the plane into the Walls of Jerusalem National Park in Tasmania. This, he said, would free the Devil and bring on the end of the world, known as Armageddon in the Bible.

After these incidents, various security improvements were made to domestic aircraft, serious upgrades from the age of innocence in which the first Australian skyjack took place. Many years after that incident, former flight attendant Janeene Christie and her husband, John Reinhold, happened to travel as passengers aboard the *John Gilbert*. The spot where Alex Hildebrandt's bullet had punched a hole in the ceiling was 'covered with a sort of corn plaster', Mr Reinhold told a newspaper in 2003.

No worries, she'll be right!

NED KELLY IN A WETSUIT

The quest for lost treasure has been the cause of many crimes. It's about financial reward, of course, but for many treasure hunters, it is the need to find the answer to riddles of sunken ships or buried loot that drives them on. Often, both these needs motivate the seekers of mysterious wealth. One man in particular was fired by this fusion of avarice and curiosity. He was known as 'Alan' (properly Ellis) Robinson and his story was a wild one. It began in 1656.

In that year, a Dutch East India Company (VOC) ship was lost off Ledge Point, around 120 kilometres north of where Western Australia's capital city, Perth, stands today. As part of a 1957 scuba dive, Robinson and his companion found a wreck Robinson believed was the VOC's missing *Vergulde Draeck* (*Gilt Dragon*). He was unable to confirm this theory because he could not later relocate the site. But six years later, Robinson was part of another dive party during which the wreck was discovered by a young Graeme Henderson. Robinson came to believe that he was not being given sufficient credit for his original discovery and so began to loot artefacts from the wreck, sometimes using dynamite.

By now, the historical value of shipwrecks along the Western Australian coast had been recognised and in 1964 the Western Australian Parliament legislated for their protection, making all artefacts public property and so stymieing Robinson's hopes of further profiting from the wreck. From this time, Robinson became engaged in a long series of legal battles with various authorities and against heritage legislation. He succeeded in his claims to the objects he had removed from the *Vergulde Draeck* prior to the 1964 legislation and continued his treasure-hunting activities.

In 1968 Robinson and others illegally salvaged artefacts from another Dutch wreck, the *Zuytdorp*, and the following year he was one of the finders of the 1622 wreck of the English ship *Trial* (*Tryall*). He was later acquitted of a charge of dynamiting the wreck to reach its treasures, real or imagined. His battles with museums, governments and ever-tightening marine heritage legislation wound on and in 1977 he was briefly successful in the High Court of Australia in a case he brought against the Western Australian heritage legislation. The High Court found that the state had acted beyond its powers in passing the laws but federal government legislation was found to confirm the validity of the state legislation. The effect of this was to confirm the control of the Western Australian Museum over all marine heritage in the state.

Robinson's private life followed a similar turbulent pattern to his legal and professional dealings. He was married with several children, though his wife grew intolerant of his increasing obsession with establishing what he considered to be his rightful claims and left him. He moved to Queensland and began a relationship with another woman, Lynette Hunter. In his memoirs, *In Australia Treasure Is Not for the Finder* [sic] (1980), and elsewhere, he complained of police harassment and was once acquitted on a charge of resisting arrest in Western Australia. Claiming that his life was in danger from police enemies he had made, Robinson went to the Northern Territory in 1981 where he established a relationship with Patricia Green. The couple had a son the following year.

The final act of Robinson's epic drama played out in a manner befitting the adventurer's extraordinary history. This time, the issue was not related to his treasure hunting, but to his personal life. In 1982, he and Patricia Green were charged with conspiracy to murder Lynette Hunter, the woman Robinson had once lived with in Queensland. Robinson skipped bail, again claiming that his life was in danger. A few months later he was arrested in the Northern Territory hamlet of Larrimah, since notorious for the unsolved disappearance of Paddy Moriarty, and eventually extradited to New South Wales to face the conspiracy charge.

While awaiting the outcome of the trial, Robinson was held in Sydney's Long Bay Gaol. He was due back in court to hear the jury's verdict on 2 November 1983. Just before half-past six that morning, warders found the lifeless treasure hunter hanging from a sheet tied to his cell window.

Had he taken his own life? Few were inclined to think so. His family and legal team said he had been cheerful the previous day and was not the type of person to simply give up. He left no suicide note and as one of his lawyers said, he was 'a vain person with a proper sense of drama—it is hard to imagine him going out in his underwear'.

Only Robinson's co-accused was in court to hear the verdict that day. The jury was not told of the death. When they returned from their considerations, the judge asked for their verdict on Green first. 'Not guilty' was their response. The judge had already advised the jury that if they found one of the defendants not guilty of conspiracy they had no choice but to also find the other not guilty. After the verdict on Green, the judge informed the astonished jurors of Robinson's death and discharged them from having to give a verdict in his case.

Robert Drewe, the writer who covered the case for *The Bulletin*, concluded 'The end of the case was as bizarre as any in recent court history, with all the participants, from the judge to Patricia Green and Robinson's counsel, having to pretend that he was still alive'. He also suggested, 'The Australian legal system may not have heard the end of Robinson'.

Alan Robinson was a colourful character, a driven man who bumped and thumped his way through a roller-coaster life. He aroused strong antagonisms, particularly among those involved in shipwreck hunting, as well as solid support. A Facebook page dedicated to his life and legend refers to him as 'A Ned Kelly in a Wetsuit', a clear sign of his ability to divide opinions and to stand up against laws he believed to be unjust, even long after his mysterious death.

CUCKOO SMURFING

'Psst! Want some dirty money?' This was effectively what global criminals have been offering to the Australian banking system. These trusted institutions laundered ridiculous amounts of tainted cash from illegal drugs, arms and other crimes, much of it dumped into the intelligent deposit machines (IDMs) available through many automatic teller machines (ATMs) in every state and territory.

Not only were these crimes enabled by banks, the crims were brazen. In 2015 a Sydney bank branch continually witnessed scruffy characters seated on milk crates as they stuffed bundles of cash into ATMs. Bank staff were alarmed and frustrated. It was obvious what was going on. Managers sent desperate emails to headquarters but no one seemed to be doing anything about it.

The extent and potential consequences of this astounding situation are laid out in Nathan Lynch's *The Lucky Laundry*, a wide-ranging investigation of the failings and fiddles of Australia's financial system and those agencies charged with ensuring its integrity. In his page-turning exposé, Lynch dissects 'the international black money hydra that has wrapped its serpentine limbs around the Lucky laundry'. One of the many cases he examines involves 'the delicate craft of cuckoo smurfing'.

A 'cuckoo smurf' is underworld parlance for a low-level operative who carries out the physical work of getting illegal funds from their source and into Australian bank accounts, from which it rapidly disappears, now cleaned of its illicit origins. The name references the cuckoo's practice of depositing its own eggs in the nests of other birds. One of these many sophisticated money-laundering operations was cracked by Strike Force Bugam, a joint operation between the New South Wales Police and the Australian Criminal Intelligence Commission (ACIC) in 2017.

Thi Lan Phuong Pham was the Vietnamese front for a large international laundering group. Her job was to recruit cuckoo

BY HOOK OR BY CROOK

smurfs in Australia who could discreetly deposit large amounts of money into local bank accounts without arousing suspicion. In Sydney, she found struggling immigrant Van Kien Do. All he had to do was receive or pick up bundles of cash from someone known only as 'the Accountant' and get them into ATMs. He was paid 1 per cent of the value of each run. It doesn't sound like much for the risk he was taking, but as the runs were typically around $200,000, Van was making easy money and doing very well thank you.

So was Mrs Pham. While Do was shouldering all the risk in Australia, she was home in Vietnam skimming off a larger percentage. It was all going very nicely. But unbeknown to the crims, the Bugam cops were onto them. When Mrs Pham came to Australia in the summer of 2016 to set up her smurf network, the police were able to tap her mobile phone. They then tracked the whole procedure, which veered between the astonishing and the farcical as Do initially blundered his way through the first attempts to deposit cash. He was unable to get the ATM to work and telephoned Mrs Pham in Vietnam for instructions. As he stood on the street with all the money, they conducted a discussion about the problem. Mrs Pham concluded that the machine was broken, laughed hysterically into her mobile and told Do to 'Cut and run'.

Practice improved Do's interactions with the ATMs. His job was to drop a little less than $10,000 of filthy lucre into each of the chosen ATMs. The amount needed to be under $10,000 because that was the point at which banks were supposed to notify the financial regulators of a suspicious transaction. The favoured bank for these deposits was the Commonwealth Bank of Australia. Their machines were available for longer hours, they could hold larger amounts than the IDMs of other banks and, most importantly, they rarely closed down suspicious accounts. Vast sums were flowing through the bank's internal systems only to reappear somewhere else as clean money that could be used for all sorts of legal, as well as illegal, transactions involving drug deals, firearms, people trafficking, terrorism and any other illicit money-making enterprise.

A favoured legal use of the funds was buying expensive Australian real estate. These mostly unoccupied luxury homes were usually owned by foreign nationals, not only as a legal asset but as potential boltholes if things went pear-shaped in their own countries. So extensive has this criminal colonisation of real estate been that it contributed to the artificial rise of Australian property values. Luxury boats, cars, jewellery, art and, of course, high-rolling casino tables were also high on the money launderers' entertainment budgets. Some money was even used to buy federal government bonds.

Mrs Pham and Do played their part in this kleptocracy with all their energy. In just six months Do laundered almost $3,000,000. The Commonwealth Bank's IDMs could swallow up to $600,000 in one gulp, any time, day or night. They were assisted by a flaw in the bank's information technology that failed to flag suspicious transactions and trigger a notification to the regulatory authorities.

In January 2017, Mrs Pham again visited Sydney to meet with Do and plan a further expansion of their rewarding venture. Bugam officers arrested them both. For their bit part in the new criminal bonanza of global money laundering, they went to prison, Do for three years, his boss for six years. When police rounded up others involved in the syndicate they found a crooked accountant, some bikies and an ex-police officer.

A broader undercover police initiative known as Operation Ironside was successful in arresting more than 200 Australian money-laundering suspects in 2021. Coordinated arrests were made in seventeen other countries in an impressive display of international cooperation. As well as twenty-one murder plots and more than 3000 kilograms of drugs, police recovered $45 million in cash and assets in Australia alone. Police elsewhere involved in the three-year operation discovered networks of crime in Asia, South America, the Middle East and Europe. A large number of outlaw motorcycle gang members were also caught in the sting. Money laundering is an essential element of these global criminal activities.

But it is not just high-profile crims enmeshed in the washing of tens of billions of dirty dollars. Despite ongoing attempts to regulate and police money laundering, Australia's financial system has been wide open to this exploitation for years. It is an important part of the black economy, a murky empire of dodgy cash that never shows up on any ledgers. Those involved in the black economy include bent cops, crooked politicians, corrupt professionals and even people in the street passing dirty banknotes in supermarkets and cafes. As the American film director John Huston reportedly said: 'After all, crime is only a left-handed form of human endeavour.'

STEALING THE PAST

One crime rarely makes the news unless an especially high-profile case is revealed. The illicit trade in antiquities is a multi-billion-dollar business carried out on a global scale by clandestine networks of 'tomb robbers' and apparently respectable dealers. Illegally obtained statues, jewellery, coins and other ancient items are filtered into both respectable and dark markets where they may be bought by private collectors but also, often, by galleries and museums spending public money on these acquisitions. When an institution is found to have purchased such dodgy items—sometimes with an apparent blindness to fake provenance documents and the reputation of the dealer—there is embarrassment and also demands for return of the items to their rightful owners. The taxpayer has also been defrauded, possibly for millions of dollars.

Away from the main European, Middle Eastern and American channels through which the trade is conducted, and with a comparatively small population, Australia was not a favoured market for illegal antiquity sales. But since the late twentieth century the country has experienced an increasing number of these transactions, including some high-profile incidents.

From around 800 to 100 BC, the Paracas Peninsula in Peru was home to a culture that produced exquisite textiles and headdresses in which they wrapped their dead. Long a target for tomb robbers, an archaeological discovery in the 1920s revealed a large hoard of funerary items, now known as the Paracas Textiles. When the dig was closed down in 1930, the site was immediately plundered and items soon began appearing on the global antiquities markets. Sweden obtained a large collection of the textiles and was eventually asked to return them by Peru, which has happened.

In 1974, the Australian National Gallery (now the National Gallery of Australia) acquired one of the Paracas Textiles from a New York dealer for $35,000 (the equivalent of more than $300,000 today). An American specialist in Paracas culture spotted the sale and alerted authorities that the item had been stolen from Peru's National Museum in 1973. The Peruvian government asked for its return in 1982. The gallery at first resisted until eventually being presented with incontrovertible evidence of the mantle's provenance. After some delay over legal technicalities associated with the newly introduced *Protection of Movable Cultural Heritage Act 1986*, the government of the day agreed to return the item in 1989. But the money paid for the mantle could not be regained as the dealer who had sold it had died.

The amount involved in this case was relatively small but a more recent case, again involving the National Gallery of Australia, involved a sum of $5 million. A 900-year-old bronze statue of the deity Shiva Nataraja was stolen from a Tamil Nadu temple. It came into the possession of a notorious New York art and antiquities dealer, Subhash Kapoor, who has since been sent to prison for running a large and lengthy illegal trafficking operation around the world. The gallery purchased the statue from Kapoor in 2008. The statue had a fake provenance, which the museum eventually realised, and subsequently handed the statue back to India. An expensive mistake that could have been avoided by examining the credentials of the seller.

In March 2022, Australia returned twenty-nine artefacts to India. They were mainly centuries-old sculptures and paintings stolen from Indian sites, in some cases more than fifty years earlier, and which had since ended up in Australian institutions. The return was related to the politics of the Australia–India relationship, its importance highlighted by the direct involvement of the prime ministers of both countries. Further returns were reportedly coming from Australia, some of which had again been acquired from the notorious Kapoor.

Australia is not only the focus of illegal antiquity sales from overseas, but it is now also the source of such crimes. Around the middle of October 1998 thieves cut an ancient Palawa carving from rock at Sundown Point in the north-west of Tasmania. It was one of many petroglyphs, as these carvings are technically known, and appeared to have been stolen to order as it was the only one of the group taken. The Australian Federal Police have been investigating the crime in concert with American authorities and with Interpol. The trail of the stolen artefact disappeared in the United States and it is still missing. It is thought most likely to have been sold on the black market and to now lie in private hands somewhere in the northern hemisphere, having been purchased for anything up to $40,000, or perhaps more. Its true value, of course, is in its significance for the first Tasmanians and its relationship to their country and traditional beliefs.

This is not an isolated case. Rock art stolen from central Australia was detected for sale on eBay in 2012 and many other sites are feared to be in danger. It seems inevitable that Australia's ancient treasures will be increasingly appealing to global antiquities traffickers. The past is not only the site of crime and criminals; it can also be the cause of illegal activity in the present and, without a doubt, on into the future.

ACKNOWLEDGEMENTS

Thanks to those who have helped bring this book into being, including Maureen Seal, Kylie Seal-Pollard, Rob Willis and the talented team at Allen & Unwin. And let's also acknowledge the crims—bad, mad or sad—otherwise not so different from the rest of us. Like it or not, their stories are our stories.

IMAGE CREDITS

Chapter 1: A Nation of Convicts

Titlepage illustration by William Ross from *The Fell Tyrant*, 1836, courtesy of the State Library of NSW.

Chapter 2: Crime Scenes

'Special photograph number 868, Phil Jeff, 9 August 1922, probably Central Police Station, Sydney', courtesy of the NSW Police Forensic Photography Collection, Sydney Living Museums.

Chapter 3: Heists and Heavies

Bertie Kidd, courtesy of Fin Press.

Chapter 4: Fakes, Frauds and Forgeries

'Amy Bock dressed in men's clothing photographed by an unknown photographer in about 1909', included in Henrietta Stuart 'Postcard albums', fl 1950s. Reference PA1-q-1020-54-2, courtesy of the Alexander Turnbull Library, New Zealand.

Chapter 5: Murders and Mysteries

'Photos from Martha Needle's prison register, vprs516 p2 volume11 page409', courtesy of the Public Record Office Victoria.

Chapter 6: By Hook or By Crook

Ronald Ryan, courtesy of Newspix.

Cover image

'Power the Bushranger' by Charles Nettleton, 1870, State Library of Victoria.

NOTES

Prologue

page 9   'him to seven years transportation': 'John Hudson. Theft: Burglary', 10 December 1783, *Old Bailey Proceedings Online,* version 8.0, www.oldbaileyonline.org/browse.jsp?div=t17831210-19, accessed September 2022.

Chapter 1: A Nation of Convicts

The First Bank Job

page 17   'a merry-meeting on the Rocks': *Sydney Gazette and New South Wales Advertiser,* 14 June 1831, p. 3.

page 18   'few of the coin boxes': Neil Radford, 'Robbing the bank: Australia's First Bank Robbery', *The Dictionary of Sydney,* 2017 at https://dictionaryofsydney.org/entry/robbing_the_bank_australias_first_bank_robbery, accessed March 2022. Carol Baxter, *Breaking the Bank: An extraordinary colonial robbery,* Allen & Unwin, Sydney, 2008.

NOTES

The Night Watch

page 18   'the colony was approaching starvation': Watkin Tench,
A Complete Account of the Settlement at Port Jackson Including An Accurate Description of the Situation of the Colony; of the Natives; and Of Its Natural Productions, G. Nicol and J. Sewell, London 1793, University of Sydney Library edn, Sydney 1998, http://setis.library.usyd.edu.au/ozlit, accessed March 2022.

page 19   'to be the fourth division': 'The night watch', *First Fleet*, University of Wollongong, http://firstfleet.uow.edu.au/s_nightwatch.html, accessed March 2022, from John Cobley, *Sydney Cove 1789*, Angus & Robertson, Sydney, 1963.

page 20   'later took to the bush': Bruce Swanton, *The Police of Sydney 1788–1862*, 2nd edn, Australian Institute of Criminology in association with the New South Wales Police Historical Society, Phillip, ACT, 1984, https://www.aic.gov.au/sites/default/files/2020-05/the-police-of-sydney-1788-1862.pdf, accessed March 2022.

The Flash Mob Goes Exploring

page 25   'his "order", will "die game".': Thomas Mitchell, *Journal of an Expedition into the Interior of Tropical Australia*, 1848, Project Gutenberg, https://gutenberg.net.au/ebooks/e00034.html, accessed March 2022.

page 26   'uniquely recruited to his expeditions': D.W.A. Baker, 'Mitchell, Sir Thomas Livingstone (1792–1855)', *Australian Dictionary of Biography*, National Centre of Biography, Australian National University, https://adb.anu.edu.au/biography/mitchell-sir-thomas-livingstone-2463/text3297, accessed March 2022.

A Child of Misfortune

page 30   'the great Disposer of events': All quotations from *Memoirs of the First Thirty-Two Years of The Life of James Hardy Vaux, A Swindler and Pickpocket; Now Transported for the Second Time, and For Life, to New South Wales*, John Murray, London, 1819.

page 31   'the government for six years': Averil F. Fink, 'Vaux, James Hardy (1782–1841)', *Australian Dictionary of Biography*, National Centre of Biography, Australian National University, https://adb.anu.edu.au/biography/vaux-james-hardy-2756/text3905, accessed May 2022.

page 31 'those of "Flash Jim" Vaux': Kel Richards, *Flash Jim—The astonishing story of the convict fraudster who wrote Australia's first dictionary*, HarperCollins, Sydney, 2021.

Gentlemen Convicts

page 34 'returned to England in 1811': National Library of Australia, 'Guide to the papers of John Grant', MS 737 https://nla.gov.au/nla.obj-290670902/findingaid#nla-obj-290672028, accessed June 2022.

page 34 'no doubt, did the whiskey': Christine Maher, 'The "gentlemen" convicts', *National Library of Australia*, 15 October 2019, www.nla.gov.au/stories/blog/treasures/2019/10/15/the-gentlemen-convicts, accessed June 2022.

page 35 'of leave-holder, his printed ticket': Charles Cozens, *Adventures of a Guardsman*, Richard Bentley, London, 1848, p. 163.

page 35 'he joined the local police': Reverend Robert Willson, 'The Gentleman Convict in Yass', *Anglican News*, Anglican Diocese of Canberra and Goulburn, 9 September 2020, https://anglicancg.org.au/the-gentleman-convict-in-yass, accessed June 2022.

An Artful Dodger

page 36 'a "cutter" and a "carpenter"': Raymond J. Warren, 'The Moreton Bay Colony, convict runaways and "the joining"', *The Warren Register of Colonial Tall Ships*, http://colonialtallshipsrayw1.blogspot.com/2012/04/moreton-bay-colony-convict-runaways-and.html, accessed January 2023; Maureen Withney, 'William Grady', *Convict Records*, https://convictrecords.com.au/convicts/grady/william/99255, accessed June 2022.

page 36 'a man's watch in 1820': 'William Grady. Violent theft: Highway robbery', 17 February 1820, *Old Bailey Proceedings Online*, version 8.0, www.oldbaileyonline.org/browse.jsp?div=t18200217-23, accessed January 2023.

page 37 'commuted to transportation for life': Matthew White, 'Juvenile crime in the 19th century', *British Library*, www.britishlibrary.cn/en/articles/juvenile-crime-in-the-19th-century, accessed June 2022.

page 38 'as reward for his services': Fiona Starr, 'William Grady: "Flash" Man, Robber, Adventurer', Hyde Park Barracks, https://sydneylivingmuseums.com.au/convict-sydney/william-grady, accessed June 2022. Using information provided by Colin Grady, a descendant of William.

page 39 'are still coming to light': David Hill, *Reckoning: The forgotten children and their quest for justice*, William Heinemann, Sydney, 2022; Graham Seal,

Condemned: The transported men, women and children who built Britain's empire, Yale University Press, London and New Haven, CT, 2021.

Red Tape and Blue Dots

page 40   'the peace and a magistrate': *New South Wales Government Gazette*, no. 8, 25 April 1832, p. 70.

page 41   'Williams in Sydney': *New South Wales Government Gazette*, no. 244, 19 October 1832, p. 816.

page 41   'on eighteenth- and nineteenth-century convicts': Simon Barnard, *Convict Tattoos: Marked men and women of Australia*, Text Publishing, Melbourne, 2016; Zoe Alker, with contributions by Robert Shoemaker, 'Convict tattoos', *Digital Panopticon*, www.digitalpanopticon.org/Convict_tattoos, accessed June 2022.

The Felonry of New South Wales

page 41   'South Wales were all ex-convicts': Lisa Durnian, 'Criminals in the courtroom', *The Prosecution Project-Research Brief 12*, 29 April 2015, https://eprints.qut.edu.au/215083/, accessed June 2022.

page 42   'other community in the world': All quotations are from James Mudie, *The Felonry of New South Wales*, self-published in London, 1837.

page 45   'in 1845 aged thirty-two years': 'William Watt', *Convict Records*, https://convictrecords.com.au/convicts/watt/william/110160, accessed June 2022; 'Jemima Chapman', *Convict Records*, https://convictrecords.com.au/convicts/chapman/jemima/87273, accessed June 2022.

page 45   'felonry of New South Wales': Bernard T. Dowd and Averil F. Fink, 'Mudie, James (1779–1852)', *Australian Dictionary of Biography*, National Centre of Biography, Australian National University, https://adb.anu.edu.au/biography/mudie-james-2487/text3345, accessed June 2022.

'I Am Not a Bad Man at Heart'

page 46   'six years . . .': All quotations from 'The Autobiography of a Convict', Empire (Sydney), 16 October 1867, p. 6.

An Habitual Criminal

page 50   'hair and light hazel eyes': Mina went by the surname of Caulfield prior to her marriage and as Jury in widowhood, in addition to her numerous criminal aliases. She was probably christened Euphemia McCauldfield.

page 51   'to get by in Melbourne': *Victoria Police Gazette*, 13 October 1868.

page 51 'fate of Roger Charles Tichborne': *The Sydney Morning Herald*, 26 July 1865, p. 1.

page 52 'whom I lent the money': *The Sydney Morning Herald*, 1 August 1873, p. 3.

page 52 'a year of hard labour': 'Mina Jury. Theft: simple larceny', 10 December 1883, *Old Bailey Proceedings Online*, version 8.0, www.oldbaileyonline.org/browse.jsp?div=t18831210-145, accessed July 2022.

page 53 'as for thefts in England': *Police Gazette* (Ireland), 2 May 1890, p. 5.

page 53 'with her surviving abandoned children': In her trial evidence, Mina claimed to have eleven living children in Australia, 'seven unprovided for', though genealogical records, not fully reliable, suggest there may have only been eight living. The relevant Australian sources are Birth Index, 1788–1922; Births, Deaths and Baptisms, 1792–1981 and Marriage Index, 1788–1950, accessed through Ancestry, November 2018.

page 53 'surviving children were ever reunited': Ancestry search for Euphemia Mercevina (Mina) Caulfield, November 2018.

Chapter 2: Crime Scenes

Murdering Gully Road

page 56 'the body . . .': 'Supreme Court', *Launceston Examiner*, 8 July 1858, p. 5.

page 58 'upon me and my family': 'Supreme Court', *Cornwall Chronicle*, 7 July 1858, p. 3.

page 58 'respectable people in the neighbourhood': 'Murder at Table Cape', *Tasmanian Daily News* (Hobart), 20 May 1858, p. 2.

page 58 'he was killed—Murdering Gully Road': *North West Tasmania*, 'Wynyard history: the story behind Murdering Gully Road', www.ourtasmania.com.au/northwest/wynyard-murdering-gully.html, accessed August 2022.

Dangerous Diggings

page 60 'bullet hit the ground': Seweryn Korzelinski, *Memoirs of Gold-digging in Australia*, trans. and ed. Stanley Robe, foreword and notes by Lloyd Robson, University of Queensland Press, Brisbane, 1979.

page 60 'by two diggers in 1862': 'Mysterious murder at Mia Mia', *Mount Alexander Mail*, 4 July 1862, p. 3.

page 61 'source is at an end': 'Amherst', *Mount Alexander Mail*, 19 December 1859, p. 3.

page 62 'of some of the trade': 'Gold swindlers', *The Argus*, 22 April 1852, p. 4.

page 63 'the fields became more organised': Caitlin Mahar, 'Crime', Electronic Encyclopedia of Gold in Australia, www.egold.net.au/biogs/ EG00181b.htm, accessed June 2022.

Sydney Coves in 'Frisco

page 64 'the 1840s and early '50s': Sherman L. Ricards and George M. Blackburn, 'The Sydney Ducks: A demographic analysis', *Pacific Historical Review*, vol. 42, no. 1, February 1973, pp. 20–31.

page 66 'determined to destroy the city': Monique Galloway, 'California gold rush: The Sydney Ducks in San Francisco', *The Collector*, 2 May 2021, www.thecollector.com/california-gold-rush-the-sydney-ducks-in-san-francisco, accessed August 2022.

page 66 'her husband to San Francisco': 'Mary Ann Hogan's examination', *Bell's Life in Sydney and Sporting Review*, 13 December 1851, p. 1. (Reported from the San Francisco newspaper *Alta*.)

page 66 'holder Michael Hogan in 1836': 'Mary Collier', Convict Records, https://convictrecords.com.au/convicts/collier/mary/87264, accessed August 2022.

Midnight in Melbourne

page 71 'is over for one night': 'Night Scenes in Melbourne', *The Argus*, 28 February 1868, p. 6; Graeme Davison, *City Dreamers: The urban imagination in Australia* (NewSouth, Sydney, 2016).

Who Was Mary Fortune?

page 72 'detective yarns in Australian newspapers': Lucy Sussex, 'Mary Fortune', *Victorian Fiction Research Guides*, https:// victorianfictionresearchguides.org/mary-fortune, accessed March 2022.

page 73 '"Avoca" printed on it indelibly': Lucy Sussex, *Women Writers and Detectives in Nineteenth-century Crime Fiction*, Palgrave Macmillan, Basingstoke, UK, 2010, p. 134 (from 'Tom Doyle's dream').

page 77 'humanity forward in interesting ways': 'The detective's dream', *Portland Guardian*, 24 December 1886, pp. 2–3.

page 78 'in a case of rape': Sussex, *Women Writers and Detectives*, p. 140 (from the *Victoria Police Gazette*).

page 78 'resting place in Springvale Cemetery': Jason Steger, 'Solved! The case of Mary Fortune, the pioneering crime writer who vanished', *The*

Sydney Morning Herald, 7 July 2016, www.smh.com.au/entertainment/books/solved-the-case-of-mary-fortune-the-pioneering-crime-writer-who-vanished-20160707-gq0u41.html, accessed March 2022.

Collingwood Crimes

page 80   'to have led the attack': 'Daring outrage at Collingwood', *The Australian News for Home Readers*, 25 June 1864, p. 11.

page 81   'had informed on his accomplices': 'The Collingwood bank robbery', *The Telegraph* (Brisbane), 3 July 1885, p. 2.

page 81   'was imprisoned for one year': 'Collingwood bank robbery', *Evening News* (Sydney), 22 July 1885, p. 3.

page 82   'coolest street in the world': Rebecca Russo, 'Smith Street has been named the coolest street in the world', *Time Out*, 10 June 2021, www.timeout.com/melbourne/news/smith-street-has-been-named-the-coolest-street-in-the-world-060921, accessed July 2022.

page 82   'reward being offered in 2017': Helen Thomas, *Murder on Easey Street: Melbourne's most notorious cold case*, Black Inc. Books, Melbourne, 2018.

Inside Starvinghurst

page 86   'God have mercy on all': 'The Song of a Prison', *The Bulletin*, vol. 30, no. 1558, 23 December 1909, p. 43.

page 88   'they stormed the old Bastille': 'One Hundred and Three', *The Bulletin*, vol. 29, no. 1502, 26 November 1908, p. 39.

At the Fifty-Fifty Club

page 91   'the morals of our youth': 'Foul blot on the city's nightlife', *Truth* (Sydney), 31 January 1932, p. 14.

page 92   'were among the few mourners': Alfred McCoy, 'The 1930s: Phil Jeffs' (from Alfred McCoy, *Drug Traffic: Narcotics and organized crime in Australia*, Harper and Row, Sydney, 1980) at *Sydney Crime Museum*, www.sydneycrimemuseum.com/crime-stories/the-1930s-phil-jeffs, accessed March 2022. 'Jeffs, Phillip (Phil) (1897–1945)', *Obituaries Australia*, National Centre of Biography, Australian National University, https://oa.anu.edu.au/obituary/jeffs-phillip-phil-13643/text24409, accessed March 2022.

True Detective Stories

page 94   'or was there something more': All quotations from Amelia Hartney (ed.), *Famous Detective Stories: True tales of Australian crime*, NLA

Publishing, Canberra, 2016. Kathleen's full name was Freda Kathleen Adele Biliski.

page 96 'opportunities than previously or since': Rachel Franks, '"A world of fancy fiction and fact": The Frank C. Johnson Archive at the State Library of New South Wales', *Peer Reviewed Proceedings: 6th Annual Conference, Popular Culture Australia, Asia and New Zealand (PopCAANZ)*, Wellington 29 June – 1 July 2015, pp. 13–24. www.academia. edu/19712973/_A_world_of_fancy_fiction_and_fact_The_Frank_C._Johnson_Archive_at_the_State_Library_of_New_South_Wales, accessed May 2022.

Murder City

page 99 'as she was usually known': 'Tragedy in Adelaide', *The Register* (Adelaide), 14 August 1906, p. 7.

page 99 'and on the suspect's clothing': 'Bristol Street tragedy', *Evening Journal* (Adelaide), 17 August 1906, p. 2.

page 100 'Habibulla died instantly': 'The doomed murderer', *Evening Journal* (Adelaide), 16 November 1906, p. 4.

page 100 'forgotten homicidal history of Adelaide': 'South Australia—crime, law and punishment', The Manning Index of South Australian History, https://manning.collections.slsa.sa.gov.au/sa/crime/murder.htm, accessed July 2022.

Chapter 3: Heists and Heavies

Pirating the Nelson

page 104 'appeared to be well acquainted': 'Piracy in the bay', *The Argus*, 3 April 1852, p. 5.

page 107 'can but weigh and surmise': Marcus Clarke, *Stories of Australia in the Early Days*, London, Hutchinson & Co., 1897, pp. 187ff.

The Crims Came by Motorcar

page 110 'separated after a few months': Rachel Hollis, 'Robbery under arms—the Eveleigh heist, 1914', *NSW State Archives*, https://gallery.records. nsw.gov.au/index.php/galleries/crime-in-the-records/robbery-under-arms-the-eveleigh-heist, accessed January 2023.

page 110 'STOLEN VEHICLE USED': 'Masked motor bandits', *The Sun* (Sydney), 10 June 1914, p. 1.

page 111 'apparently, been just as invisible': 'Eveleigh robbery recalls Brisbane outrage', *Sunday Times* (Sydney), 14 June 1914, p. 10.

Flash as a Rat with a Gold Tooth

page 111 'houses in Queensland in 1925': Tenille Hands, 'The reel-life gang-star', *National Film and Sound Archive*, www.nfsa.gov.au/latest/squizzy-taylor-reel-life-gang-star, accessed March 2022.

page 115 'a woman was somehow involved': State Library of Victoria, 'Squizzy Taylor', http://ergo.slv.vic.gov.au/explore-history/rebels-outlaws/city-criminals/squizzy-taylor, accessed March 2022. Hugh Anderson, *Larrikin Crook: The rise and fall of Squizzy Taylor*, Jacaranda Press, Melbourne, 1971.

The Shadow and the King

page 116 'am after the bigger money': 'A piece of Italian cloth', *Truth* (Sydney), 8 August 1926, p. 13, and all subsequent quotes.

page 116 'to rob Sydney's Union Bank': His words are reported differently elsewhere, though their meaning remains the same; see 'Police tell story of bank sensation', *Evening News* (Sydney), 18 August 1926, p. 9.

page 116 'before the distinctively dressed Italians': The press and police invariably referred to the robbers as 'the Italians' though, going by the names, one of the men was probably Greek.

Dapper Desire's Last Escape

page 120 'and colourful career in 1926': 'An elusive criminal', *Windsor and Richmond Gazette*, 26 March 1926, p. 1.

page 120 'the end of the war': 'Interned men escape', *The Herald* (Melbourne), 10 March 1919, p. 7.

page 121 'on which he was arrested': 'An elusive criminal'.

page 124 'next to his deceased son': 'End of the road', *Cumberland Argus and Fruitgrowers Advocate*, 19 March 1926, p. 4.

The Most Violent Woman in Sydney

page 125 'guilty on all three counts': 'Outburst in court', *The Sun* (Sydney), 1 September 1938, p. 17.

page 126 'an adjournment of their case': 'Women demand meal in court', *The Daily Telegraph*, 14 November 1939, p. 9.

page 126 'months for assaulting a constable': 'Prisoner's complaint about food', *The Sydney Morning Herald*, 14 November 1939, p. 10.

page 126   '"of my liberty," Furlong complained': 'Police sergeant's second
    wife just wouldn't stay home', *Truth* (Sydney), 11 March 1945, p. 13.

page 127   'as *Truth* newspaper put it': 'Two women freed by jury', *Truth*
    (Sydney), 3 October 1948, p. 7.

page 127   'diabetes and cancer in 1953': Fiona McGregor, 'Webber, Iris', *The
    Dictionary of Sydney*, 2015, https://dictionaryofsydney.org/entry/webber_iris,
    accessed July 2022.

Gone to Gowings

page 128   'of his life in prison': 'Quarter Sessions', *The Sydney Morning Herald*,
    13 November 1937, p. 20.

page 132   'only two men slightly wounded': Police Department, *Report of
    the Police Department of New South Wales for the Year 1946*, Parliament of
    New South Wales, Sydney, 1947, p. 6, OpenGov New South Wales, www.
    opengov.nsw.gov.au/publications/11343, accessed January 2023.

page 133   'liberty for about twenty minutes': D. McLennan, 'There's
    no escape', first published in *Famous Detective Stories*, No. 100, probably
    between 1954 and 1955, pp. 20ff., in Amelia Hartney (ed.), *Famous Detective
    Stories: True tales of Australian crime*, NLA Publishing, Canberra, 2016, pp. 59ff.

page 133   'You Made Our Lives Interesting': 'Antonio Martini', *Find a Grave*,
    www.findagrave.com/memorial/232841970/antonio-martini, accessed
    May 2022.

The Great Bookie Robbery

page 135   'girls "would end up dead"': 'The secretary of the Victoria Club,
    Mr Frank Murray, with emptied cash tins and padlocks cut with boltcutters
    by the robbers', *The Canberra Times*, 22 April 1976, p. 1.

page 135   'along with maybe $15 million': Olivia Lambert, 'Defence
    barrister Philip Dunn on Australia's most notorious robbery', *News.com.au*,
    14 February 2016, www.news.com.au/lifestyle/real-life/true-stories/defence-
    barrister-philip-dunn-on-australias-most-notorious-robbery/news-story/a1ba
    715989c6d68df7df14a918c00f35, accessed June 2022.

page 135   'the Philippines and even China': Mark Bennett, *The Great Bookie
    Robbery—Part one*, Sid Harta Publishers, Melbourne, 2016.

They Got the Lot!

page 138   'today, has never been recovered': Susan Chenery, 'They got
    the lot': The mystery of the biggest bank heist in Australia's history', *The
    Guardian*, 8 January 2022, www.theguardian.com/australia-news/2022/

jan/08/they-got-the-lot-the-mystery-of-the-biggest-bank-heist-in-australias-history, accessed June 2022.

page 138 'unable to track them down': Max Willoughby, 'The big bank job', *Timelines: Quarterly Newsletter of the Murwillumbah Historical Society Inc*, vol. 5, no. 4, April 2017, pp. 6–7.

page 139 'believing that it was impossible': Stephen Gibbs, 'Master safe-breaker, armed robber and suspected gangland killer: The untold story of Bertie Kidd', *Daily Mail Australia*, 17 November 2019, www.dailymail.co.uk/news/article-7646213/The-untold-story-Bertie-Kidd-Australias-complete-criminal.html, accessed June 2022.

page 139 'that began publication in 2019': Simon Griffin, *The Audacious Kidd, volume 1 of the Kidd Trilogy*, Fin Press, Sydney, 2019, https://theaudaciouskidd.com, accessed June 2022.

Swindling the Mint

page 141 'housed was again burned down': Stephen Pallaras, 'The Mickelberg saga and the public purse', paper to the Criminal Lawyers Association of the Northern Territory, Seventh Biennial Conference, Kuta, Bali, 27 June to 2 July 1999.

page 143 'am not proud of it': 'Anatomy of a stitch up', *Crikey*, 23 June 2002, www.crikey.com.au/2002/06/23/anatomy-of-a-stitch-up, accessed June 2022.

page 144 'very seriously, said the then premier': Jade Barker, 'Why is Australia's financial crimes watchdog investigating the Perth Mint?', *ABC News*, 19 September 2022, www.abc.net.au/news/2022-09-19/austrac-investigates-perth-mint/101438128, accessed October 2022.

page 144 'value of its gold bars': ABC *Four Corners*, 'Tainted Gold', 6 March 2023, https://www.abc.net.au/news/2023-03-06/tainted-gold:-inside-perth-mints-billion-dollar/102060270, accessed April 2023.

Chapter 4: Fakes, Frauds and Forgeries

Artists of Notes

page 147 'half were convicted of forgery': Helen Hughes, 'Forgery in eighteenth-century Britain and colonial Australian art: A case study of Francis Greenway's prison scenes', paper delivered Monash University, 28 November 2019, https://law.unimelb.edu.au/centres/iilah/news-and-events/events-2019/forgery-in-eighteenth-century-britain-and-colonial-australian-art, accessed April 2022.

page 149   'were transported for fourteen years': 'Knut Bull, Peter Smith.
Deception: forgery', 15 December 1845, *Old Bailey Proceedings Online*,
version 8.0, www.oldbaileyonline.org/browse.jsp?div=t18451215-209,
accessed February 2023.

page 149   'not an Irish State Prisoner': G.T. Stilwell, Joan Kerr and
Irene Hansen, 'Knud Geelmuyden Bull', Design and Art Australia
Online, 1992/2011, www.daao.org.au/bio/knud-geelmuyden-bull/biography,
accessed April 2022.

page 150   'open and bled to death': Rex Rienits, 'Lycett, Joseph (1774–1828)',
Australian Dictionary of Biography, National Centre of Biography, Australian
National University, https://adb.anu.edu.au/biography/lycett-joseph-2382/
text3137, accessed April 2022.

page 151   'of his death are unknown': Rex Rienits, 'Watling, Thomas
(1762–?)', *Australian Dictionary of Biography*, National Centre of Biography,
Australian National University, https://adb.anu.edu.au/biography/watling-
thomas-2776/text3947, accessed online April 2022.

page 151   'grave in the Hunter Valley': Morton Herman, 'Greenway, Francis
(1777–1837)', *Australian Dictionary of Biography*, National Centre of Biography,
Australian National University, https://adb.anu.edu.au/biography/greenway-
francis-2120/text2681, accessed April 2022.

The Lady Swindler

page 152   'her loving son and daughter': *The Sydney Morning Herald*,
6 July 1914, p. 10.

page 152   'where she was often confined': 'Hobart Town Gazette', *The
Hobart Town Advertiser*, 20 August 1847, p. 1.

page 153   'which she accomplishes her schemes': 'A Lady Swindler',
Supplement to the Illustrated Australian News for Home Readers,
26 November 1867, p. 12. Also in 'A Lady Swindler', *Leader* (Melbourne),
23 November 1867, p. 28.

page 154   'of £100 (about $12,000 today)': *Leader*, 7 December 1867, p. 5.

page 154   'often happened, was again remanded': 'Central Police Court',
Geelong Advertiser, 16 January 1868, p. 3.

page 154   'freely lent to the prisoner': *The Argus*, 27 January 1868, p. 5.

page 155   'over poverty, stigma and marginalisation': Janet McCalman,
'Hidden women of history: how "lady swindler" Alexandrina Askew
triumphed over the convict stain', *The Conversation*, 22 October 2021,
https://theconversation.com/hidden-women-of-history-how-lady-
swindler-alexandrina-askew-triumphed-over-the-convict-stain-169023,

accessed August 2022. McCalman tells the full story in her *Vandemonians: The repressed history of Colonial Victoria*, Melbourne University Press, Melbourne, 2021.

A Strange Life

page 157   'neater feet, and rather good-looking': *The Evening Star*, 26 April 1909, p. 4.

page 158   'buried in an unmarked grave': Jenny Coleman, *Mad or Bad? The life and exploits of Amy Bock, 1859–1943*, Otago University Press, Otago, New Zealand, 2010.

page 159   'overpowered me more and more': William Ray, 'Con-artist: The story of Amy Bock', *Radio New Zealand*, 12 November 2018, at www.rnz. co.nz/programmes/black-sheep/story/2018670137/con-artist-the-story-of-amy-bock, accessed March 2022.

page 159   'and easy to work on': 'The notorious Amy Bock, 1909', originally published in *An Encyclopaedia of New Zealand*, A.H. McLintock (ed.), 1966, *Te Ara—the Encyclopedia of New Zealand*, www.TeAra.govt.nz/en/1966/trials-notable/page-12, accessed March 2022.

The Magician of Mines

page 161   'mines were of immense value': 'The Northern Territories Company', *Northern Territory Times and Gazette*, 15 September 1899, p. 3.

page 161   'by his own unaided eloquence': 'Associated Financial Corporation', *Northern Territory Times and Gazette*, 19 April 1901, p. 2, quoted from the *Investor's Review*.

page 162   'out of the legal net': Peter Bell, 'Mining in the Northern Territory: A brief historical overview', Australasian Mining History Association 21st Annual Conference, Darwin, 21–25 June 2015, www.mininghistory.asn.au/wp-content/uploads/Confeence-Abstracts-Darwin.pdf, accessed July 2022.

page 163   'them his life was ruined': 'Hero or villain', *Moreton Mail* (Queensland), 4 August 1933, p. 8.

Clairvoyant Crimes

page 164   'were increasingly arrested and prosecuted': Alana Jayne Piper, '"A menace and an evil": Fortune-telling in Australia, 1900–1918', *History Australia*, January 2014, vol. 11, no. 3, p. 53, DOI: 10.1080/14490854.2014.11668531.

page 164   'legal history of the state': 'Fortune buried in tins', *Moree Gwydir Examiner and General Advertiser*, 16 April 1928, p. 2.

NOTES

page 167   'never seen either heaven or hell': 'The fortune-telling cases', *Evening News* (Sydney), 6 March 1903, p. 4.

page 168   'with claims of extra-normal powers': Samadhi Driscoll, 'Fortune-telling, family history and feminism', *Vida!*, 7 September 2016, www.auswhn.org.au/blog/fortune-telling-family-history-feminism, accessed March 2022.

The Age of Con

page 169   'other nationality—by a long shot': W. Meier, *Property Crime in London, 1850–Present*, Palgrave MacMillan, Basingstoke, UK, 2011.

page 172   'had been a commercial matter': 'Warren's arrest', *The Evening Star* (Dunedin), 10 July 1923, p. 4. According to this report, Bill netted £23,000 from Sir Walter. Dilnot, below, also says £23,000.

page 173   'of the master of craft': George Dilnot, *Getting Rich Quick: An outline of swindles old and new with some account of the manners and customs of confidence men*, Geoffrey Bles, London, 1935.

How To Be a Con Artist

page 175   'so the name has stuck': *New-York Herald*, 8 July 1849.

page 175   '(wallet thieves) and "buzgloaks" (pickpockets)': 'To the Editor of the Cornwall Chronicle', *Cornwall Chronicle* (Launceston), 29 December 1852, p. 879.

page 177   'the large amount seemingly lost': *New South Wales Police Gazette Supplement C*, 1938, p. v.

page 179   'the agents they had defrauded': Peter Doyle, *Crooks Like Us*, Historic Houses Trust NSW, Sydney, 2016, pp. 56–7.

Also Known as . . .?

page 179   'the English Riviera of Torquay': 'Hostess to Aussies at Manx home', *The Sun* (Sydney), 30 September 1945, p. 11.

page 180   'bouquet completed the lavish crowd-stopper': 'Heiress postpones wedding', *Townsville Daily Bulletin*, 10 December 1945, p. 1.

page 180   'model frock . . .': 'Sydney wedding mystery', *Barrier Miner*, 10 December 1945, p. 7.

page 181   'was remanded until after Christmas': 'Remanded', *Goulburn Evening Post*, 24 December 1945, p. 3.

page 181   'difficulties with her legal representations': 'Mrs Livesy and Council', *Barrier Daily Truth*, 9 January 1946, p. 1.

page 181   'Sessions with her Sydney solicitors': 'Mrs Livesy in Adelaide', *Border Watch* (Mount Gambier), 10 January 1946, p. 1.

page 181   'woman on a three-year bond': 'Mrs Livesy released on bond', *Advocate* (Burnie, Tas.), 23 February 1946, p. 7.

page 181   'wanted £10,000 (around $750,000 today) compensation': 'Mrs Livesy's £10,000 Action', *Examiner* (Launceston, Tas.), 12 March 1946, p. 1.

page 181   'consumed at the wedding reception': 'Mrs Livesy in Bankruptcy Court, Sydney', *Lithgow Mercury*, 31 May 1946, p. 1.

page 181   'with costs awarded against her': 'Breach of promise case abandoned', *Daily Examiner* (Grafton, NSW), 9 October 1946, p. 3.

page 182   '£3.700 and assets of £1.270': 'Legal charges excessive', *The Advertiser*, 5 February 1947, p. 12.

page 182   'be employed in "domestic duties".': 'Two months for Mrs. Livesy', *The Age*, 1 December 1950, p. 10.

Tar and Feathers

page 185   'making of a Greater Mildura': 'Notes and comments', *The Mildura Cultivator*, 6 August 1919, p. 4.

page 186   'hoped to get it accepted': 'Greater Mildura', *The Mildura Cultivator*, 6 August 1919, pp. 9–10.

page 187   'alive with excitement, all night': 'A Mildura sensation', *The Albury Banner and Wodonga Express*, 28 October 1921, p. 4.

page 187   'his journalism "foul and filthy"': Geoffrey Serle, 'Hervey, Grant (Madison) (1880–1933)', *Australian Dictionary of Biography*, National Centre of Biography, Australian National University, https://adb.anu.edu.au/biography/hervey-grant-madison-6653/text11465, accessed July 2022.

page 187   'Madison MacGlashon of New York': 'Grant Hervey', *The Northern Miner*, 30 December 1933, p. 3.

A Man of Faces

page 188   'tried, imprisoned and eventually discharged': *South Australian Police Gazette*, 1938.

page 190   'obtaining money by false pretences': 'Bogus naval officer gets six months', *The Herald* (Melbourne), 16 February 1940, p. 3.

page 190   'months for impersonating an officer': 'Posed as officer', *The Sun* (Sydney) 16 February 1940, p. 3.

Glorified Jam Labels

page 191 'be termed glorified jam labels': Richard Finlay and Anny Francis, 'A brief history of currency counterfeiting', *Reserve Bank of Australia Bulletin*, September 2019, www.rba.gov.au/publications/bulletin/2019/sep/a-brief-history-of-currency-counterfeiting.html, accessed August 2022.

page 191 'the hurly-burly of drinking sessions': 'Forged notes', *The Sydney Morning Herald*, 14 February 1940, p. 8; 'Many forged £5 notes still out', *The Daily Telegraph*, 25 February 1940, p. 5.

page 191 'of the harbour by now': Finlay and Francis, 'A brief history'.

page 193 'on the Reserve Bank's website': 'Banknote features', *Reserve Bank of Australia*, https://banknotes.rba.gov.au/banknote-features, accessed August 2022.

page 193 'be social and economic costs': Meika Ball, 'Recent Trends in Banknote Counterfeiting', *Reserve Bank of Australia Bulletin*, March 2019, www.rba.gov.au/publications/bulletin/2019/mar/recent-trends-in-banknote-counterfeiting.html#fifty-southern-cross, accessed August 2022.

Chapter 5: Murders and Mysteries

Death of a Constable

page 196 'a person or persons unknown': 'Murder', *Sydney Gazette and New South Wales Advertiser*, 28 August 1803, p. 4.

page 196 'time previous to his assassination': 'Re-examinations', *Sydney Gazette and New South Wales Advertiser*, 4 September 1803, p. 3.

page 196 '19, 1803, Aged 35 Years': *Sydney Gazette and New South Wales Advertiser*, 6 November 1803, p. 3. Luker was more likely thirty-eight.

page 199 'died in Sydney in 1833': Rachel Franks, 'The murder of Constable Joseph Luker', *The Dictionary of Sydney*, 2019, at https://dictionaryofsydney.org/entry/the_murder_of_constable_joseph_luker, accessed April 2022.

page 199 'early arrival in the hereafter': 'Sydney', *Sydney Gazette and New South Wales Advertiser*, 2 October 1803, p. 2.

From Beyond the Grave

page 201 'over herself or her family': 'The Mount Gambier murder', *The Argus*, 12 August, 1875, p. 7.

page 202 'mercy on your immortal soul': 'Local telegrams', *The South Australian Advertiser*, 7 October 1875, p. 5.

page 202   'once evincing the slightest emotion': *New Zealand Herald*, 24 August 1875, p. 3; 'The murder at Mount Gambier', *The Argus*, 7 August 1875, p. 5.

page 202   'tragedy at Mount Gambier churches': 'The Hedley Park tragedy', *Border Watch* (Mount Gambier), 11 August 1875, p. 3.

page 202   'few seconds, and twitched convulsively': 'The Mount Gambier murder', *The Age*, 28 October 1875, p. 3.

page 203   'its history of terrible crime': Hugh Fraser, 'A trip in the south-east', *South Australian Weekly Chronicle*, 15 April 1882, p. 18.

page 203   'had not accomplished his purpose': 'Mary Buchan's murder', *The Register* (Adelaide), 24 July 1915, p. 13.

page 203   'My God! My wife's dream': 'Revealed in dreams', *The Mail* (Adelaide), 16 November 1929, p. 30.

Fred the Ripper

page 204   'thieved from time to time': Barry O. Jones, 'Deeming, Frederick Bailey (1853–1892)', *Australian Dictionary of Biography*, National Centre of Biography, Australian National University, https://adb.anu.edu.au/biography/deeming-frederick-bailey-5940/text10127, accessed July 2022.

page 206   'to that of a gorilla': 'Deeming: Prehistoric man', *The Argus*, 25 January 1930, p. 6.

page 208   'The Ripper's gone away': 'Frederick Bailey Deeming', *Casebook: Jack the Ripper*, www.casebook.org/ripper_media/book_reviews/non-fiction/cjmorley/48.html, accessed July 2022.

page 208   'taken seriously by very few': Over fifty books have been written about Deeming, often revolving around the unlikely belief that he was Jack the Ripper. See WorldCat Entities, 'Deeming, Frederick Bailey 1853–1892', https://worldcat.org/identities/lccn-n2007021186/, accessed July 2022.

The Black Widow of Richmond

page 209   'mother "who feared her exceedingly"': 'The Richmond poisoning case', *The Argus*, 16 June 1894, p. 7.

page 211   'developed delusions about her parentage': 'The Richmond poisoning case', *South Australian Register*, 3 August 1894, p. 7.

page 211   'then condemned her to death': 'The Richmond poison case', *The Age*, 28 September 1894, p. 6.

page 212   'Scott had to say': 'Execution of Martha Needle', *Leader* (Melbourne), 27 October 1894, p. 18.

NOTES

page 212   'few minutes of her execution': 'Execution of Martha Needle', *Leader*.

page 213   'and the attention of others': Samantha Battams, *The Secret Art of Poisoning: The true crimes of Martha Needle the Richmond poisoner*, Samantha Battams, Adelaide, 2019.

The Baby Farmers

page 213   '"myself" people heard him say': 'A hangman commits suicide', *Truth* (Sydney), 7 January 1894, p. 5.

page 215   'moral sense of the community': Kathy Laster, 'Knorr, Frances Lydia (Minnie) (1867–1894)', *Australian Dictionary of Biography*, National Centre of Biography, Australian National University, https://adb.anu.edu.au/biography/knorr-frances-lydia-minnie-13030/text23559, accessed July 2022.

page 215   'of the babies to death': *The Age*, 16 January 1894, p. 5.

page 215   'could be no judicial mercy': Barbara Yazbeck, 'Deviant motherhood in the late nineteenth century: a case study of the trial and execution of Frances Knorr and Emma Williams for child murder', master's thesis, History Department, University of Melbourne, 2002.

page 217   'five years with hard labour': 'Trial of Mrs. Mitchell', *Western Mail*, 20 April 1907, p. 45. Stella Budrikis, *The Edward Street Baby Farm*, Fremantle Press, Fremantle, 2020.

The Man-Woman Murderer

page 217   'a ship bound for Sydney': Pip Smith, 'Friday Essay: Tall ships, tall tales, and the mysteries of Eugenia Falleni', *The Conversation*, 28 July 2017, https://theconversation.com/friday-essay-tall-ships-tall-tales-and-the-mysteries-of-eugenia-falleni-81170, accessed April 2022.

page 219   'a soft grey felt hat': 'Man-woman in court', *Evening News* (Sydney), 6 July 1920, p. 7.

page 219   'pleasantly-spoken, and good-looking young woman': 'Falleni's daughter found by police', *Evening News* (Sydney), 14 July 1920, p. 7.

page 219   'when she was set alight': 'Chatswood murder', *Daily Advertiser* (Wagga Wagga), 19 August 1920, p. 2.

page 219   'Crawford was sentenced to death': 'Eugene [sic] Falleni', *The Sydney Morning Herald*, 7 October 1920, p. 4.

page 220   'looking extremely careworn and feeble': 'Was Eugene [sic] Falleni guilty of murder?', *Evening News* (Sydney), 19 February 1931, p. 5.

page 220   'stepson over Sydney's notorious "Gap"': 'Masqueraded as man for twenty years', *The Telegraph* (Brisbane), 11 June 1938, p. 15.

page 220   'a menace to the community': 'One of strangest women criminals known to world set free', *Truth* (Sydney), 22 February 1931, p. 1.

page 220   'to be performed and publicised': 'Falleni—Australia's man–woman', *The World's News*, 11 September 1954, p. 30.

page 221   'to live as a man': Carolyn Strange, 'Falleni, Eugenia (1875–1938)', *Australian Dictionary of Biography*, National Centre of Biography, Australian National University, https://adb.anu.edu.au/biography/falleni-eugenia-12911/text23325, accessed April 2022.

The Lolly Shop Murders

page 222   '"shot—burglars"—and died in his arms': 'Tragedy at Dulwich Hill', *Barrier Miner* (Broken Hill), 2 July 1928, p. 1.

page 222   'the murderer was a woman': 'Is a woman the masked terror', *Truth* (Sydney), 8 July 1928, p. 1.

page 223   'Read it—Reading time: 10 minutes': 'The last moments of the murdered women from Marrickville', *Smith's Weekly* (Sydney), 21 July 1928, p. 3.

page 223   'legacy was over £3500 ($300,000 today)': 'Left £359', *The Sun* (Sydney), 24 August 1928, p. 13.

page 224   'reminiscing about the still-unsolved case': Hugh Buggy, 'Double murder at the sweet shop', *Warwick Daily News*, 15 September 1950, p. 5.

A Nice Girl

page 226   '*Betty Shanks* by Ted Duhs': Ted Duhs, *I Know Who Killed Betty Shanks*, 3rd edn, Boolarong Press, Brisbane, 2022. Also Ted Duhs' website, Miscarriages of Justice, www.miscarriagesofjustice.com.au/index.html, accessed July 2022.

page 227   'and returned covered in blood': Mike King, 'Betty Shanks: The geography of victimology', Mapping Evil with Mike King podcast series, https://storymaps.arcgis.com/stories/957fd041add543bd88b1e2cc4c073d61, accessed July 2022.

The Assassins

page 229   'thought to have been responsible': Global Terrorism Database, University of Maryland, www.start.umd.edu/gtd/search/Results.aspx?page=11&search=australia&expanded=no&charttype=line&chart=overtime&ob=GTDID&od=desc#results-table, accessed August 2022.

page 229   'cases, also rescued Armenian survivors': Peter Stanley and Vicken Babkenian, *Armenia, Australia and the Great War*, NewSouth, Sydney, 2016.

NOTES

page 229   'seventy murders around the world': Anadolu Agency, 'Turkish envoys slain by Armenian terrorists remembered in Australia', *Daily Sabah*, 17 December 2021, www.dailysabah.com/politics/diplomacy/turkish-envoys-slain-by-armenian-terrorists-remembered-in-australia, accessed August 2022.

page 230   'to aid the ongoing investigation': Carla Hildebrandt, 'NSW Police release audio in renewed effort to solve Turkish diplomat and bodyguard's murder in Sydney in 1980', *ABC News*, 3 August 2022, www.abc.net.au/news/2022-08-03/police-release-audio-to-solve-sydney-murder-of-turkish-diplomat/101294436, accessed August 2022.

page 231   'here suggest up to 60,000': 'Australia', Office of the High Commission for Diaspora Affairs (Armenia), http://diaspora.gov.am/en/pages/12/australia, accessed August 2022.

page 231   'Turkish-descended Australians suggest around 70,000': Nina Evason, 'Turkish in Australia', *Cultural Atlas*, https://culturalatlas.sbs.com.au/turkish-culture/turkish-culture-turkish-in-australia, accessed August 2022.

page 231   'sources give much higher numbers': 'Turkish Australians', *Wikipedia*, https://en.wikipedia.org/wiki/Turkish_Australians, accessed August 2022.

Rack Man

page 232   'was "a black gluggy mess"': Les Kennedy, 'Sinister mystery of a watery grave', *The Daily Telegraph* (Sydney), 29 August 2018.

page 233   'not enable me to say': Darrienne Wyndham, 'John Doe 1994', *Dictionary of Sydney*, 2021, https://dictionaryofsydney.org/entry/john_doe_1994, accessed April 2022.

An Enduring Enigma

page 236   'Somerton Man as Carl Webb': Meilan Solly, 'Have scholars finally identified the mysterious Somerton man?', *Smithsonian Magazine*, 8 August 2022, www.smithsonianmag.com/smart-news/have-scholars-finally-identified-the-mysterious-somerton-man-180980540, accessed October 2022; Bridget Judd, 'Derek Abbott, who helped crack the Somerton Man case, reveals how DNA helped solve the mystery—as it happened', *ABC News*, 3 August 2022, www.abc.net.au/news/2022-08-03/somerton-man-breakthrough-dna-ask-the-experts/101287824, accessed October 2022.

Chapter 6: By Hook or by Crook

Something about the Hangman

page 241 'was committed to an asylum': Ken Macnab, 'Green, Alexander (1802–?)', *Australian Dictionary of Biography*, National Centre of Biography, Australian National University, https://adb.anu.edu.au/biography/green-alexander-12949/text23403, accessed March 2022.

page 242 'I'd drink with Nosey Bob': Rachel Franks, 'Robert "Nosey Bob" Howard', *The Dictionary of Sydney*, 2021, https://dictionaryofsydney.org/entry/robert_nosey_bob_howard, accessed March 2022 and her *An Uncommon Hangman: The life and deaths of Robert 'Nosey Bob' Howard*, University of New South Wales Press, Sydney, 2022.

page 242 'income earned from his position': 'The Queensland hangmen', *Inside Boggo Road: The history of Queensland prisons*, www.boggoroadgaol.com.au/2018/07/hangmen.html, accessed March 2022.

page 242 'to anyone who would listen': 'Blay, Solomon (1816–1897)', *Obituaries Australia*, National Centre of Biography, Australian National University, https://oa.anu.edu.au/obituary/blay-solomon-22788/text36599, accessed March 2022.

page 243 'first half century of settlement': Mark Finnane and Chris Leppard, 'The hanging years', *The Prosecution Project*, Research Brief 30, https://prosecutionproject.griffith.edu.au/the-hanging-years, 9 April 2018, accessed April 2018.

The Bushranger and the Lady

page 243 'made them walk home naked': 'Harry Power', *State Library of Victoria*, http://ergo.slv.vic.gov.au/explore-history/rebels-outlaws/bushrangers/harry-power, accessed March 2022.

page 246 'hut, in the Wombat Ranges': 'Power the Bushranger', *Mornington Standard*, 23 August 1890, p. 3, contributed by 'Truth'.

page 247 'century of service in flames': Kieran Hosty and Bridget Berry, 'Convict hulks', *Sydney Living Museums*, https://sydneylivingmuseums.com.au/stories/convict-hulks, accessed March 2020.

Pilfered Pearls

page 247 'pearling ports in Western Australia': *Lustre: Pearling and Australia*, Western Australian Museum, 2015, exhibition text panels, https://museum.wa.gov.au/explore/lustre-online-text-panels, accessed May 2022.

page 249 'the sea beds vary considerably': M.F., '"Sniding", poaching and dodging on the pearling grounds', *The Daily News* (Perth), 31 March 1937, p. 10.

page 250 'a lugger worth £850': 'Pearl stealing', *The Advertiser* (Adelaide), 29 September 1917, p. 9.

page 250 '50 kilometres north of Broome': *ABC News*, 'Past workers suspected in big pearl heist', 14 September 2005, www.abc.net.au/news/2005-09-14/past-workers-suspected-in-big-pearl-heist/2103234, accessed February 2023. Also *The Age* (Melbourne), 15 September 2005.

Confessions of a Thief

page 251 'to gaol for three months': 'Central Police Court', *The Sydney Morning Herald*, 17 November 1863, p. 5.

page 251 'rolling a drunk at Redfern': 'Central Police Court', *The Sydney Morning Herald*, 27 August 1863, p. 2.

page 251 'cash box from a shop': 'Central Police Court', *Sydney Mail*, 19 March 1864, p. 11.

page 252 'or fourteen days in prison': 'Central Police Court', *The Brisbane Courier*, 30 April 1867, p. 2.

page 252 'hard labour on the roads': Mark Finnane, 'Joe Bragg: A life in crime', *The Prosecution Project*, Research Brief 19, https://prosecutionproject.griffith.edu.au/joe-bragg-a-life-in-crime, 18 December 2015, accessed July 2016.

page 252 'five-year sentence and twenty-five lashes': Bragg's partial record in New South Wales Gaol Description and Entrance Books, 1818–1930, at Ancestry, www.ancestry.com.au/sharing/29235983?h=880d26&o_xid=61784&o_lid=61784&o_sch=Email+Programs, accessed February 2023.

page 253 'prisoners were handcuffed for punishment': State Records Authority of New South Wales, 'Berrima Gaol [1]', https://researchdata.edu.au/berrima-gaol-i/164555, accessed June 2022.

page 253 'opinion he held of himself': Laila Ellmoos, 'Inside Story', *SL* (State Library New South Wales magazine for members), Autumn 2010, pp. 18ff, www.sl.nsw.gov.au/sites/default/files/SL_Autumn10.pdf, accessed June 2022.

page 254 'Joseph Bragg is indelibly tattooed': 'Telegrams', *Newcastle Morning Herald and Miners' Advocate*, 19 September 1892, p. 5.

page 254 'professing to have been converted': 'Intercolonial', *Wagga Wagga Advertiser*, 20 October 1892, p. 2.

page 254   'Wales, without carrying a light': 'Parramatta Court', *The Cumberland Argus and Fruitgrowers Advocate*, 12 March 1910, p. 4.

page 254   'Rookwood Cemetery in November 1917': 'Joseph O Bragg', *Find a Grave*, www.findagrave.com/memorial/148907074/joseph-o-bragg, accessed June 2022.

Tommy the Ambler and Bogan Billy

page 257   'and life returned to normal': 'Capture of Jones, alias "Tommy the Ambler."', *Wagga Wagga Advertiser*, 27 June 1882, p. 2.

page 258   'no known family or descendants': Michael Bennett, 'Bogan, Billy (c. 1860–1900)', *Australian Dictionary of Biography*, National Centre of Biography, Australian National University, https://ia.anu.edu.au/biography/bogan-billy-30964/text38333, accessed 1 October 2022.

Tin-pot Crimes

page 260   '"police," according to one observer': Geoffrey H. Manning, *A Colonial Experience, 1838–1910: A woman's story of life in Adelaide, the District of Kensington and Norwood together with reminiscences of colonial life*, Gillingham Printers, Adelaide, 2001.

page 260   'to prison for a month': 'Assault cases', *The Maitland Mercury and Hunter River General Advertiser*, 16 June 1852, p. 2.

page 261   'Department, Avoca, 26th September, 1859': 'The news of the day', *The Age* (Melbourne), 5 October 1859, p. 4.

page 261   'reeling with a shotgun blast': 'Tin-kettling', *Wellington Times*, 22 January 1903, p. 4.

page 261   'much larrikinism was in evidence': 'Serious stabbing affray', *The Advertiser* (Adelaide), 11 September 1903, p. 7.

page 262   'default of six hours imprisonment': 'Fined for Tin-Kettling', *The Argus* (Melbourne), 14 October 1903, p. 6.

page 262   'a charge of malicious wounding': 'Scaring off demons from the nuptial couch', *The Daily Telegraph* (Sydney), 8 March 1953, p. 46.

page 262   'and quite touched as well': 'Jo', *Momentous*, National Museum of Australia, https://momentous.nma.gov.au/stories/tin-kettling-makes-a-comeback, accessed September 2022.

Dumb Luck

page 263   'some goods—rolls of toilet paper': Vikki Campion, 'Thief caught like a rat in a cage', *The Daily Telegraph* (Sydney), 16 December 2006, www.

dailytelegraph.com.au/news/nsw/thief-caught-like-a-rat-in-a-cage/news-story/c8812946f3484504138bd714a6e269d5, accessed October 2022.

page 263   'evidence needed to charge him': Shannon Molloy, 'Alleged drug dealer's claims of innocence undone by a hilarious selfie with his huge stash', *News Corp Australia*, 31 July 2015, www.news.com.au/entertainment/tv/reality-tv/alleged-drug-dealers-claims-of-innocence-undone-by-a-hilarious-selfie-with-his-huge-stash/news-story/55e2f7b13ef1f700cde0a7aa3b5cb520, accessed October 2022.

page 263   'the headline "Claus for Concern"': *The Age*, 4 December 2018, 'Claus for concern: Man gets stuck in pharmacy chimney during alleged robbery', www.pharmacyitk.com.au/claus-for-concern-man-gets-stuck-in-pharmacy-chimney-during-alleged-robbery, accessed October 2022.

page 264   'stigmas attached to their areas': Sue Rosen, 'We never had a hotbed of crime', The 2nd Annual Marg Berry Memorial Lecture, 2006, *Inner Sydney Voice*, https://innersydneyvoice.org.au/our-projects/capacity-building-project-waterloo/annual-marg-barry-memorial-lecture/we-never-had-a-hotbed-of-crime, accessed October 2022.

page 265   'into a coma and died': 'Bullet that killed painter outside hotel meant for brother?', *Truth* (Sydney), 28 December 1930, p. 1.

Bodgie Beat-ups

page 266   'cult is based on sex': 'Sex basis of "Bodgie" cult', *Mercury* (Hobart), 5 November 1954, p. 3.

page 266   'and to complete civic irresponsibility': 'Catholic Church hits bodgie cult', *The Sun* (Sydney), 7 December 1951, p. 13.

page 266   'enthusiastically detailed at every opportunity': John Braithwaite and Michelle Barker, 'Bodgies and widgies: folk devils of the fifties', in Paul R. Wilson and John Braithwaite (eds), *Two Faces of Deviance: Crimes of the powerless and the powerful*, University of Queensland Press, Brisbane, 1978, pp. 26ff.

page 267   'sex as any other generation': Clem Gorman, 'Bodgies and African American influences in Sydney', *Dictionary of Sydney*, 2015, http://dictionaryofsydney.org/entry/bodgies_and_african_american_influences_in_sydney, accessed August 2022.

page 267   'tight trousers, and crepe-soled shoes': 'Bodgie Cult Bunkum', *The Courier-Mail* (Brisbane), 11 December 1951, p. 1

page 268   'were made during the week': John Braithwaite and Michelle Barker, 'Bodgies and widgies', p. 31. Also 'More bodgie fights feared', *The Herald* (Melbourne), 18 August 1952, p. 3.

NOTES

page 268　'known as "the Silver Bodgie"': Amanda Laugesen, 'The Silver Bodgie and Australian English', *Oz Words*, Australian National Dictionary Centre, vol. 28, no. 2, October 2019, pp. 1–2.

Skyjack

page 270　'as fast as you can': 'Bid to hi-jack airliner stopped', *The Canberra Times*, 20 July 1960, p. 1.

page 270　'but a bunch of idiots': 'Plane crew "a bunch of idiots"', *The Canberra Times*, 24 August 1960, p. 4.

page 271　'seven years in that state': Trans-Australia Airlines Museum, 'TAA Skyjacking', www.taamuseum.org.au/MuseumFront/Museum_5.html, accessed September 2022.

Ned Kelly in a Wetsuit

page 274　'a son the following year': G.C. Bolton, 'Robinson, Ellis Alfred ('Alan' or 'Allan') (1927–1983)', *Australian Dictionary of Biography*, National Centre of Biography, Australian National University, https://adb.anu.edu.au/biography/robinson-ellis-alfred-alan-or-allan-15928/text27129, accessed 1 September 2022.

page 274　'going out in his underwear': Robert Drewe, 'Bizarre death of an explorer', *The Bulletin*, 15 November 1983, p. 28.

page 275　'heard the end of Robinson': Drewe, 'Bizarre death', pp. 28–9.

page 275　'Ned Kelly in a Wetsuit': www.facebook.com/AlanRobinsonDiver/posts/a-ned-kelly-in-a-wetsuit-part-2police-and-government-persecution-lead-to-a-tragi/1841374066079699/, accessed September 2022.

Cuckoo Smurfing

page 276　'limbs around the Lucky laundry': Nathan Lynch, *The Lucky Laundry*, HarperCollins, Sydney, 2022, p. 17.

page 276　'the nests of other birds': Australian Federal Police, 'Money laundering', *AFP*, https://www.afp.gov.au/what-we-do/crime-types/proceeds-crime/money-laundering, accessed September 2022.

page 279　'also caught in the sting': Alison Xiao, 'Australian Federal Police and FBI nab criminal underworld figures in worldwide sting using encrypted app', *ABC News*, 8 June 2021, www.abc.net.au/news/2021-06-08/fbi-afp-underworld-crime-bust-an0m-cash-drugs-murder/100197246, accessed September 2022.

NOTES

Stealing the Past

page 281   'had sold it had died': Donna Yates, 'Paracas mantle returned from National Gallery of Australia', *Trafficking Culture*, 24 July 2018, https://traffickingculture.org/encyclopedia/case-studies/paracas-mantle-returned-from-national-gallery-of-australia, accessed May 2022.

page 281   'the credentials of the seller': Luca Manfredi and Bridget Murray, 'Trafficking of illicit art and antiquities to Asian and Oceanic markets', *Journal of Cultural Heritage Crime*, 12 October 2018, https://www.journalchc.com/2018/10/12/trafficking-of-illicit-art-and-antiquities-to-asian-and-oceanic-markets/#sdfootnote21anc, accessed May 2022; Duncan Chappell and Damien Huffer, 'Quantifying and describing the South and South East Asian illicit antiquities trade: Australia as an overlooked destination?', Briefing Paper, ARC Centre of Excellence in Policing and Security, no. 24, September 2013. See David Gill's *Looting Matters* blog for a list of artefacts returned from Australia to other countries, https://lootingmatters.blogspot.com/search/label/Australia, accessed June 2022.

page 282   'acquired from the notorious Kapoor': Deeksha Bhardwaj, 'Australia returns 29 artefacts stolen from India', *Hindustan Times*, 22 March 2022, www.hindustantimes.com/india-news/australia-returns-29-artefacts-stolen-from-india-101647887946746.html, accessed May 2022.

page 282   'their country and traditional beliefs': Felicity Ogilvie, 'The art of stealing', *ABC News*, 10 November 2019, www.abc.net.au/news/2019-11-10/aboriginal-petroglyphs-stolen-and-missing-from-tasmania/11663382?nw=0&r=HtmlFragment, accessed May 2022.

page 282   'sale on eBay in 2012': Tom Nightingale, 'Suspected stolen Red Centre rock art on eBay', *ABC News*, 1 February 2012, www.abc.net.au/news/2012-02-01/20120201-stolen-rock-art-on-ebay/3804694, accessed January 2023. See also Bob Brown Foundation, 'Tarkine rock art threats', https://bobbrownfoundation.nationbuilder.com/tarkine_rock_art_threats, undated, accessed May 2022.

Also by Graham Seal

Great Australian Stories

Great Anzac Stories

Larrikins, Bush Tales and Other Great Australian Stories

Savage Shore

Great Australian Journeys

Great Convict Stories

Great Bush Stories

Australia's Funniest Yarns

Big Book of Great Australian Bush Yarns

Condemned

Great Australian Mysteries

Great Australian Places